ACKNOWLEDGED
A MAN

Also by Barbara Del Buono

When Two Become One
Co-Author

Survivor of Assault in the YMCA
ACKNOWLEDGED A MAN

by Barbara Del Buono

Foreword by Allen B. Chatt, Ph.D.

THE ELLINGSWORTH PRESS, LLC

All rights reserved.
Copyright © 1998 by Barbara Del Buono

Published by:
The Ellingsworth Press, Inc.
680 Main Street
Watertown, CT 06795
Telephone: 860-274-7151
Toll Free: 877-ELLPRES (355-7737)
E-mail: ELLPRESS@AOL.COM
Website: www.braininjurydragon.com

No part of this book may be reproduced or transmitted in any form or by any means, electronic or mechanical, including photocopying, recording, or by any information storage and retrieval system, without permission in writing from the publisher, except in the case of brief quotations embodied in critical articles and reviews.

The paper used in this book meets the requirements of the American National Standard for Permanence of Paper for Printed Library Materials Z39.48-1984.

Publisher's Cataloging-in-publication
(Provided by Quality Books, Inc.)

Del Buono, Barbara
    Acknowledged a man : survivor of assault in the YMCA / Barbara Del Buono. 1st ed.
    p. cm.
    Includes index.
    LCCN: 98-73610
    ISBN: 0-9605698-1-2

    1. Del Buono, Nick, 1951—Health. 2. Head—Wounds and injuries—Patients—Connecticut—Biography. 3. Brain damage—Patients—Connecticut—Biography. 4. Assault and battery—Connecticut. 5. Trials (Assault and battery)—Connecticut. 6. Victims of crimes—Connecticut—Biography.   I. Title.
RC387.5.D45   1999
617.4/810443/092 [B]   QB199-334

First Edition
Manufactured in the United States of America
99 00 01 02 03   10 9 8 7 6 5 4 3 2 1

This book is dedicated to John Nicholas Del Buono, my loving son, John Angelo Del Buono, his loving father, and to Mary Ann Casteel, his loving sister. Grateful thanks to my grandson, Peter Casteel—only four years old when this odyssey began. Without his excellent help on the computer and his witty comments to keep me going, I would still be struggling to complete Nick's story.

A Man

Fate slew him, but he did not drop;
She felled—he did not fall—
Impaled him on her fiercest stakes—
He neutralized them all.

She stung him, sapped his firm advance,
But, when her worst was done,
And he, unmoved, regarded her,
Acknowledged him a man.

—Emily Dickinson

Table of Contents

Foreword		xiii
Introduction		xix
1	The Fateful Afternoon of June 25, 1977	1
2	Life Is in the Hands of God	11
3	Family	19
4	A Heroic Battle to Live	25
5	Discovering a Dragon	31
6	The YMCA and Joseph Tramontano	39
7	Taking Time for Prayer	45
8	Nick Needs a New Home	51
9	Kimberly Hall	59
10	The Long, Hard Road to Consciousness	65
11	Begging for Rehabilitation	77
12	Coming Home for Visits	83
13	The People vs. Joseph Tramontano	89
14	The Rehabilitation Hospital	99
15	Return to Kimberly Hall	107
16	Advocating for Justice	115
17	A Finding of Guilt	121
18	The Sentencing of Joseph Tramontano	125
19	Family Counseling	131
20	Hunting for a Trial Lawyer	139
21	Permanent Injuries	143
22	Suing the YMCA	155

23	A Previous Assault at the YMCA	161
24	An Expert Witness in Recreational Facilities	169
25	The National YMCA	173
26	Those Precious Trademarks "YMCA" and "Y"	183
27	Leaving Kimberly Hall	191
28	The Convalarium	201
29	TBI: A Newly Recognized Disability	211
30	Surviving	221
31	What's Wrong with My Body?	233
32	A Threat from Title XIX	241
33	The Governor's Task Force on Brain Injury	245
34	Support Groups	253
35	Leaving the State Support Group	259
36	The Trial	265
37	Coming Home	281
38	Caring for Nick at Home	287
	A Television Monitor	289
	Hiring Aides	289
	Daily Showers	290
	Daytime Continence	290
	Nighttime Incontinence	291
	A Waterbed	292
	A Long-leg Brace	293
39	Home Rehabilitation	295
	Speech Therapy	295
	Physical Therapy	296
	Massage Therapy	299
	Occupational Therapy	299
	Neuropsychology	299
	Operations: Gastrostomy and Tracheotomy	301
	Cranioplasty	302
	A Short-leg Plastic Brace	303
	Myofascial Release	305
	Association for the Blind	309
40	A Cocoon of Love	311
41	Dancing on the Dragon	329
42	Solving the Mystery of Angels and Devils	335

Epilogue	347
Appendix	349
Brain Injury Association, Inc.	349
State Brain Injury Associations Addresses and	
Telephone Numbers	352
Federal Programs That Help TBI Persons and Their Families	362
MEDICAID (Title XIX)	362
States with MEDICAID Waivers	363
Social Security	366
MEDICARE	367
Private and Charitable Organizations	367
The TBI Act—Prevention and Study	368
Glasgow Coma Scale	370
Rancho Los Amigos Levels of Cognitive Functioning	371
Selective Reading List	373

Foreword

It is my pleasure to welcome the reader to this story of a most successful man. Nothing unusual here, since these books appear nearly every day—usually written by, or ghosted for, the great man himself. However, this book was not self-indulgently commissioned, nor was it the result of some convulsion of public interest following a contemporary salacious and usually comparatively trivial incident. No, the effort that went into this book was motivated by unconditional love.

To quote a former vice-presidential candidate, "Who am I and what am I doing here?" Well, unless you are an inveterate reader of the esoterica of the neuronal basis of epilepsy or are one of my psychological consults, you'll never have heard of me. Why then was I asked to write this foreword? Two reasons, I suspect. First and most pleasantly, I know the man who is the subject of this book, and secondly, I too was the victim of a senseless act of violence that changed my life forever, as was the book's subject, Nick Del Buono.

I first met Nick Del Buono's parents, Barbara and John, at a birthday party in February 1994. We were seated at the same table and seemed to hit it off immediately. Barbara was attractive and perhaps the most energetic woman I'd ever met. In a matter of only a few hours, she had managed to take photographs of nearly everything of importance at this rather large gathering, talking some, eating less, then buzzing off, only to return later to repeat the process several times. Her husband was a charming, dapper, intelligent attorney in my adopted home state of Connecticut. The sometimes three, more often two of us chatted the night away over varying political, social, even philosophical issues that interested us, no doubt boring our fellow revelers. We found our most common ground, however, over a very private issue that each of us hoped would eventually receive the more general awareness we felt it deserved. That issue was *senseless violent crime* and its catastrophic effect on its victims. In fact, their passion was so infectious that I felt compelled to relate something of my personal experience with it that evening—something I had trained myself not to indulge in since its occurrence some five and a half years earlier.

In June 1988, at the age of thirty-eight, I was run over by a car driven by one of our state's more solid citizens, suffering multiple injuries that dramatically altered what some might say was a promising, perhaps even bright career in biomedical research. A fairly common, though unfortunate accident? Hardly. After a lengthy police investigation, the driver was charged with second-degree assault. Further details of the event only prolong my misery in recalling the episode itself. Suffice it to say that the incident was unnecessary and senseless, and it dramatically and permanently altered my life, both personal and professional.

Physically, the resultant injuries left me with a largely dysfunctional master hand, severe ocular damage on my right side, and a neurologically rare though increasingly well-documented condition known as reflex sympathetic dystrophy (RSD). Cognitively, a closed-head injury produced a concussion with loss of consciousness, amnesia, narcolepsy, and severe short-term memory (STM) problems, coupled with a dysphasic-like inability to recall or reproduce words with facility. Panic attacks developed; the STM deficits made reading for comprehension impossible; the inability to use my right hand cut me off from all surgical and technical skills regularly utilized in my position as a senior research scientist at the Yale University School of Medicine and the U.S. Department of Veterans' Affairs Medical Center. RSD manifested itself in constant pain, initially only to my damaged right appendage; but with the passage of time, the condition became systemic, involving my lower back and legs as well. To control the pain, significant doses of opioid analgesics were medically necessary. The totality of these insults led to my disability retirement at the obscenely early age of thirty-nine.

With time, perseverance, and the dedicated help of my wife and a multitude of health-care professionals, recovery began...but at an agonizingly slow pace. It was nearly four years before my reading for comprehension attained minimally functional levels. Extensive physical therapy and multiple invasive medical procedures, including nearly thirty surgical interventions, did not prevent my master hand from becoming dystrophic, with all but my thumb and forefinger maintaining a severe and irreversible flexion contracture. Prolonged training has allowed the return of maximum function with minimal assets: like most successful patients with handicaps, I've learned to utilize the affected structure. But despite appearances, not everything is possible. The chronic pain continues to this day. With sensitive and enlightened care from pain-management specialists, however, together with an intensive self-devised and administered physical therapy program that engages the endogenous opiate system, "normal" functioning is again approachable. Low levels of opioid analgesia coupled with high doses of NSAID (ibuprofen) on a daily basis allow me to maintain a modest consulting practice and, with the help of my wife, Gail, to direct our privately endowed nonprofit organization. However, the window on my original career had closed, and so had the window we had planned for starting a family. Over the span of a few senseless seconds on June 3, 1988, in addition to my career and our family plans, my wife's professional life was transformed from that of an internationally recognized electron-microscopist valued for her expertise by numerous scientists at Yale to a care-giver with only one patient.

Barbara and John had also had their own experience with senseless violence. As it happens, and as you will read in greater, more moving detail in this book, their son, Nick, had been assaulted some seventeen years earlier by a fellow wielding a baseball bat. This guy was exceptionally good at what he was doing; their son received head injuries massive enough to make even seasoned emergency room professionals cringe.

This chance meeting in Washington, D.C., of victims of these senseless acts of violent crime led to my becoming involved in their son's case as a consultant. Amid all my quiet sorrows, amid unfulfilled dreams, amid my struggles to cope with the injustices inflicted on me and mine, came Nick Del Buono, my patient, my friend.

To know Nick Del Buono is to know "Phoenix Rising." Nick's injuries were more severe than mine, his losses greater, his future invisible, his strength Herculean, his courage heroic, his spirit indomitable. And Nick Del Buono has survived. He has done more than that...he has succeeded. Nick Del Buono was severely beaten about the head by a person whose concept of success was very different from his own. Nick Del Buono never boasts of the money he has made nor that he'll make next year, nor of the cachet of his new sports car, nor that he can drink the next guy under the table. He never brags about conquests he's made, how clever he was in closing that latest deal, how beautiful, intelligent, or successful his children are. Why? Because Nick Del Buono has no job, he doesn't play the market, he has no car, the conquests he's made wouldn't be interesting to the "power lunch" crowd, he's closed no deals, and sadly, he has no children.

But Nick Del Buono is an extremely successful man. He has beaten his beater, he is loved by all and hated by no man and he has created life. Money means nothing to him, nor does power; he has created life by enhancing beyond any reasonable expectations my life and the lives of all others who have known him. Does Nick Del Buono hate his oppressor? I doubt it. Nick has no time for such un-Christian nonsense. You see, Nick Del Buono was severely beaten about the head by a person whose concept of manhood is greatly different from his own. He is busy coping with the vagaries life has thrust upon him and focusing on his assigned mission: *to inspire*. No braggadocio, Nick Del Buono doesn't remind you, even subtly, of his accomplishments. He leads from strength of character. By dealing for more than twenty years with challenges that would have brought most of us to our knees, *he inspires.*

That he inspires is fact. *How* he inspires is what this book is about—that, and the story of a devoted mother whose drive to tell her son's story these past twenty years has been heroic. And of a family of one brother and six sisters, nieces and nephews, a strong and loving father, all of whom have come together as a family unit in a manner no novelist could ever have conjured. And the character required to engender such behavior from others has been, is, and will continue to be embodied in one Nick Del Buono.

Our lives are defined by our impact on others. Using this criterion, Nick Del Buono has made his parents, siblings, doctors, caregivers, and me better able to cope with the vagaries of our lives. I wrote earlier that Nick Del Buono was my friend. I pray that I am his.

And as you read this story of a life, of many lives, transformed by senseless violence, don't despair for Nick Del Buono. Nick Del Buono has been acknowledged a man, not an invalid. In fact, he may be the most successful man I know.

—Allen B. Chatt, Ph.D.
Executive Director & Consulting Psychologist
The Phoenix Fund for the Neurologically Challenged
Tallahassee, Florida, and Madison, Connecticut

P.S.: Oh, that birthday party! It was for former President of the United States Ronald Reagan, himself a victim of senseless physical violence in 1981 and now, sadly, a victim of senseless biological violence as well.

Dr. Allen B. Chatt

Before injuries forced his retirement in 1990, Dr. Chatt was a research associate professor of neurology at the Yale University School of Medicine in New Haven and a senior research psychologist at the Veterans' Administration Medical Center in West Haven, Connecticut, where he was engaged in biomedical research. He has also held faculty positions at The Florida State University in Tallahassee and The University of Texas Medical Branch in Galveston. He has contributed to more than fifty publications in professional journals and to three books on the basic brain mechanisms involved in both pain and epilepsy.

Throughout his career, he has received invitations to deliver guest lectures at the UCLA, University of Pennsylvania, Yale University, SUNY at Buffalo, and the University of Maryland Schools of Medicine, the Mt. Sinai and Upstate Medical Centers in New York City and Syracuse, respectively, and annual meetings of the American Academy of Neurology, the American Epilepsy Society and the Society for Neuroscience. In 1987, he was invited to be a visiting professor of neuroscience at Beijing Normal University in the Peoples Republic of China and has been asked to fill a similar position in the Institute of Physiology at Glasgow University in Scotland. His research has revealed insights into the neuronal circuitry involved in the onset, spread, and potential pharmacologic and surgical control of epilepsy, as well as an improved neurosurgical technique to control the devastating effect of the chronically painful clinical condition known as reflex sympathetic dystrophy.

Dr. Chatt has been elected to *American Men and Women in Science* (1989), *Who's Who in Science and Engineering* (1994), *Who's Who in the East* (1995), and most recently to the prestigious *Who's Who in America* (1997).

Currently, he is founder and executive director of The Phoenix Fund for the Neurologically Challenged, a privately endowed philanthropic organization committed to the support of neuroscience research, training, education, the promotion of several community-based outreach programs, and direct financial assistance to select individuals with special needs due to neurologic pathologies. Further, he is a consulting psychologist for the fund specializing in behavioral, referral, and case-management services for patients with disabling neurological disorders. He also sits on the advisory boards of several non-profit organizations.

Introduction

There are many reasons for writing this story, and I have tried to include all of them in the chapters of this book. The most important reason, though, is to tell the story of an extraordinary man, John Nicholas (Nick) Del Buono.

He was brutally brain-injured at the age of twenty-five in a YMCA weight-lifting room and was expected to die by the medical personnel who dealt with him. Even his mother and father made preparations for his funeral. None of us who became a part of his "new" life were prepared to meet the incredible spirit of a man who loved life too much to give it up.

Nick has matured from age twenty-five to a man of forty-five, and in these years he has taught all of us who have chosen to become a part of his life the meaning of courage. Despite being a traumatically brain-injured person, he has displayed the motivation to conquer every obstacle life has placed in front of him and the stamina to endure the work before him when it seemed impossible to do.

To become truly a man, one must be tested by adversity. Nick has gone through the fiercest battles a man can be required to fight and has met every test with courage and fortitude. His life is so inspiring I wanted to share his story with the world and to show everyone an example of a man who met life's most formidable challenges, overcoming some and dealing with those he could not conquer in a positive way. John Nicholas Del Buono is truly a man and must be acknowledged one.

But there were three other important reasons for writing this book. Once we were confronted with the terrible crime committed against our son, we slowly became aware that a three-headed dragon had reared its ugly heads in our lives. Those three heads were represented to us as the criminal and civil justice system, the Young Men's Christian Association (YMCA or Y), and the medical profession. All three heads of this dragon had to be fought simultaneously, and the fight consumed years of our lives. We will never be entirely rid of our dragon, but we have subdued it to where we can live with it.

Though the criminal justice system has changed in recent years to give victims the right to speak before a judge at a sentencing, there is still little "justice" to be had. Justice is often only a mirage, and victims new to the system are led to believe that punishment will fit the crime. But when they arrive at the courthouse, they find the system badly flawed to the point of meting out little or no punishment at all. As a result, we have become less civilized in our society because crime is not punished so that the penalty becomes a deterrent.

The civil court system is so slow in its handling of cases that injured persons are victimized again by delays that consume years before judgments can be made. Waiting for the relief that a decision may bring through this system becomes a torture. This can result in a new injury to the victims, but it may also become a weapon in the hands of the accused negligent persons. Some use it skillfully and without conscience.

Another reason for writing this book is to talk about the YMCA organization. It began as a Young Men's Christian Association and is now widely known as the Y. Its past affiliation with Christ and His teachings has little, if anything, to do with the present organization. This is a significant change that has taken place, and, in my opinion, this change is reflected in the way Y's are managed all over the world.

Further, I believe most people think, as I did, that the local Y's programs and standards are directed and guided by the national organization. The trademarks YMCA and Y lead the public to think this is true. It is not.

Nick was injured as a result of joining one of the YMCA's programs for weight lifting. I believe Nick's injuries were the result of his joining a YMCA and lifting weights in one of its programs where, in my opinion, there was no responsible person in charge, and he did not know it. I want his story to be told so that parents who send their children to such programs, and adults who participate in them, will look closely at who is running them. Not all YMCA programs are bad, but don't assume that because it is in the Y it will be properly run.

One of the crucial reasons for writing this book is to alert the public to the unavailability of medical treatments to many brain-injury victims and their families. The medical system for handling the immediate trauma in major hospitals has improved since Nick was injured. Better equipment and more thoroughly trained medical personnel now exist in this setting. However, it is still the "luck of the draw" as to whether a brain-injured patient will be able to access one of these trauma centers in the first crucial hours of the injury.

Rehabilitation therapies are now at least available. When Nick was injured, there were none. He has personally been a catalyst in helping develop some of these programs, which now benefit countless others who have had their lives changed dramatically in an instant. This is another way Nick's life has been used for good.

I cannot stress too strongly the *need* for neuropsychological testing of anyone who has been a victim of brain injury. Cognitive testing can help determine abilities and also lack of them. Without this help, the road map for future life may be badly routed. Those dealing with the brain-injured person need this information as much as the victim does. They need it because without it they may incorrectly evaluate the person they are trying to help. Behavioral problems often result in such persons being placed in mental hospitals or prisons because no one understood or knew how to deal with the injured victim. Neuropsychological testing is one of the most-needed therapies, but it is one that is often ignored.

Brain injury is for life. Few studies exist on what happens years after the brain injury occurs. Nick's life is positive proof that improvements can occur many years after the injury was sustained. For this to happen, others must devote their lives to help rehabilitate the injured person.

For those brain-injured persons who are living their lives out in a long-term situation, very little has changed since Nick was injured. Therapies are often not available because it is believed that little progress can occur. Persons left with severe deficits have a very hard time trying to find a place to live. Some group homes exist for such people, but they are far too few. Many times families cannot afford the cost that such places demand, and insurance does not cover their expense. Therefore, the only resource they have is to beg for help from society for their loved ones through government programs. Parents are left wondering what will happen to their injured sons and daughters once they die.

The Brain Injury Association, Inc. (formerly known as the National Head Injury Foundation), and the brain injury associations in almost every state advocate for changes that will enable traumatic brain-injury persons to receive better treatment. As a result, Congress passed the TBI Act in July 1996, and fourteen states have been approved for a Medicaid waiver that will help many TBI persons (see Appendix). None of these organizations existed when Nick was injured. My husband, John, and I helped start the one in Connecticut.

Anyone wishing information about brain injury can receive it by calling the Brain Injury Association in Alexandria, Virginia, or one of the state associations. A list of these is included in the appendix of this book.

Nick's story is an important lesson to all of us because brain injury can happen to anyone at any time, and it occurs in an instant. From that moment on, life changes forever. If it happens in your family, may you meet a new person in your life who displays the love, the courage, the determination, and the will to live that I have met in my beloved son. I wouldn't have missed knowing him for anything in the world.

I hope that what Nick and we have learned together will be of help to other traumatically brain-injured persons, their families, their friends, and especially the medical personnel they come in contact with.

ACKNOWLEDGED
A MAN

1
The Fateful Afternoon of June 25, 1977

The hands of our kitchen clock were moving from 3:30 PM to 4:00 as my husband, John, and I sat on the deck in our back yard relishing a rare Saturday afternoon alone in our home. Only three of our eight children were still living with us, and they were out enjoying activities of their own. The insistent ring of the telephone bell lured me from the deck into the house.

A female voice casually inquired, "Is this Mrs. Del Buono?" "Yes," I replied.

"Do you have a son named John?"

"I have a son John Nicholas. We call him Nick."

"Does he go to the YMCA?"

"Yes," I answered, a bit put out.

Her tone was still calm, but mine was becoming tense.

"This is the emergency room at St. Mary's Hospital. Your son was in a fight at the YMCA, and we need you to come down and sign some papers."

"I'll be right down."

I told John about the call, and we prepared to leave. Nothing in the woman's voice indicated that this was anything other than a minor incident. Neither of us was alarmed or felt a sense of urgency, but we were a bit annoyed at having our quiet time at home interrupted.

Nick was our second child and oldest son. He was twenty-five, a former Air Force sergeant who had recently returned from California to work with us on a book-publishing venture. This afternoon, June 25, 1977, he had gone to the YMCA to do his weight-lifting routine. Now that date is forever burned in our memories. Future time and events in our lives will always be measured by it.

We drove straight to the hospital, and I got out at the emergency room entrance while John parked the car. Upon entering, I told the nurse who I was and that I had been called to come down. She arose immediately, which surprised me, and led me to a hallway where a police officer, Anthony Massaro, was waiting for me. I still was very calm and totally unprepared for what I was about to hear.

Officer Massaro directed me to one of the empty examining rooms and asked me to sit down in the only chair in the room. Fear started to surge through my body. Once I was seated, he told me bluntly, "Your son has been hit in the head with a baseball bat." The words stunned me. Silently, I wondered, "A baseball bat? Why would anyone hit him in the head with a baseball bat? At the YMCA?" Officer Massaro interrupted my thoughts.

"Do you know someone by the name of Joseph Tramontano?" he asked.

"No, I never heard of him."

At that moment, John was escorted into the room by a nurse. He shook hands with Officer Massaro, but when he looked at me he knew something serious had happened. "What's the matter?" he asked. The story was repeated for him. If possible, he was more shocked than I had been. Unnerving panic attacked us both. I was breathless and gasping for air.

"Why?" The thought kept racing through my mind. John asked to see Nick, but Officer Massaro detained us by asking questions and giving us more details. He told us they were trying to find the man who had assaulted our son.

"Find him?" we asked. "Did he escape from the YMCA?"

"Yes," Officer Massaro answered.

While we were still trying to understand his answer, a nurse came

The Fateful Afternoon of June 25, 1977

to usher us into another room where there were a desk and chairs. Another nurse entered carrying a clipboard. She made some remarks about a paper that had to be signed, handed the clipboard to John, and asked him to put his signature on a specific line on the page.

"When can we see Nick?" John asked, ignoring the clipboard.

"The doctor is with him; you can see him soon."

She insisted that the paper she thrust in front of him had to be signed. John, an attorney, started to look it over (as if he were capable of reading it at that moment).

"What's my signature for?" he asked her.

"It's authorization for treatment and financial responsibility for the bill."

"I don't want to sign authorization for treatment until I have been advised what treatment will be given. We need to see our son and talk to a doctor."

"Are you refusing to sign the paper?" she asked, a touch of impatience in her voice.

"I want to see our son and talk to a doctor," John said forcefully.

She took the clipboard from him and briskly left the room.

In a few minutes, a wiry, middle-aged man with short, thinning, ash-blond hair came in the room. He was dressed in white tennis shorts, a polo shirt, and tennis shoes, and he carried the clipboard, but his appearance suggested it should have been a tennis racket. He sat on the edge of the desk positioned directly in front of us, obviously irritated, but feigning calmness as he peered down at John.

"What's the matter? Why are you doing this?" he asked.

"We want to see our son and be advised as to what treatment will be given before I sign the paper," John said.

"Do you know who I am?"

"Yes, I know who you are. You're Dr. Robert Sturman. I've had you on the witness stand."

"Then you know I am a neurosurgeon."

"Yes, I know. When can we see our son?"

The doctor's arrogant attitude diverted my attention from the shock and numbness I had been feeling. I became angry over the way the doctor spoke to John, and I'm sure it showed as I glowered at him. However, I decided to keep quiet. John had the situation under control.

"What is the name of your family physician?" Dr. Sturman asked.

"We don't have one. We've always used a pediatrician, Dr. Thomas Monagan, for our children," John said.

But Dr. Sturman was not satisfied and kept trying to get the name of a family physician from him. Then he stated bluntly, "I cannot treat your son until you sign this authorization."

Clearly irritated, John put his signature on the form. "Can we see our son now?"

Dr. Sturman's tone changed dramatically. "I'll advise you of what treatment will be given when I know what treatment is appropriate," he promised in a friendly voice. He left the room with the clipboard and another assurance that we could see Nick soon.

After what seemed like an interminable length of time, Dr. Sturman returned and escorted us into a large room with white cabinets on the wall and a couple of examining tables on wheels in the center of the room. A nurse was busying herself at the counter with her back turned to us so as to avoid our gaze.

Nick was lying on one of the tables, propped up in a semi-sitting position with several pillows under his head. The white sheets and pillow cases were spotted with red blood, which seemed to leap out at me from the white background.

He was bleeding from the mouth and nose. His entire face was so disfigured he was hardly recognizable. When I saw him I felt like someone had punched me in the stomach. I wanted to lie down on the other table, curl up in a ball, and scream. Being told that Nick had been hit in the head with a baseball bat was hard enough, but seeing his bruised and swollen face made me feel like vomiting. "Nick, Dad and I are here," I said at his bedside. I spoke soothingly to him because he couldn't see through his swollen eyes. He tried to rise up on the table to a full sitting position, and the nurse approached him as more blood gushed from his nose and down his face.

"Aspirin, aspirin," he pleaded.

Dr. Sturman came to me and said, "Why don't you go home?"

The Fateful Afternoon of June 25, 1977

His words infuriated me. All the anger I felt over Nick's horrible condition and everything I had suppressed in the other room spewed out.

"Go home and do what, doctor?"

"Well, if you want to stay here and crucify yourselves, go ahead."

"Well, if you don't mind, doctor, I think I'll stay here and 'crucify' myself for at least five minutes."

The nurse heard it all. She turned her head in embarrassment as the doctor backed away. I held Nick's hand, and soon Dr. Sturman came and put his arm around me.

"I'm sorry," he said.

Tears were rolling down my cheeks as I asked, "What would you do if it were your son?"

"I have a son the same age, and I would do just what you are doing."

We were told that they could not give Nick anything for the pain because it might mask his injuries. Nevertheless, he kept crying out. He tried to sit up, but blood kept gushing from his mouth and nose.

I spoke to him, trying to calm him, but I sobbed as I asked, "Do you know the person who did this to you?"

"Joey—Joey Tram. He hit me four or five times with a bat," he stammered. "Surgeon, surgeon," he begged, in a loud voice.

Dr. Sturman came to the table and tried to calm him.

"What are my chances?" Nick asked.

"You're going to be all right, son," Dr. Sturman reassured him.

Nick lapsed into something like sleep. We stayed, trying to comfort him, but unable to really comprehend what had happened: we were too numb with shock. At no time while we were with Nick in the emergency room was he either medicated or monitored with any machines. He just lay on the table suffering terrible pain, and we suffered with him.

About a half hour later, Dr. Sturman returned and reported that Nick had sustained two fractures of the skull, one on each side of the head. He had a fracture of the jaw, and there were lacerations on his forehead and on the back of his head. The doctor said he was going to admit him to the intensive care unit (ICU). John and I were horrified by the enormity of what he told us.

Acknowledged a Man

The nurse quickly called me to her work station and handed me a plastic bag. In it were Nick's clothing and shoes, with blood all over them, and his wallet with his ID in it. She was preparing to take him to the ICU.

We were told that we could wait or go home and they would call us if there was any change. We certainly could not leave, so we waited. About 5 o'clock, there was a call for us on the intercom from a Dr. O'Donnell. We tried to reach him but were told he had left the hospital.

As we sat on a bench in the hall waiting for Nick to go to ICU, we remembered our children; they would be wondering where we were. One of us had to make a telephone call. I went to the phone and called home. Our seventeen-year-old daughter, Sally, answered. She suffered the same shock we had endured and asked the ever-present question, "Why?"

"Sally, tell Debbie and Cathy and go to Joe's and let him know what's happened," I told her. Our son Joe was married and lived a few miles from us. "I'll call again as soon as I know more," I promised.

It was nearly 5:30 when I returned to John, and we just sat in silence for a while. "How could a thing like this happen in a YMCA?" I thought to myself. Then I said out loud, "Wasn't there anybody in the YMCA to stop this? Nick said he had been hit four or five times."

As I said this, Officer Massaro came to us and said he was still investigating the case. He explained that he had just come from the police station, where he had talked with a fellow from the YMCA by the name of Paul Ford who was in charge of the building that day. Officer Massaro remarked that while he was talking with Mr. Ford, Tramontano entered the room. Officer Massaro was amazed at how frightened Mr. Ford was of Tramontano, even in the station house with all the police around. Mr. Ford told Officer Massaro that Tramontano had been "acting up for a few days." We had no idea what that meant, but it disturbed us very much.

The waiting seemed to go on forever. The only thing we could talk about was why this had happened and the fact that a bat had been used that had caused fractures on both sides of Nick's skull and a broken

The Fateful Afternoon of June 25, 1977

jaw. This had to mean serious injury, all to the head. Would he be brain damaged? Endless questions flooded our minds. We knew the situation with Nick was critical, but at least no one had mentioned dying. We could only hope for the best. About 6 o'clock Nick was taken to the ICU.

We followed the nurse who took Nick upstairs and were told to wait again, this time in the ICU waiting room. We heard the "Code 3" call (emergency status) and asked a nurse if it was for our son. "No," she said. But it was, because another nurse told us so later. We wondered where Dr. Sturman was. We hadn't seen him for a long time. About 7:00 he finally came into the waiting room where we were seated, along with several other people. He was dressed in baggy green operating-room clothes and had a green cotton cap on his head. He again wore tennis shoes, but I couldn't help noticing that this time they had blood on them.

His words were directed to us, but everyone in the room heard him say, "We're going to operate on your son, relieve the pressure on the brain. He's gone into a coma. You have to understand he may not come out of this alive." The words were spoken quickly and were the ones we had dreaded to hear.

"Is there any alternative?" John asked.

"If we don't operate, he'll certainly die."

"Then operate."

(This delayed operation was the beginning of a series of brain injuries that Nick would suffer, one after another, as the clotting inside the sac surrounding the brain swelled.)

The doctor left, and the room resounded with silence. No one would say a word as the other people in the room diverted their attention away from us. John and I looked at one another in horror. Our helplessness was overwhelming. I hated being in this room with these people who could see our grief and observe our most intimate emotions. I wanted to be alone with John and have him hold me while I cried.

It seemed impossible that earlier in the day, we had enjoyed the peace and quiet of our home. Now that atmosphere was shattered, and it seemed like it had happened a million years ago. I felt as though it would never return.

We realized we had to let our whole family know the gravity of Nick's condition. His older sister, Mary, was in New York visiting her in-laws. June 25 was her husband Tom's birthday, and they had gone to his parents' home in Queens to celebrate and attend the wedding of a friend.

Our family had been to Mary's home for a party the night before. Nick had attended, looking very handsome. It was Friday night, and he was going out after he left the birthday party. He said goodbye to all of us. It was the last time we saw him before the brain injury changed him forever. Mary had to be called to come home. Nick's sister Joan was in Colorado, and another sister, Susan, was in California. They would want to come home too.

When Joe and our three daughters were told that Nick might die, they came to the hospital immediately. About 9:30 PM, Dr. Sturman appeared and informed us that Nick had survived the operation, but cautioned that his condition was still critical and he was still in a coma. We asked to see Nick and were given permission to go in for a few minutes, one at a time.

I went to his room first. His head had been shaved, and it was bandaged except for his face. The white bandages emphasized the bruises of every color—purple, yellow, blue, green—covering his swollen face. He was not recognizable as the son I loved. His eyes were swollen shut; wires, tubes, and machines were attached to him everywhere. His whole body was in constant spasms. These spasms would start at the upper part of his torso and work their way down to his feet, then begin all over again in a rhythmic fashion. (These were Jacksonian seizures, which show a tendency to "march" up and down the body.) His hands were clenched in fists, and he had an ugly grimace on his face. He was a frightening sight.

I was apprehensive about the rest of the family seeing him, especially his three youngest sisters. Yet how could I ask them not to come when I could not stay away?

Nick's father, brother, and three sisters went in one by one and came back devastated, crying with helplessness and anger. We felt alone in our grief, though we were in the midst of others in the ICU

The Fateful Afternoon of June 25, 1977

waiting room. Only the numbness of shock kept us from falling apart emotionally.

We waited for hours and hoped that Nick would come out of the coma that night, that we would be there and he would wake up and say something to us. We took turns returning to his room. As the evening wore on, though, it became clearer and clearer that it was not to be. Our children left first, and by 11:30 John and I decided to leave too.

When we arrived home, our house seemed barren and cold. The peaceful atmosphere we had enjoyed in the afternoon was completely gone. It was as if we were in someone else's home, and we hardly knew how to act or what to do.

Sally, Debbie, and Cathy couldn't sleep, so we talked and tried to comfort and console them. Debbie was particularly overwhelmed and couldn't stop weeping. We finally persuaded them to try to get some sleep so we could be with Nick the next day.

About 1:00 AM, John and I lay down in our bed, but sleep wouldn't come. Our bodies were rigid, our minds numb, no longer able to reason. Our bleary eyes remained wide open. Our feelings were so intense that we couldn't even share them with each other. All we could do was hold hands.

Soon John got up, dressed, and said, "I have to go back to the hospital."

2

Life Is in the Hands of God

John could cope with his rage easier alongside Nick's hospital bed than at home. Also, he was engulfed in fear because it was obvious that Nick's life was in grave danger.

A nurse offered John a reclining chair in the hallway outside Nick's room, but he refused it, preferring to stay in the room holding Nick's hand. John was terrified of losing him.

As he stood beside Nick's bed, Nick's breathing became very difficult. His chest heaved up and down as he tried to get air into his lungs, but he wasn't succeeding. John knew Nick had to get help; he could not go on gasping for breath. (He didn't know Nick was suffering from hypoxia, a partial deprivation of oxygen that could signify another injury.)

A young, diminutive black-haired nurse stood nearby watching the whole scene, her eyes looking straight into John's. A respirator machine was close to Nick's bed, but she didn't move to put him on it. John called her attention to Nick's labored breathing, alarmed that his next breath would be his last. He asked her to hook him up to the respirator, but she only looked at John quizzically. More than a moment passed without a word being said between them, and then she brought the life-sustaining machine to Nick. As it pumped air into his lungs, Nick's breathing became normal.

Had John not been in Nick's room at that moment and requested the respirator to sustain his life, he surely would have died. It was our impression that Dr. Sturman had left instructions with the staff that there was to be no further "Code 3" for Nick: no heroic measures were to be taken to save his life.

The early morning hours wore on, and there was neither sleep for me at home nor any for John at the hospital. About 5:00 AM Mary called from New York. She was near hysteria and desperate to get home. I cautioned her husband to please drive carefully. About 6:00 AM, I phoned the airport and made arrangements for Susan and her one-month-old baby, Jason, to board a plane in California that would stop over in Colorado. Joan could then board the same plane and they could fly home together.

John returned home from the hospital, and we attended the 10 o'clock Sunday Mass at our parish church. Memories of Nick flooded through my mind: his First Holy Communion, his Confirmation, his graduation from grammar school. All these had been made in this church.

First Holy Communion.

I remembered a scene when Nick made his First Communion. There were black-and-white rectangular tiles on the floor designed in an angular pattern, and I remembered seven-year-old Nick in procession coming down the aisle dressed in navy blue trousers, white shirt, and white tie, head down, hands folded in prayer, walking the pattern of those tiles, which made him step with his toes turned outward like a duck. When I saw him doing this, I couldn't help smiling, but the memory of this scene caused me to start crying uncontrollably. People began to stare, so I left the church.

The headline of an article on the front page of the Sunday edition of the *Waterbury Republican American* newspaper read: "Man hit with bat at city Y critical."

The story reported:

An argument in the YMCA weight room Saturday afternoon left a Waterbury man in critical condition, after reportedly being beaten on the head with a baseball bat, and an Ansonia man arrested and held under $50,000 bond....The injured man was identified as John Del Buono.

The relatively high bond was placed on [Joseph] Tramontano pending the outcome of Del Buono's surgery....The two men reportedly had been arguing for about 45 minutes before the baseball bat was used. Police did not know exactly what the argument concerned.

A spokesman said the YMCA's weight room was sealed off, also pending the outcome of surgery....A hospital spokesman said Del Buono suffered head injuries and multiple bruises. Police interviewed several witnesses in headquarters late Saturday afternoon and reportedly will interview more witnesses today.

This seemed so unreal to us. How could such a situation last forty-five minutes without someone stopping it? Who was this Tramontano fellow? What was the argument about? Questions, questions, questions, but no answers. We were so engrossed in Nick's medical condition that we knew nothing of what the police had learned concerning this horrible tragedy, and they did not contact us.

In the early afternoon, I went to the hospital to be with Nick. The ICU was a very large room that had several cubicles with a patient in each one. Nick's was the nearest to the entrance door of the room, so other families coming to see their loved ones had to pass by his bed. He looked so monstrous that he could not help being a grotesque curiosity. People stared at him in disbelief and embarrassment and then hurried past him. I wanted to take Nick in my arms, to shield him from their shocked attention, but I could only gasp for breath to allay my tension and anxiety. I turned my gaze against the wall so as not to see anyone nor let them see me.

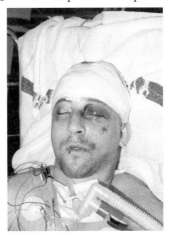

Nick in ICU—five days after the assault. Most of the multi-colored bruises have faded.

The nurses in ICU were mostly young women about Nick's age. Some had gone to school with my children. They were very attentive to each machine guarding Nick's vital signs. The steady beep at every heartbeat was reassuring until the rhythm speeded up or slowed down. Any change would bring a nurse quickly to his bedside. Liquid feedings poured into his veins through tubes in his arm; a respirator helped him breathe; a suctioning machine drew a ghastly looking greenish liquid from his throat. Though it appeared his life was slipping away, it was actually being renewed as he lay in a deep coma. The spasms, or seizures, were incessant, and that grimace persisted on the ugly mask that had become his face.

We went home earlier the second evening, about 10 o'clock. We were utterly exhausted from lack of sleep and shock. Around midnight, our rest was interrupted by a phone call from Dr. Sturman. He was inquiring whether we would allow Nick's kidneys to be donated to another patient for a transplant operation! He explained that there was a twenty-six-year-old man who desperately needed one.

"Doctor, you're hitting me like a Mack truck. Do we have to make the decision immediately?" John asked.

"No," Dr. Sturman answered.

I could see John sinking in the chair, so I took the phone from him and explained, "John is afraid Nick is going to die."

"Well, I'm afraid he won't die, and if he lives, he'll be like an infant in a crib; a grown man, but just like a baby in a crib." There was no way my emotions could handle what Dr. Sturman was saying. Unable to make a response, I dropped the receiver in its cradle.

John and I were so upset we couldn't sleep, so we dressed and went to the hospital. We had to see Nick. He appeared to us to be no better, but no worse. The spasms were continual. Dr. Sturman's question about Nick's kidneys would have to remain unanswered.

The days of the first week that followed Nick's injuries were spent in handling crisis after crisis: medical ones for Nick and emotional ones for all of us. Our daughters had returned from New York, Colorado, and California. My family in Oklahoma, Texas, and New Mexico had been called. My brother, Don, and sister, Mary, flew to Connecticut from Oklahoma to be with us. John's family came by our house for visits.

Life Is in the Hands of God

The newspaper carried daily accounts of Nick's condition, so friends and relatives called and dropped by the house with gifts of food and flowers and sympathetic understanding. I slept very little. I would wake up in a cold sweat and stare into the darkness for hours. The mornings could not come too soon for me.

On one such morning, I arose early; my brother was already up. Don and I decided to go out for breakfast. It had been a long time since we had an opportunity to talk alone. Don spoke of times when he had been close to death himself, and of his faith in Jesus. He gave me a cross from his pocket for Nick and a prayer he had composed on the airplane bringing him to Connecticut.

I talked about Nick when he was a child and of his beautiful, simple faith in God. I told Don that Nick believed his prayers would be answered as much as he trusted that supper would be on the table at night. When he wanted something, he simply asked God for it and never doubted that he would get it.

Nick with the fish he caught for Joe's birthday.

I remembered the occasion when Nick was about ten years old and it was his brother Joe's birthday. Nick wanted to give Joe a live fish that he caught himself. He came home from school and announced that he was going to a brook nearby to catch his brother a fish. The nuns had taught him to pray for the souls in purgatory; when those souls were in heaven, they would remember the ones who had prayed for them. He was now going to cash in on all of those prayers: he wanted a fish for his brother, and the souls from purgatory would help him get it.

Within the hour he came screaming through the park behind our house carrying a live fish. He had really caught one! We put it in the bathtub, and the birthday party ended up in our bathroom while the children watched the fish swim in the water. The next morning, his father, his brother, and he took the fish to the brook and threw it back in. They couldn't bear to kill it.

Don loved the story and laughed. I remembered another occasion when I took Nick with me to buy a present for his sister, Mary, to celebrate her First Holy Communion. We went into a store where there was row upon row of statues of saints. I was looking for one that would be appropriate for Mary and asked six-year-old Nick to help me pick one out. He spied a small statue of Our Blessed Mother Mary dressed in blue with her arms outstretched; he had to have that one for himself. I insisted that his turn would come next year, but it did no good. He would not leave the store without the statue. I bought it and have always been glad that I did. It remained in his room all the time he was growing up.

On one of the occasions when he came home on leave from the Air Force, he walked into his room and grabbed the statue and said, "Here you are. I promise I will never leave you again." Then twenty years old, Nick took the statue with him when he left our home to return to George Air Force Base in California.

Nick's kidneys became the subject of much conversation during the first week he was in the hospital. The doctors and nurses continually tried to prepare us for Nick's death and made it seem as though donating his kidneys would be the humanitarian thing to do. Their approach was subtle, yet the question bothered us enormously. We talked about it, considered it, but we couldn't help asking, "What would Nick want?"

I remembered having gone with him to the Motor Vehicle Department to renew his Connecticut driver's license when twenty-five-year-old Nick came home from California only six months prior to his injury. We had talked about organ donation, and Nick had refused to put an "X" in the box on his driver's license for that purpose. He always wanted to have control of his own life. I told John about this episode.

We had a dear friend who was a priest in Oklahoma. Reverend Kenneth Fulton had baptized Nick when he was an infant, so I felt that I could talk with him heart-to-heart about the matter. Father Fulton was appalled when I told him about Nick, but his counsel was that it certainly would be morally correct for us to donate his kidneys to be used for a transplant. Nevertheless, the decision to do so should be strictly ours.

Several days into the first week after Nick was injured, Dr. Sturman brought the subject up again. John explained to the doctor that there were three aspects of the matter that greatly bothered him. One was that if he authorized him to do this, Joseph Tramontano could use the decision as a defense to a murder charge. Another was that in the event of a civil lawsuit, a similar argument could be used in the assessment of damages. But it was the final aspect that really gave John the most trouble. The question haunted him: "How will I know when Nick is really dead if I do this?"

John knew that Nick would have to be declared "brain dead." A Massachusetts case had held this reasoning to be legal. Dr. Sturman explained it to John.

"I'll look at your son's brain wave pattern on an EEG and determine whether or not he is 'brain dead.'"

"But how will I know Nick is dead?" John asked.

"I'll tell you," Dr. Sturman replied.

"That's not quite good enough," John quickly responded.

I frequently stayed at the hospital very late at night to be with Nick. The nurses arranged for a recliner chair to be put by Nick's bedside so that I could hold his hand and still be sitting down. One evening a nurse came to me and suggested that I go with her into the nurses' room for a cup of coffee. Two other nurses were already in the room having their coffee break. All three nurses engaged me in conversation about Nick. Their approach was to make me aware that he was going to die and that it would be a wonderful gesture if his kidneys could be used for some young person who badly needed them. They related to me the torturous life of living on the dialysis machine. They explained that they knew a young man who needed a transplant and what it would mean to him.

I listened, registering nothing but the fact that Nick's death was imminent. That was all their conversation meant to me. I couldn't wait to get back into Nick's room and hold his hand.

When John told me of his talk with Dr. Sturman and explained to me that Nick's heart would still be beating if an operation to take his kidneys was performed, I resolved to oppose the procedure, euphemistically called "harvesting." It was the first time I had been told this, and it made the decision easy for me. Thereafter, I found the entire transplant concept repugnant to think about.

John felt the same way, but he did not want to tell the doctor of our decision at this time. Justified or not, John and I felt that if we were to agree to the kidney transplant, it would affect decisions regarding Nick's medical treatment.

We agreed that if the topic were ever mentioned again, we would tell the doctor firmly that he had only one responsibility, one patient, our son. We did not want even the hint, in our minds, of divided loyalties between recipient and potential donor. We wanted our son to be the doctor's only concern, doing everything in his power to save his life.

We believed that our son's life was in the hands of God and that the doctor was not a god.

3
Family

The summer of 1977 should have been the beginning of a season of fun and relaxation for our family. However, it turned into a nightmare of unending crises. The catastrophe visited on Nick was too much for any of us to handle, but it was particularly hard on our three youngest daughters, Sally, Debbie, and Cathy.

These teenage girls were having their high school years scarred badly by this tragedy. In addition, they lived at home and were more keenly aware of what John and I were going through than some of their siblings. This affected them almost as much as what happened to Nick.

Nick was the one who had been injured, but our family was hurting too. We were anxious, often in tears, and feeling helpless. We also felt rage toward Joseph Tramontano and feared that Nick would die. Our world had been turned upside down without warning. Our family floundered under the enormity of what had happened to us.

The trauma was especially rough on fifteen-year-old Deborah. She was very close to her injured brother. The ten years that separated them were bridged by their kindred spirits. Both were sensitive, artistic, charming people with outgoing, vulnerable personalities. They shared dreams and made plans for the time when Debbie would finish high school. They thought about going on the road together with their own "act." Debbie was taking dancing lessons and was quite good, so her "dreams" were firmly grounded. She was a very attractive, dark-haired, dark-eyed beauty. Nick had been studying cinematography in college, so he was headed toward the "show business" world too. When Nick came home in 1976, he took a personal interest in all that Debbie did. They attended movies, plays, concerts, and dances together throughout that winter and spring.

When Nick was beaten so viciously, Debbie's ability to cope was tested to the limit. Every day she looked at Nick in a coma in the hospital, his body bruised beyond recognition. Then she would go to school and try to function in the world of high school teenagers. Though Sally and Cathy faced the same circumstances, they did not have the same intense relationship with their brother that Debbie did.

Mary and Nick licking the cake bowl and becoming friends for life.

Sally was seventeen, a junior in high school. She was a quiet person with a demure personality that was very appealing. She had long brown hair and an elegant way of wearing clothes, and was always smart in school without working too hard to get good grades. She and Nick were opposites, though, and their personalities often caused them to disagree. Therefore, when Nick was assaulted, Sally suffered all the pangs of guilt one might expect.

Cathy, our youngest child, was fourteen, a freshman in high school. She was a darling child, the apple of her father's eye. She had just graduated from grammar school the year before. She was a very attractive girl with long, blond, naturally curly hair. Her cheerful personality shrugged off any unhappiness.

How does a fourteen-year-old girl react to seeing her brother beaten and bruised and lying in an intensive care unit? For Cathy, the trauma was too much to handle. She withdrew from the situation nearly to the point of denial. I know she felt neglected during this period and, of course, she was.

Our oldest daughter, Mary, was twenty-six, just a year older than Nick. She was an attractive blonde with outstandingly good facial features and beautiful greenish-brown eyes. She was married and had two children, Peter, four; and Amy, two. She had always been very close to her brother Nick. They shared many happy memories of walking home together from grammar school, double-dating through high school, and always staying in touch with one another when he went away.

They were working together on a joint business venture when Nick was injured. They spent time with each other every day. They had shared a lifetime of personal experiences, and Mary was thoroughly shattered when her brother was so brutally beaten.

To her husband Tom's credit, he understood what she was going through. He readily accepted a new reality of coming home from work and finding dinner on the table and Mary at the door ready to go to the hospital. It made a real father out of him as he supervised the children through feeding, bathing, and bedtime, while Mary visited her brother. This pressure on their marriage seemed to draw them closer, though I know they had many problems dealing with all the trauma they were experiencing.

Nick—Two years old.

Our daughter Joan was twenty-four, a year younger than Nick. She too had shared his younger years in a very special way. She had followed him through the trails of the park behind our house and reenacted all the battles of World War II with him, which he loved to do. She could climb trees every bit as well as he could, and she was always his sidekick in everything he did, when he would let her. She was diminutive in size but not in personality. Her popularity in high school was due, in part, to her outstanding ability to make friends and to be one in return.

Joan left Connecticut to attend the University of Colorado. She had graduated at the time Nick was injured and was teaching school. She flew home to be with Nick, but could remain only a week. Her burden was in trying to deal with her feelings long distance.

Nick's brother, Joseph, was twenty-three. He was a tall, handsome, all-American young man. His common sense was his trademark, and he loved Nick though they were different in talent and temperament. Joe and Nick shared a bedroom through all their childhood. They got along very well, seldom ever fighting. When Nick was injured Joe was married and had a two-year-old daughter, Kristen. Nick admired and envied Joe tremendously for his beautiful child.

Nick's Graduation.

Nick had a very special reverence for life and was in awe of women who were pregnant. When Mary was carrying Peter, he used to hold her stomach to feel the baby kicking and enjoyed the miracle taking place within her. When Peter was born, Nick literally danced with joy at the news of his birth. He felt the same way when Amy and Kristen were born.

Our daughter Susan was nineteen. She was tall and thin with naturally curly ash-blonde hair. She loved the outdoors and animals. She took horseback riding lessons and was very good at it. Our dog, Chipper, followed her everywhere. When she finished high school, she set out to fulfill a dream of working outside with animals. She went to Colorado to be with her sister and got a job working with horses by taking people on trail rides through the Garden of the Gods. Later she went to California to be with her best friend in high school and to be near the man with whom she had fallen in love. They had a son, Jason, just one month before Nick was injured.

Susan returned from California with her newborn son. She was always a joyful child. Now, her happiness was shattered as a result of the assault on her brother's life. She felt it deeply, though her own family responsibilities consumed most of her time. We were all coping with the catastrophe in our own ways. Sally came home from the shopping

Family

mall outraged because her friends had pointed Tramontano out to her as he blithely walked along the promenade, clearly unconcerned about the wrong he had done to Nick. Many times, Sally and Cathy were bombarded with information from their high school friends about Tramontano, none of it good.

John had very special problems at this time too. In addition to trying to save his law practice from ruin as a result of spending so much time with Nick, he was bombarded with the problem of paying enormous medical bills. John had signed papers in the emergency room accepting responsibility for these bills, but it quickly became apparent that they were going to amount to staggering sums of money which he was totally incapable of paying.

He investigated the details about the Title XIX Medicaid program and found that Nick would be eligible for it if he had less than $600 in assets. I had been typing Nick's checks for him and knew that there was only $200 in his account. He didn't own a car or real property, so John decided to see if he would qualify for the program. His disappointment came when he discovered it would take months to process the application, and he could only hope that the hospital would wait for this to be decided before pressing him for payment of the bills.

Nick in the Air Force.

Shortly after Nick was injured, John was at the Superior Court when a representative of the Veterans Administration (VA) was there also. Though Nick's disability was not service-oriented, John decided to talk to him about Nick's case. He discovered that Nick would have rights to a pension if he was not at fault for the injury and had no other income.

Payments on the pension would be retroactive to the date of application, so it was necessary to find Nick's papers regarding his discharge and service record. When I found a file folder with "Jesus Is My Friend" scrawled across it in big letters, I collapsed on the floor and cried. Inside were all his papers pertaining to his military service. The VA accepted his application pending the outcome of the criminal case. If it was determined that Nick was not at fault, he would be eligible for the pension.

Nick had worked since high school days, so there might be some rights under Social Security. I filed an application to see if he would be entitled to these benefits too. After checking his records, the Social Security office notified me that Nick had not worked enough quarters to be eligible for disability under this program.

There was no quick financial relief in sight. We would have to wait and see. John and I were spending almost all our time, money, and energies trying to help our son. It would eventually put us in great debt.

Looking back on this period of our family life, it does not seem possible that human endurance could stand the strains under which we were functioning. Yet there is a power that comes to us when we need it most. John and I knew in our hearts that God was watching over our family and listening to all of our prayers for help.

4

A Heroic Battle to Live

The first week in the ICU was a twenty-four-hour-a-day crisis. Nick was in a desperate battle for his life. No one on the medical staff expected him to live, and his condition remained critical. Yet Nick refused to die. The persistence of the ugly facial grimace and the pattern of the rhythmic spasms in his body made me wonder if he were not in such a rage over what had happened to him that he was too angry to die.

He remained in a profound comatose state, intubated with a tracheostomy tube and monitored every moment. His temperature rose to 107 degrees. He was placed on an ice mattress, and when that was not effective, he was "sandwiched" between two mattresses. His whole body became reddened from the cold, yet his temperature rose another six-tenths of a degree. He looked so pitiful, so cold, I couldn't help but hate this treatment. I just wanted them to let him die in peace. The ice treatment was working, though.

One week following his injury, in the early hours of the morning, we received a phone call from an ICU nurse. She told us that Nick could not live another eight hours.

John and I felt resigned to his death, so we called the rest of the family and went to the hospital. One by one, each of us went to Nick's room to spend a few last moments with him. John and I decided to go to the chapel and pray for Nick's merciful death or that God would grant him a miracle. We truly felt that he would die, though, because we discussed funeral arrangements for him.

John asked the nurse if Dr. Sturman had been notified of his condition. "He has been made aware of it, but he is not coming to the hospital," she said. This only confirmed for us the fact that Nick was dying. We believed that Dr. Sturman was not bothering to come to the hospital because he knew Nick could not make it through the night.

This was not the case, however, as we later learned. Dr. Sturman was not alarmed because he had deliberately treated Nick with the ice mattresses so that his temperature would not only return to normal but drop below that point. This was the method he chose to prevent more brain damage by reducing the amount of oxygen needed by his brain. However, he failed to notify the ICU nurse of his strategy! The nurse interpreted Nick's falling body temperature to mean that he was dying.

Our family were the unwilling victims of this incomprehensible lack of communication. It strained our emotions to the breaking point. We returned home to nervously await the next crisis.

Feeding Nick intravenously became a serious problem. The veins in his arms were collapsing from all the punctures. The nurses would pound on them trying to find another life-sustaining vessel. After two weeks of injecting needles into his arm veins, it was decided to incise the ankle on the right foot, making it easier to place a catheter. Two days later the ankle on the left foot was also incised. These wounds are still prominent on his ankles today.

After a few weeks, this treatment too was discarded, as it was decided that a gastrostomy tube had to be placed directly into his stomach so that feedings could be poured from a can directly into the gastrostomy tube. Nick's heroic battle to live was confounding everyone. However, this decision meant another trip to the operating room and another warning to us that he might not survive the operation.

When the surgeon, Dr. Joseph Reynolds, exposed the stomach lining, he found that Nick had suffered a ruptured peptic ulcer due to trauma. Dr. Reynolds explained to us that there was a great deal of pain associated with this condition, and we couldn't help wondering if Nick felt that terrible pain. Hopefully his comatose state prevented it, but we will never know for sure. Certainly his facial gestures, that terrible mask, could have indicated extreme pain. John believed he was reliving the original beating and told the staff so.

This unexpected development meant that the stomach tube had to be used for insulin medication to cure the ulcer condition rather than for intragastric or tube feedings. This took a few days. Then Nick was taken off intravenous feedings and began to receive his nourishment through his tube.

Nick continuously turned his head to the left, no matter what position he was placed in. He would do so even if pillows were put in his way to prevent it. His eyes were not moving in concert, and his pupils were nonresponsive to light stimulus. (This was evidence of seizure activity, which we did not understand at the time.)

He began to have foot drop on both feet. Slippers called "booties" were put on his feet and a footboard added to his bed. These measures were taken to prevent a condition referred to as "angel feet," wherein the toes permanently drop below the heels and may prevent the person from ever walking normally.

Nick was engulfed by tubes and equipment. The only touches of home in the cubicle were the "get well" cards covering the wall at the head of the bed and the stand with the Blessed Mother Mary statue on it.

There was no time or place where John or I could express our emotions or show the grief we felt. At the hospital, we were constantly observed by medical personnel. At home, we had to be strong for the sake of our children. John practiced law in an office just a few blocks from the hospital, and I worked in the office with him. We were constantly on guard in the office not to let our personal situation with Nick interfere with our work.

John found that he could not walk on the street without someone stopping him to ask about Nick, because the story of what had happened to him and his medical condition was frequently reported in the newspaper. This was emotionally draining for John, though it was kind of people to ask about our son. He developed a monotone response, which was the only way he could handle the conflict of replying to friends who were showing their concern and his own difficulty in talking about his brutally injured son.

After Nick had lived three weeks in a comatose state on the brink of death, Dr. Sturman decided it was time to do an angiogram to see if there had been some clotting or swelling that had not been relieved. He explained to us the dangers of such a procedure. About one in 1,500 persons died from it, and in Nick's condition this was a strong possibility. Furthermore, there was no CT scanner in either hospital in Waterbury, making the angiogram the only alternative. Our "luck of the draw" on receiving state-of-the-art medical treatment for Nick was extremely poor.

One scanner for Waterbury had been approved, but the administrators of both hospitals were contending with each other to get the machine. Dr. Sturman was chief of neurosurgery at both hospitals, and he told us that the neurosurgeons in town thought that it should be at Waterbury Hospital. He asked John to use the situation with Nick and whatever influence he might have to break the deadlock. A CT scanner was finally approved for Waterbury Hospital. Within five years one was approved for St. Mary's Hospital as well because of the extremely heavy use of one machine.

While CT scanners were available in both Hartford and New Haven, Dr. Sturman made no move to transport Nick by ambulance to either town. He did not discuss the matter with us, but we later felt that he should have given us the choice of whether to risk such a trip in Nick's precarious medical condition.

John and I were at the hospital on the afternoon that Nick was moved from the ICU to the cardiac lab for the dangerous and inevitable angiogram. It was a scene straight out of a horror movie. Nick's face was swollen and bruised. The rest of his head was wrapped in white bandages. Five people in white hospital gowns were at the head, foot, and center of his bed, supporting bottles and machines attached to Nick by needles and tubes. They rolled the table slowly down the hall, trying not to jar Nick or the equipment. We wondered if this would be our last view of him.

I had the privilege of shaving Nick that morning before the operation. It felt so good to do something meaningful for him. However, the orderly who permitted me to shave him was reprimanded for doing so, probably because of some legal precautions.

Dr. Sturman came to us immediately after completion of the angiogram. "I want to operate on your son as soon as possible. The angiogram revealed a lot more clotting than I originally thought," he said. "I'll lift up the entire frontal section of his skull to see what is there. It is another major operation, and I have to warn you that he may not live through it."

The operation was scheduled for July 19, twenty-four days after his injury.

We will never know the extent of the serious brain damage that occurred in those fateful three weeks while Nick lay in coma in the ICU!

5
Discovering a Dragon

I arrived at the hospital early in the morning before the scheduled operation. As I entered the ICU, the curtains around Nick's bed were drawn, but not all the way. An orderly was shaving his head, and Nick was protesting the only way he could, with a grotesque, terrified look on his face that was so frightening it made me withdraw from the room immediately.

I was sick to my stomach and couldn't return to his room. I went to the ICU waiting room and lingered for a long while. It took all my strength to compose myself and return to Nick. I was convinced by this episode that he could feel and express pain, even in coma.

John soon joined me to wait for Nick to endure another operation and the possibility of death. The frustration we felt was not easy to deal with, but we had no choice. We were apprehensive every moment as we sat scanning magazines and trying to engage in light-hearted conversation to relieve the tension. The waiting was painful, every second of it, but we realized that as long as we were waiting, there was still hope; Nick had not died.

The operation lasted three interminable hours. Finally, Dr. Sturman entered the waiting room and said, "He's holding his own in the recovery room. It's a good thing I operated. He had the longest clot I have ever encountered in all my years as a neurosurgeon. I have never read of a longer one in any medical journal. It extended all the way across the front of his brain."

Dr. Sturman explained that the clotting would cause brain damage, because there are only a few centimeters of space between the skull and the sac that surrounds the brain. Swelling could fill this space and crush the sac around the brain, or push it down in such a way as to damage the brain stem.

Clotting in the brain means expanding blood mass that occupies space between dura and skull. Any expansion beyond the few normal centimeters would result in pressure on the dura and underlying brain, because these surfaces are compressible while the skull (cranium) is not (or nearly not). Any swelling of the brain from this pressure or any swelling that accrued due to cerebral edema secondary to temperature would only make this compression worse causing more damage on the surface of the brain and damage to structures deeper in the brain.

Nick wasn't injured once; he was injured over and over and over again. Treatment was not given or withheld or delayed for many explainable reasons. He was not taken to a trauma center with state-of-the-art medical equipment to handle this kind of injury. The belief that he would die, or even should die, may have caused decisions to be made that delayed use of those measures which were available to save him from more damage.

When Nick returned to ICU from the recovery room, he remained in deep coma. His fever rose again, so he was placed on another ice blanket. One day, I entered his cubicle, and again the curtains were partially drawn. I looked through the opening and saw Nick's body actually vibrating on the bed. He was covered in ice cubes, and an ice mattress was both underneath and on top of him.

I was sick all over again. I ran to the bathroom and heaved, but nothing came up. I went to the ICU waiting room because I couldn't return to his room. In a moment of weakness, I sat there praying he would die and wanting the pain to be over for all of us. But my strength returned and hope took over as it had before, and I went back to his room asking God for a miracle.

Nick got pneumonia, and the pulmonary therapists trekked into his room to thump on his chest to loosen the secretions. They turned him in every conceivable position to perform their task. He recovered from this bout of pneumonia, but the high fever continued to be a problem. He got pneumonia again, and his chest was routinely pounded and medications renewed.

I was sure Nick could not survive another round of this torture and equally sure I could not. Yet every time my mind lingered on a merciful death, I couldn't help praying for a miraculous recovery. I could no more think of giving Nick up than he could give in to dying. Surely there was a heroic battle to live going on inside his bruised and mangled body.

In spite of his struggles, he was unable to achieve a level of awareness that would convince the medical staff that he was anything but profoundly comatose.

Unreality is a common phenomenon in brain injury. The mind does not want to convey the enormity of what has happened to the injured person, and the medical profession is as subject to this as is the family. Everyone tends to float in a state of unawareness. In my heart, I knew Nick was aware of my presence and understanding some of what was going on around him and what was being said to him.

Yet my unreality showed about a month after Nick was injured when I asked Dr. Sturman, "Should we drive Nick's car?" I wanted some confirmation from the doctor that one day Nick would be whole again and drive it himself. Dr. Sturman, always a man of few words, looked at me incredulously and said bluntly, "Well, Nick will never drive it again!"

Nick's car had been parked in the lot behind the YMCA on the day he was injured. John picked it up and parked it in our garage where it remained. We decided we had better use the car, as it was not good for it to sit idle. When John opened the trunk he found a sales slip dated the day of the assault and a box for an AM-FM radio. But where was it? I called the YMCA and was told that there had been a radio in the weight room but the police had taken it. I called the police station, and it was there that I picked it up.

After the episode with the radio, I realized Nick must have had his gym bag with him at the YMCA. He always took it. His wallet contained an envelope where he had checked his valuables, and there was a key chain, but I couldn't tell if one of the keys was for a gym locker. I called the YMCA again and made arrangements for our son-in-law, Tom, to stop there on his way home from work and pick up the gym bag.

When Tom arrived, he was told that the man I had arranged to have him meet was not there and would not be back that night. I made new arrangements, and again the bag was not available. At this point, my suspicions were aroused about what the YMCA was doing with his gym bag. I had to get it back.

I called the Police Department and talked to a detective about the problem. He listened patiently and told me he would call me back. He did, with instructions about when I was to go to the YMCA and pick up the bag. I couldn't go down to the men's locker room to identify it, so Joe went with me to the YMCA. I sat down on a chair in the lobby and looked around while Joe went downstairs.

It had been many years since I had been there. Nick and Joe had learned to swim at this YMCA when they were young boys. I looked at the front desk in the lobby. A man was sitting behind it with his back to the entrance, watching a TV set. The wooden reception enclosure allowed only his head to show while sitting in the chair. There was clearly no protection to be had from him should someone want to enter the lobby and walk past him with a dangerous weapon.

I felt increasingly angry as I sat in the lobby. This was the place where Nick should have been protected from the assault he endured. Why should any person be permitted into this YMCA building carrying a baseball bat in his hand? They certainly didn't play baseball here. How could a thing like this happen in a YMCA? Furious, I fully understood why John could not bring himself to walk through the front door of this place. Joe soon returned with the familiar bag, and we quickly left. All I could say on the way home was, "Thanks, Joe. I'm glad we're out of there."

Nick's painful treatment in the ICU was incessant. An intern, performing one of these procedures, looked at John one day and abruptly stated, "You know he's going to die, don't you?"

"I know no such thing," John said.

John prayed continually for a miraculous recovery or a merciful death, whichever was God's will. Nick was our son on earth, but God's child in eternity. He alone would decide when Nick would leave this earth. Our belief in God was our salvation throughout this ordeal.

The battle for survival continued with ice blankets and tubes, with constant fever and bouts of pneumonia. A lounge chair on wheels was brought into his cubicle, and Nick "sat up" for a while each day after being lifted into the chair by the orderlies, who carefully arranged the tubes connecting him to support systems of one kind or another. This was done to prevent pneumonia. It gave us great pleasure to see him sitting up, and a little more reason to hope.

Nick had been in ICU for more than a month and was still in critical condition. We believed he would remain in ICU until he became at least well enough to respond to our presence. We hadn't considered the fact that he would leave before his medical condition was stable. However, Dr. Sturman came to us and said that although Nick was still on an ice blanket, he did not need the constant monitoring that the ICU staff routinely performed. He told us he was going to move him to the neurology ward.

This news frightened us because Nick was still attached to many tubes, and he would no longer have the constant attention that the ICU staff provided. John had to ask Dr. Sturman, "Is there a doctor anywhere who can help Nick?"

"If there was, I would have consulted him," Dr. Sturman replied.

"What about Yale-New Haven Hospital? It has an international reputation in the field of medicine."

"I'm on the teaching staff at Yale-New Haven."

"What about Dr. Francis O'Brien? I know him, and he's a renowned neurosurgeon in this area."

"I share an office with Dr. O'Brien, and I have consulted privately with him since the beginning, but I'll ask him to examine Nick before he leaves the ICU."

To Dr. Sturman's credit, he understood John's need to ensure Nick had every opportunity to receive the medical help he needed. John asked for Dr. Robert Good, an ophthalmologist, to examine Nick's eyes and for Dr. Henry Merriman, an otolaryngologist, to test his hearing. Dr. Sturman consented to all these consultations.

John and I were at the hospital when both Drs. Good and Merriman finished their examinations. I shall never forget the looks of utter gloom and despair on both their faces. The unspoken message was that Nick would die, and this was something we would not accept. Both explained that Nick's comatose state made their tests difficult, if not impossible. I'm sure they left us never expecting that Nick would live, or if by some miracle he did, it would certainly be in a "vegetative" state.

The one word connected with brain injury that I hate the most is "vegetable" or "vegetative." I'm sure it is the correct medical term for a human being in deep coma, but it's an insensitive description of someone you love very much.

Dr. O'Brien came from a sick bed to see Nick. He spent well over an hour talking with us and Mary after examining Nick and his medical records. He talked about the heroic medical attention given to Nick and discussed his chances of coming out of the coma. He explained that there were two favorable factors that should help Nick: one was his youth, and the other was his excellent physical condition prior to injury. Dr. O'Brien told us that if Nick did improve, it would be in slow, almost imperceptible stages over a long period.

He spoke about the brain, how it operated, and about brain cells that had been damaged and would not regenerate. He was certain that if Nick did come out of the coma, it would be a slow process, and that we couldn't expect that Nick would ever wake up and say, "Hello, Mom."

"Should we give up any hope of his improving?" John asked. After a long pause, Dr. O'Brien responded, "I wouldn't close the door on that. God is good."

Dr. O'Brien felt that Nick's condition was stable enough to schedule a trip to Hartford Hospital in an ambulance for a CT scan of his brain. He also felt it would be helpful to have periodic EEG exams to test for changes in Nick's brain waves.

This talk with Dr. O'Brien was the first time that a medical person had sat down with us and taken time to explain what was happening to Nick and thus console us in our yearning to know the truth, even if we had a hard time accepting it. It would be the only time until, many years later, we met Dr. Stephen Sarfaty.

I've come to believe that many doctors fear the patient's family, and many families are distrustful of doctors. Neither trusts the other to be real and forthcoming about what they "know" about the patient. I also believe that both doctors and family members "know" something that the others may be afraid to hear.

The doctors know the human body and the medical facts that affect it. They also know the consequences, which can be crippling and even fatal, when any part of that body is injured or diseased. And they know that family members do not want to hear the bad news when they are told that the body of their family member is no longer blessed with health. After all, it is their mission in life to heal, and they are vulnerable to the family when they are unable to restore lost health.

But family members know the person and are familiar with the spirit that resides within. That spirit gives them a special kind of hope that the doctors don't want to rely on. Too many times they are afraid to count on that spirit and the hope it brings because it sometimes disappoints us all. Nevertheless, that spirit contains a power that the doctor cannot produce, and it must not be dismissed. It comes from God, who is the Ultimate Healer.

Nick remained in the hospital encountering one battle after another while he refused to give in to dying. We suffered with him through all these ordeals as we became more and more aware that brain injury is an injury to the family as well as the victim. What we were discovering for sure was that we had a monstrous dragon with three heads in our lives, and the "medical" head of this dragon was eating us alive.

6

The YMCA and Joseph Tramontano

On that fateful Saturday afternoon, June 25, 1977, the police arrested Joseph Tramontano at his place of employment, not the YMCA. Paul Ford, the man in charge of the YMCA that day, had deliberately instructed the staff not to detain him from leaving the building, with his baseball bat in his hand, though he had committed this terrible crime inside the YMCA.

Tramontano went to work at Century Brass as if nothing had happened, as if he had committed no wrong. He was supposed to be at work at 3 o'clock that afternoon, but he remained at the YMCA arguing with Nick and then beating him over the head with his bat. The inhuman callousness of the man was incredible.

"Who is this fellow Tramontano?" we wanted to know. Within a few days of his assault on Nick, information began to trickle in from persons who knew him and us. We learned that Joseph Tramontano had been in the Marines, was thirty-two years old, had been married but was now divorced. Most revealing, though, was his direct connection with the YMCA.

On the Monday following Nick's injury on Saturday, a friend of Nick's, Mark Guerrera, came to the hospital to see him. Mark and Nick had struck up a friendship after meeting at a billiard parlor. Nick was such an excellent billiard player that he would entertain people by putting on padded gloves and hitting the billiard balls with his fist instead of a cue stick.

Nick was also an accomplished weight lifter, and he often met Mark at the YMCA weight-lifting room. On the Monday I met Mark at the hospital, he told me he had made plans to meet Nick at the YMCA the previous Saturday afternoon but had been unable to do so. He was grief-stricken with guilt, thinking maybe he could have done something to help if only he had been there.

"Do you know someone by the name of Joseph Tramontano?" I asked Mark.

"Sure," he said, "he's in charge of the weight room for the YMCA."

When Mark told me this, I was sitting down. His words so startled me that I jumped right out of my chair. I couldn't believe the implications of what I was hearing. We talked for a few minutes more, but I was totally unaware of what was being said. I excused myself and went to a telephone booth to call John.

I hardly knew how to tell him what Mark had said. We had no idea Tramontano was anyone other than a patron of the YMCA. When John answered the phone I just blurted out, "John, Tramontano was in charge of that weight room for the YMCA."

"What? Who told you that?" he asked incredulously.

I repeated my conversation with Mark, and John was dumbfounded. If this information was true, the YMCA might be responsible for Nick's injuries.

As the first week went by, relatives of other patients came to the ICU. One was a former client of John's who worked with Tramontano at Century Brass. He talked about him and said that as far as he was concerned there was something wrong with this man, that he was the kind of person you instinctively avoided. He told John about weird handwritten signs that Tramontano had made at Century Brass. He said Tramantano intended to put them up in the weight room at the YMCA to "make sure those slobs pick up after themselves." He also confirmed Mark's information that Tramontano ran the weight room for the Y.

More stories flooded in to other members of our family about

Tramontano: he had beaten his dog so badly in a public street that the police were called; neighbors were afraid of him; he had been accused of whacking a fellow employee in the stomach with a two-by-four at Century Brass.

Young men came to our daughters in high school with stories about Tramantano standing at bars with brass knuckles on. One said he had worn them at the YMCA. Another related that he always carried a bat in his car as well as chains.

We learned that his ex-wife, Christine Tramontano, was a legal secretary in Waterbury, and I wanted to talk with her. After a few inquiries, I learned that she had worked for attorney John Greco. I called his office and talked with Renie Altieri, an insurance agent who shared an office with him. She was heartbroken about Nick, but volunteered the information that Christine Tramontano had worked for Greco and related how Tramontano had abused and beaten Christine so much that she constantly wore long-sleeved blouses to work to try to hide her bruise marks.

I felt a compelling need to talk with her, and she agreed to meet me for lunch. Before we could meet, however, Christine telephoned and said, "I've been having second thoughts about going out with you. What was it you wanted to know?"

I told her frankly, "I don't know, except that I just want to try to understand why this happened to Nick. I thought maybe you could help me understand it, since you were married to the man." She sounded very apprehensive on the phone and told me that the best thing for me to do was to get a transcript of her divorce proceedings.

We ordered the transcript and found that the divorce had occurred on June 25, 1972. That date, June 25, caught our attention. It was exactly five years prior to the day Tramontano assaulted Nick. Testimony from the transcript told a brutal story. Christine testified that shortly after they were married, her husband began beating her. When she became pregnant with their child, he kicked and punched her constantly, every week. She said that she always had black-and-blue marks on her body.

On the night she came home from the hospital with their son, he beat her again, and pictures were taken of her bruised body. She testified that this occurred the whole time they were married, that he had a very violent, mean temper and that she was on the verge of a nervous breakdown when she separated from him.

Upon reading the transcript, we were beginning to understand that the man who had tried to kill Nick had been violent for a long time. Wasn't it predictable that he was going to hurt someone as badly as he hurt Nick? It almost happened to his wife! Hadn't people at the YMCA become aware of his bad temper?

We also learned from the divorce papers that Tramontano had not seen his young son for almost two years. Then, on another June 25, he went to court to get visitation rights. Christine Tramontano fought him bitterly, but in the end, a judge permitted visitation even though the youngster became hysterical when around his father. The court records also showed, through his financial affidavit, that Tramontano had paid a psychiatrist.

The divorce was granted on *June 25,* 1972, exactly five years to the day prior to his assault on Nick. On another *June 25* he went to court for visitation rights with his son. We couldn't help wondering: *Did Tramontano become upset each year on the anniversary of his divorce?*

Why did the YMCA personnel permit someone like Tramontano to run their weight-lifting room? His violent temper was so well known that they couldn't have been blind to it. Christine Tramontano told me that the Waterbury YMCA was his second home, that he practically lived there. She made it clear that he had devoted many years of service to the YMCA and said, "They knew him."

Now I understood why she was afraid to talk to me. Tramontano was out on bond and still had visitation rights with her son. By order of the court, she had to turn her young son over to him regularly. What fear must have gone through her each time, knowing what he had done to Nick!

Nick's father had to look at Nick in his horrible condition every day. John was approached twice by well-meaning individuals with suggestions that revenge should be taken for what Tramontano had done to his son. John was being goaded over and over by others that if that were their son Tramontano would be dead. It was John's steadfast Christian beliefs and his professional regard for the law that kept him from taking Tramontano's life.

At his first bond hearing, Tramontano was out of jail. When he was arrested, a $50,000 bond had been ordered. On his first appearance in court, it was reduced to $10,000. This happened while Nick was still in the ICU, and we were being continually told he was not expected to live.

What could have possessed a judge to reduce his bond to such a low amount? If Nick died, wouldn't there be a murder charge? The judge's order meant that for a bond amount of $1,000, Tramantano could be released onto the streets.

The court stenographer provided the answer to our question. She told her sister (a good friend of ours) that the attorney general for the state of Connecticut, Carl Ajello, was in the courthouse on the day the bond was reduced. He was Tramontano's uncle by marriage!

The law firm of Ajello, Sponheimer and Hoyle was indeed defending Tramontano on the criminal charge. Attorney John Sponheimer appeared in court to argue for the bond reduction, but Attorney General Ajello was in the Waterbury courthouse that day, not in his public offices in Hartford, when Sponheimer argued Tramontano's case. A curious coincidence? I didn't think so!

My sense of the law's fairness was crushed. My ability to trust the criminal justice system to act with an even hand was stretched beyond the limit. The judge who reduced the bond was a political appointee. The same governor who appointed him also appointed Carl Ajello. There appeared ample chance for undue influence to be used to get Tramontano off, even though five men had witnessed the attack on Nick. I couldn't help asking myself, "What was the attorney general for the state of Connecticut doing in the courthouse in Waterbury when his law partner was already there arguing the bond reduction, if it was not for the purpose of putting pressure on the prosecutor and judge in favor of Joseph Tramontano?"

I was so upset over this matter that I went to the courthouse to see the prosecutor, Mary Galvin. She agreed to talk to me as soon as she was told who I was. Her tone was considerate, but wary. Once in her office, I couldn't help crying as I asked, "How could the bond on Joseph Tramontano be reduced to such a small amount? Do you know my son's condition?"

"I do," she replied. "I explained it to the judge. I opposed the bond reduction, but it was granted over my strong objections." Knowing Carl Ajello had been in the courthouse, I certainly didn't wonder why.

In 1977 there was no victim's advocate we could turn to for help. Our fear that political influence would be used, and Tramontano would not be punished for the crime he had committed against our son, was real. We now knew that we would have to start fighting for justice by taking an active role in seeing that Tramontano was punished for the crime he committed against our son in order to counteract the possible political influence that the attorney general could bring to bear on this case.

We discovered that another head of the dragon that we were fighting was "criminal justice," and we were being drawn into a mighty battle we did not expect to have to fight.

7
Taking Time for Prayer

It felt like we were leaving one world and entering another when Nick left the ICU. One of the most satisfying aspects about the move was that he was now in a private room. This meant we could have precious moments alone with him without being watched.

In the ICU, every move we made toward Nick could be seen by a nurse behind a glass enclosure. We felt like we were always on display. But now I could talk to Nick without anyone hearing me, and I spoke to him constantly. It mattered not at all whether he could hear me. I regaled him with stories about his childhood and told him of the extraordinary pleasure of having him for a son.

Before Nick was transferred from ICU, I asked a nurse if we should have private-duty nurses on with him in the neurology ward. "Probably not, since he's comatose and not likely to move around," she said, a tone of disbelief in her voice. Once again, I felt she was criticizing me for being unrealistic. She said the nursing staff on the neurology ward was quite good, but if I was concerned about it, I should talk with the doctor. I got the hint, though, and was not about to approach Dr. Sturman after her reaction to my inquiry.

Nevertheless, while Nick was on the neurology ward, Mary called me one evening and told me a bizarre tale about how Nick had fallen out of bed one night. I was stunned. I had not been told of this, although it was recorded in the nurses' notes. Mary related how one of the nurses had told a friend of hers about the fall. The friend knew Mary and told her. Otherwise, we might never have known.

When we investigated the incident, we learned that Nick was missing from his bed one evening when the nurse went into his room to perform a medical procedure. She immediately initiated a code calling for security. I was told that the nursing staff jumped to the conclusion that John and I had come to the hospital and had taken Nick without consent. How ludicrous! Nick was a coma patient! How could we remove him from the hospital without being noticed? Nevertheless, they immediately began a search of the hospital for him.

Finally, someone on the search team had the good sense to check his room again. Nick was found lying on the floor on the side of the bed, which could not be seen from the door of his room, with tubes attached. He was lying in the area between the bed and the wall where the sink, the cabinets, and the telephone were located. Upon entering the room, you would not have been able to see him unless you went around the bed and looked on the floor. Why this was not done before security was called is still a mystery to me.

Orderlies were called to pick him up and place him back in his bed. A doctor was reportedly called to examine him, but it was not Dr. Sturman. When I learned of this episode, I promptly called him at his home. He was as shocked as I had been. I wanted x-rays of Nick's entire body, and they were done. Nothing had been broken. But we'll never know what trauma Nick suffered!

It was reported that the side rails were up on the bed, and Dr. Sturman surmised that he had "slipped down" past the side railing and just "slid" out of bed. All of this while he was unresponsive in a coma? I found this explanation to be preposterous. I don't believe the side rails were up. If they had been, Nick could not have fallen out of the bed.

When our daughter Debbie learned of this incident, she told me that she had called the hospital that night hoping a nurse would answer the phone and talk to her about Nick. She let the phone ring a very long time, but no one answered. Did Nick hear the phone ringing and ringing and try to get out of bed to answer it?

Unfortunately, we will never know what really happened on that night. However, I like my hypothesis better than the one proposed by Dr. Sturman. It gave us a little hope to think that Nick might be able to respond that well. Besides, this story has the added virtue of being more likely.

Once we learned of this incident, though, we were very distrustful of the staff, and someone from our family was with Nick night and day until he was transferred from the hospital. His aunt took the night shift, and the family covered the day shifts. This was the beginning of our participation in Nick's care that has never abated.

Word spread all over the United States about Nick through the grapevine media of friends and relatives. Letters and cards flowed back and forth. Prayers were being offered for him everywhere there was a relative or friend. The religious order of the Daughters of Wisdom, who taught at the grammar school Nick attended, offered prayers for him daily.

One of the nuns of that order, Sister Ann Whitty, and I had become very good friends. A few days after Nick was injured, she called me, without having read anything in the newspaper about him. My voice revealed my emotional state, and she immediately knew something was wrong. I told her about the assault on Nick, and she came to see me immediately.

It was summertime, and she was in a career crisis herself. She had been informed by the pastor that her teaching services would no longer be needed at the parish grammar school the coming year. She had taught there for nine years, so it was an emotionally trying time for her too. Her only recourse was to find a job on her own, or she would have to accept one assigned by the order.

She became a frequent visitor to Nick in the hospital, and his plight helped her put her own situation in perspective. Compared to Nick's problems, hers was a small one. She and I spent many hours together during that summer of 1977 helping one another through our respective crises.

During Nick's stay on the neurology ward, Sister Ann Whitty

learned of John's great desire for Nick to have the sacrament of Anointing of the Sick. He had received this sacrament previously, but John wanted it done at a time when the family could be present. She contacted a friend of hers, a priest stationed in Boston, to travel to Waterbury to give Nick this sacrament. Arrangements were made for the family to be present.

We gathered in Nick's room, and Father Jim tenderly anointed Nick's body (and our souls) in a beautiful ceremony that touched us deeply. We kissed and hugged one another and felt a family love that only such a moment can bring to the surface. Afterward, Father Jim came to our house for a home Mass. This surely is the closest mortal beings can come to the loving presence of Christ. Jesus was literally present in our home, comforting and caring for us.

I had converted to Catholicism before I was married, but my family upbringing was Southern Baptist, and I had many relatives writing and phoning to tell me of their private prayers, as well as the prayers of their church groups. This wonderful offering of concern and friendship coming quietly from Christians in so many parts of the country offered enormous hope and consolation in our lives.

A particularly moving spiritual experience for Nick came when a layman, Mr. Kennedy, from the Catholic Church in Bethlehem came to pray with him. Mr. Kennedy arrived on one of those occasions when the comatose Nick was "sitting up" in his special chair in his room. I watched as he prayed aloud, holding Nick's hand. The moment came when I felt certain Nick was hearing his prayers. Nick moved slightly, as if he were trying to lean forward! It startled Mr. Kennedy and me. The look in Nick's eyes was strange and eerie. He was listening! He was hearing! Something great was happening! I felt it and so did Mr. Kennedy.

After the ecstasy of the moment waned, Mr. Kennedy and I talked. He explained that praying with people like Nick was his gift both to and from God, and that God often did his best work when man could no longer help.

Our dear friend, Father Fulton, came from Oklahoma to pay a visit to Nick too. He brought another friend, Father Wilkemeier, who had also visited our home years before. They stayed with us again, blessing our home and blessing our lives with their presence.

No blessing was ever given with more meaning and power than Father Fulton standing beside Nick's bed at St. Mary's Hospital making the sign of the Cross while looking down on that bruised and broken body of a man, the body of the child he had baptized twenty-five years earlier.

My eyes filled with tears as Nick received his special blessing. The room was filled with a power that could not be seen, nor adequately described, but it was everywhere. It was the power of love filling the room, and it made me cry. It was a scene that has been played over and over again, century after century, as this ritual reminded us once again, "See how these Christians love one another." Prayer is just a word until it is experienced in this way, and then it becomes a reality of just how powerful a God it is that we worship.

Some people might ask: "Why does a powerful God allow such tragedies to happen?" The answer is, He doesn't. Humans commit these atrocities, and God uses them to teach us beautiful lessons and wonderful truths that we would not learn any other way.

In many of his healing acts, Jesus told us over and over that it was the soul that was important, not the body. To prove this He cured people of many diseases of the body that kept them from being just like all of us who are not crippled in our bodies. He always warned, however, that He was doing this to teach us that the effects of sin cripple our souls just as disease can cripple the body.

As Nick's life progresses in a body crippled by brain injury, I have had the extraordinary opportunity to witness the perfection of a soul. I have watched Nick's soul blossom and soar within his crippled body, and the truth that Jesus taught has become a living one for me. Watching people deliberately cripple their souls with sinful acts is a very hurtful thing.

Nick is living proof of Christ's teaching. Though he must hobble through life in his body that does not function as well as ours, he has joined with God to perfect his soul. He begins his day with God on his lips, he goes to sleep at night whispering His name, and when he awakes in the middle of the night, he can always be heard calling out to God.

Nick, in his crippled body, is the living example of the condition of a soul crippled by sin. Such a soul functions no better than does Nick's body. In truth it is far more limited in its ability to cope with life than is he in his ability to use his muscles to work his body.

8
Nick Needs a New Home

Nick was in ICU for two months but within three weeks of his being moved to the neurology ward, we were called to the social worker's office to discuss his discharge from the hospital. I was shocked and appalled when she began to speak about the subject. Dr. Sturman had never mentioned the idea to us, and I was totally unprepared for the fact that the hospital would consider discharging a patient in Nick's condition. Neither John nor I was ready to accept this new challenge.

I felt compelled to call Dr. Sturman and ask him what Nick's chances were of coming out of the coma. Dr. Sturman's abrupt, harsh, hope-killing response was, "Absolutely zero."

I was so stunned I couldn't say another word. I wasn't expecting such a drastic prognosis. As a result, that old familiar feeling of unreality about Nick's medical condition returned, and numbness began to set in. It seemed the medical staff was giving up on Nick, and they thought we should do the same.

The social worker was the liaison between the doctor, the family, and the utilization committee, whose job it was to monitor patients who could no longer benefit from the acute care given in the hospital setting. The purpose was to keep hospital costs down. Nick's move to the neurology ward was partially to give the hospital personnel a dignified amount of time to move him out of the hospital and to try to get the family to accept the inevitability of his condition. But we didn't know that at the time. The problem with this arrangement was that the job became impossibly difficult with the patient still in a coma and in need of skilled nursing and medical attention.

At another meeting with the social worker, we told her that Nick was a veteran. Perhaps the Veterans Hospital would take him. Its answer was, "No." There was a waiting list of at least half a year. A hospital in New Britain had a wing for patients in coma. Maybe it would take Nick, but its answer was, "No beds."

A convalescent home was suggested, but I found the idea repugnant. The social worker mentioned the name of one where two of my children had worked while they were attending high school. Joan had become so disgusted with the treatment of the patients that she turned in a complaint to the Connecticut Department of Health and quit. I shut the door fast on that suggestion.

Nevertheless, the social worker persisted that arrangements had to be made to move Nick; he could not stay in the hospital. She suggested another convalescent home that had a bed available immediately. She insisted I go there, see the room, and tour the facility.

It was a dingy, small room with two beds and no sink. There was barely enough room for one bedside chair between the two beds. I didn't even bother to look in the bathroom. I thought of all the equipment Nick would need, especially the suctioning machine for his breathing tube, and the need for a sink nearby. I left filled with feelings of disgust, loneliness, helplessness, frustration, and rage. Back in my car, I resolved that Nick would never be put in a place like that.

The social worker was dismayed and upset. I told her I would find my own place for Nick. I spoke with Dr. Sturman again. I was shocked when he said he knew nothing about where to move coma patients like Nick. The medical profession had made no provisions for people in coma! It couldn't be true—but it was.

When John and I talked, he suggested I take as much time from work at his law office as I needed to personally go to nursing homes in the area for interviews. We wanted Nick near home, and we had to come to grips with the fact that a nursing home was our only recourse.

I went to Hartford and spoke with the man in charge of nursing homes in the state. I had no appointment, but he graciously granted me an interview. He said that Connecticut had no facilities other than nursing homes for the care of young persons like Nick. He decried the situation but said he could do nothing about it.

I inquired about what services would be available to me if I brought Nick home. They were so meager and inadequate that it really was not an option I could choose. Furthermore, he spent a great deal of time persuading me not to think in that direction. He was sure it would be utterly destructive to our family life and might be a threat to our marriage. He told me that though he was a registered nurse himself, he would not consider such a thing even if it were to happen to his own child. Without recommendation, he mentioned a place in Windsor, Connecticut, that I rejected because it was forty-five minutes from home.

I traveled to almost every nursing home within a half hour's driving distance from our home. In some places I entered, the smell of urine was so strong I would walk out without even talking to anyone. I encountered every reaction imaginable: caring concern, respect, politeness, wariness, disinterest, and great hostility to accepting brain-injury patients.

I was getting positive recommendations regarding one specific facility: Kimberly Hall, in Windsor. It was far from home, but I was becoming weary after three full days of searching. But I knew I had to do something. I had told the social worker I would get my own place for Nick, and I knew he was not wanted at the hospital.

John and I were with Nick one night when the surgeon who had performed his stomach operation came in. We spoke with Dr. Reynolds, and he invited us into a room for a cup of coffee. He was friendly but quite frank. He told us that the doctors were hoping Nick would die during one of the times he had pneumonia, probably out of a sense of compassion for Nick and us.

We had encountered this attitude so much that it was not the shock it should have been. I believe it was a terrible thing for him to say and it fortified our resolve to get Nick out of the hospital as quickly as we could.

Sister Ann Whitty knew of our dilemma and contacted one of the nuns in her order who now worked in a social agency in Hartford. Both of them had taught some of our children at the grammar school they attended in Waterbury. She too recommended Kimberly Hall in Windsor. I decided I had to go and see this place myself, so I called and made an appointment for the next day.

That afternoon, I received a phone call from the social worker. She was obviously upset and said, "Reports have been coming to me that you are saying I am pressuring you to get your son out of the hospital."

"Well, you are, and I will get my son out of your hair as soon as I can," I replied.

We had started out with caring, considerate medical personnel and were now dealing with one who had an impossible job because there were no facilities for people like Nick. The relationship had deteriorated into such a distrustful one on both sides that we wanted to be rid of each other.

John and I were called to the hospital's business office on several occasions to talk about the payment of the bill. The gentleman in the office was considerate and understanding and willing to wait for an answer from Title XIX.

Two months after being admitted to the hospital, Nick was accepted on this program, but John had to sign papers that Title XIX would be reimbursed out of any judgment or settlement Nick might receive from a lawsuit. John quickly signed the papers.

We still had not heard from the VA regarding Nick's potential pension rights, because the criminal trial had been delayed and any fault Nick might have had was not determined. However, I was reluctant to accept the decision the Social Security office had made, so I decided to check the quarters they were counting. They had not included the time he had worked for our publishing company. This was what was needed to qualify for Social Security disability benefits. At least two sources of financial help had paid off for Nick, but we still had the problem of what to do with him now that the hospital would no longer keep him.

I went to see June Buttryman at Kimberly Hall in Windsor. On the way, I prayed that God would lead me in the right direction for our son. But even if this was a good place, it would be so far from home that it would be difficult for members of the family to see him often.

I followed the directions carefully and turned into a long driveway leading to a two-story brick and frame structure of beautiful design and a meticulously kept lawn. I was impressed before I walked into the building.

I went directly to Mrs. Buttryman's office and sank into a large white leather chair. She was as gracious as the building's appearance suggested she would be. Her kindness overwhelmed me after the treatment I had encountered elsewhere. I burst into tears, and she understood what was happening to me without my having to say a word. She allowed me the time I needed to compose myself and then suggested a tour of the facility.

She took me down an immaculate corridor to a private room adjacent to the nursing station. It had a large bathroom and two big, sunny windows in the bedroom. I couldn't believe what I was seeing, so I reminded her that Nick was a Title XIX patient. She said she knew that, but his condition warranted a private room near the nursing station. This would be his room if he were accepted and we wanted him to come here.

I was introduced to a friendly nurse, Mary D'Agata, and then to Connie Nelson, the director of nurses. She was a pert, lively woman with short, curly red hair and an infectious smile. Their manner was in such pleasant contrast to what I had been experiencing that I was awed.

I left Kimberly Hall in a happily dazed state with the agreement that they would check Nick's records and let me know about admission. I went home ecstatic about the place, vowing that Nick must go there. The family accepted my judgment of Kimberly Hall with joyous relief.

I believed it was imperative that nothing be done to place Nick in any facility other than Kimberly Hall until its staff had time to act. In my earlier interview with the man in charge of nursing homes, I had learned that the hospital could not discharge Nick to a nursing home I did not approve. Of course, I could not withhold consent capriciously, but now I knew what I wanted in a facility, and I knew how to get it. I had been told to keep careful notes of all the places I visited and the time I spent on interviews. I had my report ready if needed.

I enlisted the help of Dr. Sturman to keep Nick at St. Mary's Hospital until we found a place suitable to us. However, he began making inquiries on his own and learned that another comatose patient on the same floor as Nick would be going to Kimberly Hall. Her name was Linda, a young girl injured in an automobile accident. When we told him of our desire for Nick to go there, he quickly agreed that Kimberly Hall was the place to go.

Within a few days, Mrs. Buttryman, Connie Nelson, and Mary D'Agata came to Waterbury to see Nick and Linda and review their records. They agreed to accept both of them, and arrangements were made for Nick's discharge on September 21, just eighty-eight days post injury.

By this time Nick was controlling his body temperature without the assistance of the ice mattress. He was being tube fed through the gastrostomy; he was still being suctioned daily for adequate breathing; and he was still comatose. But incredibly, he was beginning to respond to my commands on occasion.

During Nick's last week at St. Mary's Hospital, I was positive that he could hear me, and I told the physical therapists and nurses about the intentional, not reflexive, responses I was getting. On a few occasions, in their presence, I had been able to get Nick to move his left arm or leg by asking him to do it.

By September 1, the therapists were making notes in the chart about it, which pleased me very much. I felt that if they were willing to write it in the chart, they really believed Nick was doing it on command.

I told John about my success in getting some movements from Nick, but he was skeptical. He had not seen anything to indicate a voluntary response, and Dr. Sturman's "absolutely zero" prognosis still rang in his ears. He was so accustomed to being told that every movement was due to involuntary reflex that he began to believe it.

Nick Needs a New Home

As we were leaving the hospital lobby one evening, I challenged John concerning my belief that I could elicit a voluntary response. I asked him to return to Nick's room and watch while I attempted to do it. "If you can do that, I'll believe it," he said.

We took the elevator back to Nick's room and were alone with him. I talked to Nick for a moment and then asked him to lift his leg. The left leg rose slowly off the bed, and John was thrilled. Nick restored his hope in an instant. There would be no giving up on our son by either of us from that moment on!

When the day came for Nick to leave the hospital by ambulance for the trip to Kimberly Hall, Dr. Sturman came for his final visit and talked with me as Nick was placed on the stretcher to leave. "Put him in the convalescent home and go home and tell yourselves you have done everything you can for your son. Go on with your lives," was the advice he gave.

My response was quick and immediate. As they wheeled Nick out of the room wrapped in ambulance blankets, I said firmly, "I am not leaving here with a corpse. He is my son and he is alive and I will do everything I can to help him."

These two philosophies, meeting head-on that day, would be encountered time and time again as Nick struggled for a conscious life.

We left St. Mary's Hospital as attendants wheeled the bruised and unconscious body of Nick past curious eyes to the basement where an ambulance was waiting. Sensations of fear enveloped me as the unknown future loomed before me. It seemed unreal that Nick and I were on our way to a convalescent home that was forty-five minutes from our home and family.

John and I vowed that day that we would do everything in our power to see to it that no father or mother would ever have to leave an acute care hospital with a comatose child and no place to go except a convalescent home for the elderly.

9
Kimberly Hall

Fear accompanied me all the way to Windsor in the ambulance with Nick as I contemplated the future. Yet, as he was wheeled down the corridor to his room, I could see the blackboard on the wall opposite the nursing station. In bold chalk letters it said, "Welcome Nick."

Connie Nelson accompanied the ambulance attendants into the room, and Nick was made comfortable in his bed while I waited outside. When I went into his room, I noticed another "Welcome Nick" sign posted on the closet door. Nick was dressed in a bright blue hospital coat instead of the white he had worn for three months. These simple touches gave me a great psychological boost and allayed my fears about Nick's care. I felt assured my decision to bring him here was the right one.

Connie Nelson was hovering over Nick's bed when I walked in. She was greeting him by asking him to say "Hello" back to her. In a few minutes, Nick made some sound, and we were both sure he had said "Hello."

Mrs. Nelson lingered in Nick's room to talk to me. She wanted to know everything possible about him before he was injured: his likes and dislikes, his temperament, his interests, where he had been, and so forth. We chatted for a long time. It was a relief to tell someone about the Nick that I knew.

Acknowledged a Man

Nick was of medium height: he had dark-brown hair, hazel eyes, long eyelashes, good Roman facial structure, and a physically fit body. His personality was his greatest asset. He was an extrovert with charm to spare. He made his own decisions regarding everything and did not follow the crowd. This trait often led him to investigate ideas that he later rejected, but not before he knew why.

He did not make friends easily, but when he did they were good ones. This was true of male and female friends. He was as normal as any other teenage young man, and his shyness came to the surface around young women. He would talk with Mary endlessly about whether or not she thought a girl would go out with him if he asked. He was vulnerable enough to be easily upset at a refusal. Even when Mary knew that a certain girl would like to have him call, he would go through torture before making the phone call.

His greatest fault was that he would not tolerate stupidity in anyone. His first impressions of people tended to be permanent, but, to his credit, he was usually right. He admired common sense and could put someone down unmercifully if they failed to display it. His father used to say that his worst quality was that he always fought like a gentleman when his opponent often did not. That was not like his father. When someone attacked John by putting him on the defensive in a situation where he could not exit the scene, it was a fight to the death, and one of them would go down with no holds barred.

When someone would ask Nick the time of day, he would say, "The time is right now." "How are you?" would be answered with a quick question, "Compared to what?" He would not listen to people complain about anything. "Get over yourself," he would say, and mean it. He strongly believed that everyone had the power to change their lives if they wanted to. He was blunt and to the point with everyone, and it was one of the traits Sally didn't like in him. "Sally, get a haircut" hurt her deeply. She was very proud of her long brown hair, which almost touched her waist.

Connie Nelson's request caused me to remember a lot of things about Nick: how he liked swimming, billiards, tennis, and jogging. He hated waiting, even for a bus, and would walk five miles home rather than stand at a bus stop. He loved old movies and watched them endlessly for camera quality and unusual shots. He had taken me to a movie, *Black Sunday*, the previous Mother's Day. He pointed out all the scenes with difficult camera angles in them and told me how they were made. Attending a movie with him was not an ordinary experience. It was his Mother's Day gift to me.

One Friday night shortly before he was injured, John and I took Nick to dinner and on the way home passed by a night club John and I sometimes attended on Saturday evenings when they played ballroom dance music. The three of us decided we'd like to go in, but when we got to the door the attendant looked at my graying hair and then at John's and cautioned us that Friday was disco night. We might not like the music.

Nick really wanted to go in, so we did. John and I had no trouble having a good time, but Nick was alone and too shy to ask a girl to dance. He asked me, and I went out on the dance floor with him. He started performing some really sharp California disco steps, and I started imitating them. We had a marvelous time. When the music stopped, several couples came over and complimented us. Nick's eyes were shining as he said, "Thanks, Mom, for making me look good." He had no trouble the rest of the evening getting dances with any girl he asked. This is a memory of Nick before injury that I shall always treasure, but remember painfully.

Nick was an avid reader, willing to tackle a book on any subject. He especially liked history and science fiction. He was anxiously awaiting the release of George Lucas's movie, *Star Wars*, and had read everything he could about the special effects wizardry performed in it.

Obviously, Nick liked weight lifting, or he would not have been at the YMCA that fateful Saturday. He had begun this in basic training in the Air Force. He is one of the few persons I have ever known who loved this period in the service. He was surprised at how well he felt with all the exercise and swore he would never let his body get out of shape again.

His taste in music ran the gamut from Zappa to Beethoven. He had bought every record Frank Zappa had released. (Later he would get very upset at hearing any of his records and ask us to stop playing them.) One day he came home from the library with a Beethoven album exclaiming, "Mom, you have neglected my musical education. Listen to this record." It was Beethoven's "Ode to Joy." He had placed an order for this recording at the local record store on the day he was injured.

In the Air Force, he had gone to photography school after basic training. I mentioned this to Mrs. Nelson.

She asked me, "Do you have any of the pictures Nick took?"

"Yes, some of them are at home," I told her.

She wanted me to bring them to Kimberly Hall and put them on the wall in his room in hopes that he might see one and recognize it. She also asked for a photo album of Nick so the nursing staff could become acquainted with as much of his life as possible.

For the first time, I had the feeling that things were going to be better. The atmosphere at the hospital had been so gloomy and pessimistic that I had forgotten what hope felt like. I was invited to have lunch in Nick's room and was brought a tray of delicious food. I learned that in convalescent homes the main meal of the day is served at noontime. How I wished Nick could taste the food as I sat eating in his room.

I spent the afternoon with Nick, Mary D'Agata, and the aides who would be taking care of him. Not one person had mentioned death. Their attitude was one of hope, in sharp contrast to what we experienced at the hospital. For the first time, we were in an atmosphere where Nick's recovery was discussed. Their attitude was so upbeat that I couldn't help inquiring about it.

I was told that the staff considered Nick (and Linda) a challenge to their nursing skills that they otherwise did not get taking care of geriatric patients, which was their primary mission at Kimberly Hall. Furthermore, the administration felt that they could keep a more qualified staff if their nurses were challenged to provide the kind of attention that Nick and Linda required. They would not be so likely to quit in favor of working in a hospital where their skills would be kept up to date. It was comforting to hear this.

John came to Windsor to pick me up. I told him how impressed I was with Kimberly Hall and the people who would be taking care of our son. He was pleased with what he saw too and we stayed with Nick for a long time before leaving.

There are no words that can adequately describe the terror that grips a mother and father who must leave a comatose son in a nursing home. The pain in the pit of your stomach doesn't stop hurting. It is the beginning of a nightmare from which there is no awakening. However, the welcoming Nick received and the kindness shown to him and to John and me made it possible for us to leave with some semblance of peace.

10
The Long, Hard Road to Consciousness

Medical personnel and machines had saved Nick's life and revitalized him, but now it was time for the family and a new rehabilitation team to act.

Someone from our family made trips to Kimberly Hall several days a week to be with Nick and help in his therapy. His needs were unending, and we could not provide enough time to fulfill them. Nevertheless, there was a newfound peace in being with him, because we could at least assist in his recovery and were encouraged to do so by the Kimberly Hall staff.

We needed to learn a lot about coma recovery quickly, but there was no one to teach us. Our own intelligence and that of the staff were the only guides Nick had in his struggle for consciousness. We had to assist Nick in his efforts to move his limbs again, to stimulate his mind to function, to help him speak again, even to hold his head up by himself. So we spent every available moment performing exercises with him.

Time spent on the road traveling to and from Kimberly Hall turned out to have one valuable aspect to it: attitude adjustment. This was a very necessary part of being able to work with Nick. We needed time, en route, to mentally adjust ourselves to enter his new world. On the way home, we needed time to shift our thoughts to be able to return to our daily routine. The trip home was frequently filled with tears. Only those who took the time to be with Nick in his brain-injured world could ever really relate to him in his new life.

Coma is a world of its own, a planet where lost people grope their way out of a darkness the rest of us cannot imagine. Someone must find the person and hold their hand while they gently feel their way along unfamiliar paths, not really comprehending why they are there and what has happened. Usually, the memory of what brought them to this place has been erased, and they are left to wander through this darkness with only a familiar or friendly voice to guide them along. Not everyone is capable of handling the trauma coma patients present, and others cannot give the time that it requires to slowly bring forth the person so lost.

The principal persons in Nick's brain-injured world turned out to be myself, John, and Mary. No former friends and few family members would make the sacrifice of time and life to provide Nick the assistance he needed. Mary gave time, help, and love to her brother, even though she carried heavy responsibilities at home for her husband and two pre-school-age children. Peter and Amy learned to play at Kimberly Hall as if it were their living room.

The first nine months at Kimberly Hall were full of paradoxes: Nick continued to be a very sick young man, though he was getting better. His weight had dropped to *eighty-five pounds,* down from one hundred sixty pounds when he was assaulted. He had been so proud that he had increased his weight from the one hundred thirty five pounds he weighed when he came home from California. He had accomplished this through diet and weight lifting. His waist size remained the same, so he looked terrific in the new suits he bought for his job. Now, however, he could not eat or exercise. He lay unconscious on his bed, looking like a victim of starvation.

We quickly learned that the left side of Nick's body was more capable of response than the right. He began to move his left arm and leg on request without difficulty. With this much movement, we were able to develop a "yes" and "no" language by asking him to lift his left leg for "no" and his left arm for "yes." This method was our first crude communication with him.

He still could not move his head in any manner that could be used for this purpose, nor could he blink his eyes voluntarily. Coma patients have periods of sleep and of being awake. They may move their arms and legs, even thrash about. They do not lie still with their eyes closed at all times. Though they may not be able to communicate, they may hear and even understand words or conversations. Nick's arm and leg movements led us to believe that he not only was hearing what we were saying to him, but understanding it as well. Clearly, some part of his injured brain had to be working in order for him to perform these minimal tasks.

These small accomplishments seemed monumental triumphs to us until someone would ask how he was doing. When we would say that he was able to move an arm or a leg, their reactions brought us back to reality. We were on such a roller coaster of emotions: elation when we were with Nick, depression when we talked about him to others.

On November 25, 1977, Nick had a generalized convulsive (grand mal) seizure that lasted seven minutes. It was a whole-body seizure that caused him to shake uncontrollably. When I heard about it, I was glad I had not seen him in this condition.

Persons suffering from brain injury are often subject to such seizures. If they reoccur, a diagnosis of post-traumatic epilepsy may result, and anticonvulsant drugs may be ordered to try to control the seizure activity. Though it may or may not be known exactly what is causing the seizures, it is an indication of malfunction of the electrochemical processes in the central nervous system. It may or may not be easy to treat or eliminate the seizure activity.

We would later learn that this seizure activity may have been the beginning of a phenomenon in Nick's new life that would not abate for a very long time. I believe that this seizure was the first awareness in him that something very terrible had happened to him.

Dilantin was ordered for Nick. It is a drug that must be carefully monitored by blood sampling to keep it at a proper level. Dosages are increased or decreased to control the blood serum level between a figure of ten and twenty. For the majority of persons, a level above twenty could be toxic, and a level below ten might not prevent recurrent seizures.

As with all drugs, Dilantin has side effects. It was prescribed by Nick's attending physician at Kimberly Hall. One side effect is that it promotes the growth of gum tissue in the mouth. Unless there is vigorous brushing of the teeth on a regular basis, the tissue can grow down over the teeth. The other is that it can have a deleterious effect on the liver. Nick was subject to both these side effects. No mention of them was made to us, though we found out about them soon enough.

The suctioning machine remained beside Nick's bed for several months, but by December 1, 1977, it was seldom being used. Nick was beginning to handle his saliva in a normal way.

The Foley catheter was removed by December 23. The nursing staff was satisfied that his daily output of urine was sufficient, and leaving it in posed a risk of infection to the urinary tract. Taking it out, however, meant that he had to be diapered.

Every gain seemed to have an accompanying loss. All the problems were hard to accept. While denial was preferable, acceptance brought the only peace of mind I could find. With even a small degree of acceptance, I could muster the courage to help Nick in his world of utter helplessness.

Nick made sucking motions, which bothered Mary very much. She felt that he was trying to tell us that he was hungry; she wanted to give him something, even a lollipop to suck. The nurses agreed to let her try it, because she could hold onto the stick and get it out of his mouth at any time. They were already cleaning his mouth with lemon-flavored sponges on sticks, so the lollipop idea was not too drastic to try.

It worked! He licked it! What a relief it was to be able to put something into his mouth that he clearly enjoyed.

After the success with the lollipop, Mary wanted to try baby food. She did, but Nick would keep his mouth tightly closed and his teeth clenched. She tried pulling his lip down just enough to put a bit of baby food in the space between his lip and teeth. He could slowly feel the food melting in his mouth, and he swallowed it. This procedure did not last long, however, for when Nick tasted food, it was the beginning of a new life for him.

Within days, he was opening his mouth each time a spoon was placed on his lips. He ate with relish the pureed food that was brought to him. Everyone was overjoyed that he could have something to eat, even if it had to be baby food. In no time, he was eating everything fed to him, and wanting more.

I was in Nick's room one evening at dinner time when the aide came in to feed him. The tray had a small dish with two canned pear halves on it. *Solid food!* I knew this was a mistake, and assumed that she did too. Before I could say a word, however, she cut off a piece of pear and placed it in Nick's mouth. He chewed it and swallowed! He ate the whole dish of pears!

I rushed down the hall, looking for a nurse. When I told her what had happened, she was as happy as I was, and from then on, some new solid food was introduced to his diet each day.

By December 6, Mary's birthday, Nick's tube feedings had been diminished and he was eating regular meals, indicating likes and dislikes. What a birthday present for Mary! Three times a day, trays of food came down the hall to Nick's room, and he ate every bite.

On December 9, the nurse noted that he was smiling when the conversation turned to birthdays, Christmas, or cookies. She also noted small-muscle coordination in his left hand.

As early as December 11, 1977, Nick was able to move his head in a "yes" or "no" fashion. This was a tremendous improvement in communicating with him. He also developed gestures, with which he could indicate many of his needs—including the need for a bedpan. However, in the slow-motion world of brain-injured persons, it is impossible, in a nursing home, to attend to bowel and bladder needs in this way. If Nick was placed on a toilet, he had to be watched constantly. It would often take him a half hour to have a bowel movement or even void. Thus, the diapers were continued.

By December 20, he was using his left hand to help raise his right one. He could not move the right hand without this assistance. The muscles in the right arm and hand were very contracted. However, when Nick was in deep coma, we could do all range-of-motion exercises with the right arm without any difficulty.

On Nick's 26th birthday, December 20, 1977, he was using his lips and tongue to manage food so well that we planned a party for him. Several members of our family traveled to Windsor in the evening to celebrate with him. The administrator of the nursing home gave us the recreation room on the second floor for privacy. Mary gave Nick a beautiful gold cross on that first birthday in his new life. Sally made him a pint of shrimp Newburgh as a present. He ate every bite of it, so much that I was frightened he would vomit. We had a cake, of course, but I allowed him only one bite.

Nick loved eating so much that by December 31 he had pulled out the gastrostomy tube for a second time. He made gestures to indicate he did not want it reinserted. It was not.

By January 9, 1978, he was holding bread and cookies placed in his left hand and finding his mouth, albeit with difficulty. It was his first small step toward some sort of independence.

Nick was sometimes making other responses that revealed he was not always in a profound coma. However, there were other times when he would fall into a deep slumber and it would make no difference where he was or what he was doing. No amount of stimulation would bring him to a responsive state.

We would later learn that there were different levels of coma. The deepest and lowest state would be defined as the inability to be aroused, to become aware of surroundings, or to act in an intentional manner. When coma occurs, it means that the "power supply" to the brain has been damaged.

The Glasgow coma scale numerically rated such things as the ability to open one's eyes, to verbalize, and to follow commands. This scale would rate patients from three to eight in coma, and a rating of nine or more would be given for consistent consciousness. In the future, the Rancho Los Amigos Hospital in California would develop a Scale of Cognition with levels of recovery from I to VIII (see Appendix).

We did not know the full extent of damage to the muscles in

Nick's body. Certainly, the motor control section of his brain had been badly damaged, as was evidenced by his inability to perform so many motor activities. He was getting range-of-motion physical therapy on a limited basis. We had been taught many of the exercises by the therapists at the hospital so we could do them whenever we visited him.

When Nick was in bed, the right hip was rotated outward and the leg was bent at the knee. The hamstring muscle pulled the lower part of the leg and foot under the knee almost to his buttocks. This is called a flexion contracture and it results from a disruption in the normal balance between muscle flexor and extensor. In such an imbalance, the flexor muscle is nearly always more powerful. Hence, the flexor wins, and you get a flexion contracture. Efforts to straighten it out were not fruitful.

The physical therapist tried standing Nick up. This was accomplished by having one person on each side protecting and assisting him. There was no tilt table for Nick to slowly get used to the sensation of being upright. Rehabilitation for brain-injured persons in Connecticut did not exist in 1977. Unfortunately, Nick would be one of the persons who caused it to come about.

Slowly, Nick was able to put weight on his left leg and foot, but the right leg was still bent at the knee in an awkward position. It simply would not straighten, and attempts to pull it into a correct position caused Nick excruciating pain.

Up to this time, Nick had made no consistent sounds, although we tried to get him to speak. With the onset of this pain, he began to make rasping or groaning sounds. Though this was very upsetting, it indicated to us that Nick's voice box might work to some degree. Nevertheless, he could not make any recognizable speech sounds. This may have been partially due to the fact that the opening in his throat from the tracheotomy had not closed on its own. As a result, he would lose air through the hole in his throat.

The paradoxes were present again. He was breathing without the aid of any machines; he was handling his own saliva; and he was swallowing food and liquids. All these gains signified great accomplishments, but his intake of air was so inadequate he could not make meaningful sounds.

We quickly learned how precious it is to be able to take a deep breath, fill the lungs with air and let it out slowly in sounds of speech, song, or even screams of pain and shouts of joy. What marvelous muscle coordination this takes!

Nick's handicaps constantly, and painfully, reminded us what a wonderful creation is the human body and that God's creation of man is truly the greatest miracle in the world.

Nick experienced another grand mal seizure on January 3, 1978, which lasted four minutes. His dosage of Dilantin was increased in an effort to control the seizure activity.

I knew Nick could understand and respond to simple requests I made of him, so I constantly devised ways to prove to others that he was intelligent and not just a mass of bone and tissue, sitting in a chair. I would ask him to touch different parts of his body with his left hand. He could respond to commands to: touch your eyes, ears, nose, hair, chest, knee, other knee, even esophagus. He could do these exercises by using his left hand with amazing success.

I often practiced these with him in the hallway, because he was more at ease and evidenced far more pleasure in this setting than in the quiet of his room. The corridor near the nurses' station was busy all the time, and it was stimulation for him to be in the atmosphere where conversations were taking place. He often reacted to these with shrugs or a sign he would make that signified, "Right on," from the old days before injury. Sometimes there would be the attempt at a half smile or a little noise that sounded like a laugh.

One day, the speech therapist saw us and came over and asked, "What are you doing?" I demonstrated for her his ability to recognize parts of his body. "I think he should have speech therapy," she said.

She talked with Connie Nelson about it to obtain the necessary order from the doctor for her to work with Nick. When the doctor approved, I spent an hour going over Nick's records with her and answered all questions she had. She began speech sessions with Nick in February, and they would continue for a long time.

Nick's eyes looked normal, but they did not respond to light stimulus and only occasionally seemed to follow someone in the room. We held up pictures and asked if he recognized any of them. He made no response. I bought a pad of colored paper, and Mary D'Agata would hold up sheets from it and ask him to respond "yes" or "no" to questions about their color. Nothing we tried indicated that he could see.

We asked for an ophthalmological examination. The doctor came to Kimberly Hall when we were not there. The nurse related to us that testing had been difficult because Nick could not hold his head in such a way as to look straight into the examining instruments. The diagnosis was that Nick was totally blind in the left eye and had only minimal light perception in the right eye.

This news really hurt. It was hard to accept as truth. John was particularly devastated and wanted another opinion. But Nick's bed was turned so that his right side was near the window where he would receive the benefit of any light coming through it.

Nick was eventually moved to a new room, a private one on the same unit. It was large, with a private bathroom, but as far from the nursing station as possible. Nick could not push the button to call the nurse because he had no fine finger control of either hand. Furthermore, there was the question of whether he could remember that a call button was present.

Someone else needed Nick's room, but this fact didn't keep John and me from being upset that Nick was so far from the help he might need. In this new location, there was no way he could receive the attention that he had been used to getting.

We tried everything we could think of to be sure the nurses would hear him if he needed help, but nothing worked. Finally, we tied a string of bells to his bed rail. Unfortunately, he didn't seem to remember they were there. Our only hope was that the nursing staff would check him regularly and that the bells would ring to signal the nurse if he had a grand mal seizure.

Though we were unhappy over this situation, I don't believe there is another nursing home in the state that would have been as generous with a Title XIX patient as were the administrators at Kimberly

Hall. The private room was a gesture of generosity we have always deeply appreciated.

Efforts to straighten Nick's right leg were going badly. When he was standing, the leg would drop due to gravity, but this would only happen for a few minutes each day. When he sat in a chair, it looked almost normal, as the knee would naturally be bent. However, the right leg would still gravitate toward the left one in a scissorslike position.

An orthopedic surgeon was called to look at Nick's leg and advise the therapist. He suggested a splint be applied for short periods of time, a half hour at most, because Nick would suffer pain while wearing the splint. The splint was made and applied regularly until a nurse left it on for an entire night, resulting in Nick's leg being rigid. He refused the splint thereafter by pushing anyone away who tried to apply it. The pain he endured was excruciating, and he could not even scream for help!

The doctor then suggested that the staff tie the leg to the bed rail with a sheet while Nick was asleep. However, Nick would always find a way to work the leg loose or scoot down in bed until he was comfortable.

This problem persisted until the therapist came to me almost seven months after Nick was admitted to Kimberly Hall and told me he was not going to pull the leg down to straighten it anymore, as Nick was in so much pain the therapist could no longer stand it. He told me that his muted screams were more than he could tolerate, that if it were his own son he would not permit it.

By January 2, 1978, Nick was responding faster to requests we made but not as quickly as we thought he should. We would ask him to do something, but, thinking him helpless to respond, would move on to something else. Then he would respond to our first request while we were talking about another subject or asking him to follow through on a new command.

It is difficult to imagine what went on in his mind with all of these crossed signals. What concentration it must have required to perform these simple requests! His frustration level must have been at its peak.

People often spoke in front of Nick thinking that he could not hear or understand what they were saying. Sad to say, this was particularly true of professionals. I firmly believe that Nick heard and understood every word by January 1978, just a little over six months from injury, but he was not considered fully conscious and out of coma.

Dr. O'Brien's prediction that Nick would not suddenly wake up and say "Hello" was coming true. His return to a conscious life was a very slow process. The terror I felt for Nick was that when the strange feelings of his new life slowly engulfed him, he would have to come to a state of awareness in which he was a blind man who would never again see the light of day. How would he be able to comprehend or understand this?

Though he might yearn with all his might for the life he remembered with friends, family, work, and play, that world would never be available to him again. Too much had been broken. Brain cells had been killed or damaged beyond repair.

The pity of it is that as he came out of coma into a conscious life, he could not remember or understand what had happened to him, and we could not understand what he was trying to tell us about his feelings.

11
Begging for Rehabilitation

John and I were impressed with Nick's progress toward full consciousness. He was alert most of the time now, and we believed he needed to go to a rehabilitation center where the medical staff would know more about how to help him recover whatever faculties he still possessed. This would never happen, though, unless we could get a doctor to recommend it.

I made an appointment with Dr. Sturman. I hoped he would examine Nick again for the purpose of referring him to a facility for rehabilitation. I felt certain Dr. Sturman would be impressed with the fact that Nick was out of the coma. In the car on the way to the doctor's office, I was so full of emotion about the outcome of this interview that I alternately cried and prayed, pleading with God to move Dr. Sturman to give Nick a chance for more expert treatment than what he was getting in the nursing home.

Dr. Sturman listened patiently and then promised to go to Windsor to examine Nick. This was more than I had hoped for! However, after two months of futile waiting, I called him and asked if we could bring Nick to his office. I assured him we would take the precaution of using an ambulance. He apologized for not getting to Windsor and agreed with the suggestion.

On the morning of the long-awaited appointment, I drove to Kimberly Hall to ride in the ambulance with Nick to Waterbury. John met us at the doctor's office, and Nick was wheeled into the waiting room on a stretcher. He was then transferred into a wheelchair we had brought from the nursing home so that he could go into the examining room in a sitting position.

Dr. Sturman looked at Nick and then began to examine him while he sat in the wheelchair. He tested his responses to light stimulus and arm and knee jerks. But this is all he seemed to want to do. John and I were becoming nervous. He didn't want to try to talk with Nick or get any of the responses from him that we had worked so hard to elicit. His reaction to seeing Nick was not what we had expected.

Both of us made a point of talking to Nick so the doctor would know that he was understanding and responding, through gestures, to what we were saying to him. We wanted Dr. Sturman to realize these were voluntary and not conditioned responses, but he did not seem impressed.

Finally, in desperation, I asked Nick to make the sign of the Cross, which I felt necessitated abstract thinking, and I thought Dr. Sturman would realize this and know that his brain was functioning on this level. When Nick made the sign of the Cross, Dr. Sturman asked, "Is this something he has been taught over and over, like Pavlov's dog?"

He said this right in front of Nick! I was astounded, and, once again, unable to respond to this brutally unfeeling statement from this great neurological technician who seemed to have no sense of compassion for his patient. The answer to his question was, "Yes!" Nick had been taught this sign when he was a very young boy, and certainly he had been gesturing this prayer over and over most of his life.

When Nick first arrived at Kimberly Hall in coma, I pondered every method I could think of to prove to myself and others that Nick could still hear, think, and respond. One day, I leaned over his bed and started whispering in his ear about the first prayer I had taught him as a child. I reminded him that he didn't even have to try to say it, just *sign* it. Without another word, Nick's left arm slowly went to his *forehead,* then to his *chest*, then to the *left shoulder* and then the *right:* the familiar *sign of the Cross!* I was thrilled when he did this and showed the nurses his new accomplishment. They were as pleased as I was, but now Dr. Sturman had relegated the sign of the Cross to a Pavlovian dog response!

The exam was very short, and we were quickly given the same diagnosis about his eyesight: light perception in the right eye, but not enough to distinguish objects. He said that the part of Nick's brain that stored memory of what a door or window was had been damaged, and even if he could see those things he would not know what they were.

Years later, I asked Nick if he could think of one word to describe a window, and he slowly said, "P-p-porthole." I thought that a brilliant one-word description and couldn't think of a better one myself. He certainly had to use the part of his brain where memory of a window was stored to describe it as a porthole. So it was not destroyed! Others I had asked to do this for me couldn't think of a one-word description, and they were not brain-injured.

Nevertheless, Dr. Sturman reluctantly agreed to recommend an evaluation at Gaylord Rehabilitation Hospital in Wallingford. I think he did this just to satisfy us, because as we started to leave his office he cautioned us strongly, "Even if your son makes the best recovery possible, he will never be the son you knew." But Nick was going to have a chance at rehabilitation, and no amount of caution could dampen our spirits. We had the doctor's referral order, and this is what we wanted.

John had made arrangements with the ambulance drivers to take Nick to our home for a short visit. This trip meant a great deal to John; to him it signified the fact that Nick was getting better if he could come home, even on an ambulance stretcher.

The family was waiting when the ambulance came up the street and they all came out on the lawn, cheering, as Nick was wheeled into the living room. No soldier ever had a sweeter homecoming, and he had truly fought a great battle to get there. I often wonder what impression all this made on the young grandchildren who witnessed it.

The ambulance drivers were pleased and slightly embarrassed at all the fanfare. They gave us a telephone number to call when we were ready to go back and told us to take our time. It was a nice gesture. We feasted and laughed and cried, and Nick seemed to take it all in.

Of all the things that had happened to us since the assault, this was the most significant for our family. John had been right to insist on it. As he said, "There is nothing like coming home." Our hopes, our spirits, and our resolve received a boost from this trip that nothing would ever dampen.

I went back in the ambulance with Nick and gave the happy news to an elated staff at Kimberly Hall. They felt as though their efforts were being rewarded at last.

While we waited for Nick to be admitted to Gaylord, he became more and more alert. He was dressed in his own clothes each day and put in a gerichair (a heavy chair with four wheels that can be moved easily around the room or hall by the staff or the patient). Nick maneuvered the chair so well that he could push it with his left foot and go from one end of the hall to the other.

We knew a wheelchair would be easier for him to manipulate, so we decided to buy one especially adapted to his needs. One like this was not available to him in the nursing home. The Campaigners for Christ had given us $100, which was the only contribution we ever received. We applied it toward the purchase of a wheelchair with a left-wheel drive. We were hopeful that he could learn to push the wheel with his left hand. It was fully reclining with a head rest. The cost was $1,000. We paid the balance.

In this wheelchair, Nick could travel up and down the hall and maneuver it so well that he could go behind the nurse's station where Mary D'Agata was sitting. He always wanted her attention and had grown to know the sound of her voice. This was done slowly, of course. The sad part was that he would use his left foot, not his hand.

However, this posed a new problem for Nick: he couldn't see where he was going and became a danger to himself and other patients, as he could easily bump into them or objects in the hallway. His skills and abilities were being tested by everyday experiences, and his progress became his cross.

With his ability to move about, Nick made friends of some of the residents and enemies of others. Those who were capable of understanding the great tragedy that had happened to him were patient and kind to him. Others who were suffering from diseases themselves were unable to comprehend anything but the fact that he was a nuisance to them. Nick suffered some humiliating remarks from these people, but I suspect it was not their fault.

However, one of the finest compliments I have ever received came from a wonderful gentleman who was particularly kind to Nick. He just looked at me and said: "You're a wonderful mother."

Another lady told John, "I wish I had you to help me in my recovery." She marveled at the way he never gave up and always prodded Nick along no matter how difficult the task. She heard John as he often told Nick, "You fight from the inside, and I'll fight from the outside."

John meant exactly what he said. He believed Nick was caught in the belly of a dragon and it would take both of them to rescue him from this many-headed monster: Nick fighting from the inside and John fighting from the outside.

12
Coming Home for Visits

Nick was dressed in his own clothes each day and looking much better. He was gaining weight, and we felt very good about this. We became confident enough in his progress to start taking him home every Saturday and Sunday, weather permitting.

Nick could transfer from the wheelchair to the car by standing on his left foot with his arm around someone's neck. He would then pivot his entire body to the position for sitting down in the car seat. His legs would then be lifted into the car and the seat belt fastened.

Either John, Mary, or I would make the trip to Windsor early Saturday morning, bring Nick home to spend the day, and then take him back in the evening. We would repeat the trip again on Sunday, spending three hours on the road each day. It was worth this enormous effort because the time at home with Nick was precious and wonderful.

These visits were a time of relaxation in our lives that we had not recently experienced. Those who wanted to be with Nick started "hanging out" at our house on the weekends, and we were together as a family. Nick was treated as a son and brother and not as a patient. In this setting, Tom grew to know Nick and became confident enough to volunteer to drive to Windsor many Saturday mornings to bring him home and thus save John, Mary, or myself one of the trips.

On one of our return trips to Kimberly Hall with Nick, we learned that his sweat glands didn't work properly. When we were stalled in a traffic jam in a car without air conditioning, Nick's temperature rose to an alarming degree. When we finally arrived at the nursing home, Mary and I spent the next hour wrapping and re-wrapping his entire body in cold towels and filling him with liquids to get his temperature back to normal. We always traveled in air-conditioned cars after that experience.

Nick became so alert that he knew where we were going when we were in the car ready to take him back to Kimberly Hall. He didn't want to leave home and would wave his left hand over to the driver's side of the car, indicating that he wanted to go back home. It was heartbreaking each time he did this. It made it very difficult to handle the driving and Nick too.

Now that he could be transported, we wanted to take him to an eye doctor for an examination in an office where more sophisticated equipment could be used. John searched for the best place and learned that the VA hospital in Newington had eye specialists coming in weekly to do exams; their equipment was first rate. We made an appointment for Nick to be examined there.

We picked him up at Kimberly Hall and drove to Newington. Upon arriving, we encountered the inevitable "wait" and learned how terrified Nick became when out of his usual surroundings. The unfamiliar noises bothered him a lot, and my voice was not enough to comfort him. I had to hold onto his hand tightly every moment. Once we were in the examining room, we watched as the ophthalmologist tried in vain to help Nick place the front of his head on a bar designed to keep his head straight while the doctor looked through the retinoscope into Nick's eyes. When Nick was asked to open his eyes, we saw his body muscles tighten. He was trying with all his might but could not voluntarily open or close his eyelids. With every request he tried harder, as the muscles in his face tensed and his arms flexed. He simply could not focus his eyes or adjust his head to look into the doctor's equipment.

We were unaware of all these limitations until this moment and were shocked once again at the horrible extent of Nick's losses. I hated what Joseph Tramontano had done to Nick more than I ever had before.

Nick's responses to "yes" and "no" questions seemed eternally slow in this "normal" atmosphere. The doctor was initially patient but gradually became irritated with having to slow down to Nick's level. He finally tried turning off the lights so that the room was totally dark, then turning them on (a "diffuse field" test). Though Nick tried to answer whether it was dark or light, he was obviously guessing and really didn't know.

The prognosis was the same: some light perception in the right eye and totally blind in the left. He had what the doctor termed "doll's eyes": eyes that move opposite to manual manipulation of the head. His eyes looked perfectly normal. They moved about and even looked straight at you, but they saw nothing. He had optic nerve damage that could not be repaired with any kind of known treatment. The hurt in the pit of my stomach was excruciating. It was bad enough that he was brain damaged, but blind too, with no known treatment for his condition. John was utterly devastated.

The doctor explained that there was one other test that might be done with Nick. He said there was even more sophisticated equipment at the University of Connecticut's John Dempsey Hospital. In particular, there was a machine that would register light waves coming through Nick's eyes (visual evoked potentials) without his having to make a response. Arrangements were made for this test to be done, but it would be a long time before we could get an appointment.

When we returned to Kimberly Hall, the nursing staff was as saddened by the news as we had been. Nevertheless, the diagnosis of light perception in the right eye gave us some cause to hope he might someday improve, or that a way to repair optic nerve damage might be discovered.

Much effort had gone into trying to get Nick to visually recognize objects, pictures, colors, and so on, but now we all knew it had been for naught. He had been blind and couldn't recognize them. It was almost as if we had been taunting him with his loss of sight. It caused all of us to have another let-down and some guilty feelings over yet another injury that we did not know was there.

This is one of the saddest parts of brain injury. Doctors cannot tell what the consequences are until the person tries to perform a function and is unable to. Then it becomes apparent that the part of the brain that controls that function has been damaged beyond repair.

Mary D'Agata told us that when Dr. Lucas came for visits, they tried to get Nick to make the responses they saw every day. Nick would never respond when the doctor was in the room. They devised a scheme whereby the doctor was stationed in the room without Nick's knowledge. They put him through several tests for responses, and he did each one perfectly. From this they discerned that, for some reason, Nick would not do anything in the doctor's presence. I believe the reason was that Nick still retained that old attribute of testing people he dealt with, and Dr. Lucas came up wanting. Nick would do nothing for him.

Several people had come to us with news about a Catholic priest in Worcester, Massachusetts, Father Ralph Diorio. He conducted healing services. "Have you taken Nick there?" they would ask. At first the idea seemed preposterous, and John was very skeptical about the whole thing. However, I got more information about Father Diorio and his services and decided I wanted to take Nick to one of them. John suggested I go there first and see the service myself before trying it with Nick.

I went and was very positively impressed. Father Diorio made it abundantly clear that he was not a faith healer. In fact, he would get very upset at the suggestion. Any healings that took place, he insisted, were because God had chosen to use him as a channel through which the healing grace of the Holy Spirit would operate.

At the beginning of his service he never knew who would be helped. As the power of the prayers said by a church full of people began to be felt, something happened in the auditorium. I could never have imagined spending three or four hours singing, praying, and really enjoying the time spent so much that I was sorry to see it come to an end. Yet that was what happened.

People claimed to be healed of minor and major ailments and diseases. The most obvious outcome, though, was the healing of spirits. There was an unimaginable peace that enveloped you. Joy was everywhere. The early Christians must have known this feeling. I asked myself, "Why couldn't services like this be offered everywhere?"

I returned home certain we should take Nick to one of Father Diorio's services, in spite of the fact that he was in a wheelchair. There were many stairs leading to the church, but men volunteered to carry people up the stairs and considered it a privilege.

John was not so eager. He remained pessimistic and skeptical. Finally, he agreed to go with me to a service. He returned from it feeling just as I had.

We made plans to pick Nick up at Kimberly Hall and drive to Worcester with him on a Sunday. We had to make sure we had a supply of diapers, see that he was dressed properly, put him in the wheelchair, take him to the car, transfer him to the car seat, put the wheelchair in the car, and begin the trip to Worcester. We had to stop for food on the way and transfer Nick to the wheelchair for the trip into the restaurant, and then put him back in the car for the rest of the trip to the church.

When we arrived, Nick was carried up the stairs in his wheelchair by volunteers. They placed Nick in front of one of the first pews. I was allowed to stay in the front pew right behind him, but John had to sit elsewhere.

When the service began, Nick paid attention, listening and trying to sing. The songs were simple ones, melodies played over and over, especially one in which "Alleluia" was sung several times. This was the easiest sound for him to attempt, and he really tried. At one point during the service, Father Diorio asked the audience, "Raise your hands if you love Jesus." Nick's left hand shot upward and remained there long after everyone else had lowered theirs. He couldn't see, so I told him to put it down. Finally, Father Diorio approached all of the persons in wheelchairs. When he came to Nick, he placed his hands on his forehead and gave him a blessing.

After the service was over, people came by and touched Nick as if he were a holy person, and some made the sign of the Cross as they passed him. One lady asked Nick to pray for her. It was wonderful to be in an atmosphere where Nick was treated as someone special.

We had spent about three hours in the church, and Nick needed a diaper change badly. We stopped at a restaurant and went through the ordeal of transferring him to the wheelchair again and into the restaurant. I told the waitress about our problem of having to enter the ladies' room with Nick to change him, and she stood outside so that no one would enter while we were cleaning him. Then we had a very happy, peaceful meal and went back to our car for the trip home.

Though there were no miracles for the body, our spirits were one thousand percent better. We were very pleased that we had gone and would gladly do it again, though it was physically exhausting for all of us. We took Nick back to Kimberly Hall and arrived at our home thirteen hours after we left.

We now anxiously awaited the day when Nick would be transferred to the rehabilitation hospital. It finally came in May 1978, almost one year after Nick was injured. Nick had struggled for an alert, conscious life for more than seven months of that time.

13

The People vs. Joseph Tramontano

A year had gone by, and "the People" seemed not to care that Joseph Tramontano was still on the streets, unpunished for the terrible crime he had committed in view of five witnesses. Even Nick had identified him in the emergency room when he stammered, *"Joey—Joey Tram. He hit me four or five times with a bat."* The police had taken statements, but still there was no action taking place in the criminal court. The case was not even scheduled for trial!

Becoming actively involved in the criminal matter was an unwanted challenge. The charge was "assault in the first degree." That sounded so innocuous. "Assault with intent to kill" was a much better description.

John intended to file a civil lawsuit, and we were working every spare moment on the writ that would have to be filed in court to start it. He wouldn't file it, however, until the criminal case was finished, as there might be information revealed in it that he would need for the civil suit. Also, the VA was still awaiting the outcome of the criminal matter before acting on Nick's pension application.

The state's attorney, Francis McDonald, called John and me to his office on only one occasion. He wanted to learn from us what punishment we thought ought to be given to Tramontano. John responded quickly, "That's up to the state to handle."

My response was not so humane, but given just as fast. "I want Joseph Tramontano to be locked up in prison just as long as my son is locked up in the prison of his body that no longer works."

Mr. McDonald heard me, loud and clear. He understood that I wanted a stiff punishment, but he said, "You know that's impossible."

Nevertheless, he knew I was determined that Tramontano would have to go to prison for what he did to Nick.

The Waterbury Police Department had acted swiftly in arresting Tramontano. They had taken statements from some of the witnesses and had made their reports. Though no one would ever hear from Nick what happened on that fateful afternoon in June, we were beginning to be able to piece together a scenario of the events that had taken place in the YMCA weight-lifting room.

We knew from the statements taken by the police that there were five men in the room: John M. O'Donnell, an intern doctor at St. Mary's Hospital; John Delaney, a Waterbury fireman; Steven Topazio, a seventeen-year-old high school student; Michael Carter, a college student and former employee staff person for the YMCA; and Oscar Anderson. Oscar Anderson successfully avoided every attempt made by the police to get a statement from him.

The first police report stated that when Officers Massaro and Cote arrived at the YMCA, they talked with Dr. O'Donnell. They learned that he had given first aid to Nick, and the officers stated in their report that Dr. O'Donnell told them "that he saw what happened but that he was not going to say any more about what happened or give any more information because he was not going to get involved because he, John Del Buono's father, was a lawyer and that a long dragged-out civil suit was going to take place and he was not getting involved."

When it became apparent that this was a serious criminal case and that Nick might not live, the police had called their photographer to come to the YMCA and take pictures of the inside of the weight-lifting room, where there was blood on the floor and on a large iron weight, indicating that this was the area where the assault had taken place.

The foreman at the Century Brass Company called the police and said that he had heard they were looking for Tramontano, who was an employee at Century Brass. He suggested that Tramontano come into the police station after 11 o'clock, when his shift was over. Lt. Bochicchio told him they wanted to speak with him now. The foreman put Tramontano on the phone, and arrangements were made to meet him at Century Brass.

Detectives Bouley and Murray and Sgt. Messina went to Century Brass about 4:55 PM and drove into the parking lot, where they waited for about ten minutes. They then saw a white Ford Pinto driving out of the lot headed for the guard shed and blew their horn to get the driver's attention. Sgt. Messina got out of his car, approached the driver, and showed him his identification. Sgt. Messina determined that it was Tramantano who was driving the car. While he was talking to him, he noticed a Louisville Slugger bat on the floor of the Ford Pinto in plain view.

At the Detective Bureau, Tramontano was advised of his constitutional rights. The only thing he said pertaining to the assault on Nick was that Nick kept arguing with him, and he struck him with the bat. He was quick to mention that he was working six days a week at Century Brass, and that both his mother and father were very ill with cancer.

Tramontano refused to give a written statement but said he would talk with the police about what happened. He claimed that he and Nick argued over the signs he had put on the walls of the weight-lifting room, that they fought in the mat room, in the hallway adjacent to the weight-lifting room, and in the weight-lifting room. Nick had started to pull some of the signs down from the wall. Tramontano had told Nick to stop, and they fought again out in the hallway.

Tramontano stated that he went out to his car, which was parked in front of the YMCA, got his bat, and placed it outside the weight-lifting room. When the argument started again, he stated that Nick was holding some iron weights in his hand and that Nick threatened him with them. He told the police that Nick kicked him in the groin, and he then got the bat he had brought into the YMCA and hit Nick over the head with it, after which Nick fell to the floor.

Tramontano was booked for assault in the first degree, under Section 531-59 of the Connecticut General Statutes, and placed in the lockup.

The first voluntary statement was taken by Lt. Bochicchio of the Detective Bureau from Paul Ford. Ford stated that he worked for the Waterbury YMCA as a program director and was the YMCA senior person on duty on June 25, 1977. At about 3:00 PM, he was talking to a clerk at the YMCA, Judy Heitman, at her desk. He saw John Delaney run by him, and then Steve Topazio shouted to one of the employees to call the police. He then went to Topazio and asked him what was going on. Topazio said, "Joey hit someone with a bat." Ford knew Topazio was talking about Tramontano, because everyone at the YMCA called him "Joey."

Ford told an employee to call the police and then went to the men's locker room. When nothing was amiss there, he started for the weight-lifting room, as Tramontano was a weight lifter. On his way he saw some guys talking to Tramontano, and he was leaning on a bat. Ford asked Tramontano if someone was hurt downstairs and Tramontano said, "No, what gave you that idea?"

"Someone mentioned it to me," Ford replied.

Tramontano had on a light-colored shirt, and it looked like there was blood on the front of it. When Ford started to walk away, Tramontano said, "Where are you going?"

Ford replied that he was on duty and making his rounds. He said in his statement, "I did not want any trouble with Joey, and he did have a bat in his hands."

When Ford arrived at the weight-lifting room, he saw a man on the floor with blood all over him, thrashing around a lot. Blood covered his face, and Dr. O'Donnell was trying to restrain him. Dr. O'Donnell told Ford to make sure the ambulance was coming and to bring some Valium. Ford went to the pool area and called 911 and then returned to the weight-lifting room.

The ambulance arrived. The attendants worked on the bloody man and then removed him on a stretcher. When they washed the blood from his face, Judy Heitman recognized him as John (Nick) Del Buono, and then Ford recalled having seen him around the YMCA lately.

What startled us most about this statement to the police was that Paul Ford, the man in charge of the YMCA on that day, was afraid of Joseph Tramontano!

The second voluntary statement was also given to Lt. Bochicchio, by Steven Topazio. He told the police that he had gone to the YMCA that day by himself and arrived about 2:30 PM. He changed clothes and went to the weight-lifting room, where he saw Nick, but he did not know his name. He noticed that Nick had scratches on his neck and face and asked, "What happened?" But Nick did not say anything. John Delaney, Dr. O'Donnell, Michael Carter, and Oscar Anderson were in the weight room at this time.

Tramontano then walked into the weight-lifting room with a baseball bat in his hand. When Nick saw him with the bat, he picked up a metal bar, and it looked like there was going to be a fight. Tramantano told Nick, "I am not going to hit you," so Nick put down the bar, and Tramantano put the baseball bat outside the room.

Nick and Tramantano started to argue again. Topazio reported to the police, "Joey takes care of the weight room and he had put up signs, one of which said, 'You slobs put the weights away after using them.'" Nick had taken down the sign. He thought Tramontano worked for the YMCA, and Nick said to Tramantano, "How can the hired help treat paying customers like this?"

They argued, and Nick said to Tramantano, "I will fight you at the Libra Athletic Club, just set a date."

"Joey and Nick were pushing each other around in the hallway," Topazio's statement continued, "and when I looked out, Nick had Joey around the neck with his arms. Michael Carter was watching and told Nick, 'Let Joey go,' and Nick let him go. Nick returned to the weight room, and Joey got the bat and hit Nick over the head with it. Nick was right in the weight room, near the doorway, and Joey was in the doorway when he hit Nick over the head with the bat, causing him to fall to the floor. Joey then stood over Nick and swung the bat twice more, striking Nick in the head each time." Topazio then ran out of the room to the desk and asked for the police to be called. He returned to the weight-lifting room and helped Dr. O'Donnell hold Nick down by holding his legs. When the ambulance crew arrived, Topazio left the YMCA and returned home.

Of the five witnesses to this terrible assault, the young Steven Topazio and his parents were the only ones who were considerate enough to try to help us by allowing John to take his statement. Topazio was also the only man in that room who had given any assistance to Dr. O'Donnell after the assault had taken place. We shall always be grateful to Dr. O'Donnell and Steve Topazio for their assistance to Nick, and to Topazio's parents for allowing their son to help us know what had happened to Nick on that life-shattering day.

John Delaney also gave a voluntary statement, but it was so innocuous I could hardly believe he actually saw this terrible beating occur. His apparent need to run from the YMCA and escape involvement in this incident has lasted to this day.

The fourth voluntary statement was obtained from Michael Carter. He repeated much of what had previously been said, but with some additions. He stated that Tramantano and Nick were arguing because Nick did not like the signs that Tramantano had put up in the weight-lifting room. He said the sign that got Nick mad was the one that said, "This is to all you slobs, keep the room clean." The word slob really made Nick mad, and he felt that Tramantano had no right to put up a sign saying that the members were slobs, though agreeing that maybe signs were needed.

All of a sudden Nick said, "Gentlemen, forgive my actions, but there comes a time when a man just has to stand up for what he believes in."

Carter stated that after more arguing, Nick pushed Tramantano out into the hallway, where the two men tussled. Nick got behind Tramantano and grabbed him around the neck with his arm. In his statement, Carter said,

> Joey could not get free. Joey said that he could not breathe and slipped to the floor. I believed that Joey was going to pass out. He was weak, so I reached down and grabbed the guy's [Nick's] arms from around Joey's neck and told [Nick] to let go, and he did let go of Joey.

I was still looking at [Nick] when Joey walked by me real fast, and hit [Nick] over the head with the bat, and he fell to the floor. While [Nick] was on the floor, I remember Joey hitting him with the bat a few more times and then I saw Joey kick [Nick]. I think he kicked him in the groin.

The doctor yelled to get Joey out of the room, so Oscar Anderson and I took Joey out of the weight-lifting room. Joey still had the bat in his hand, and the doctor closed and locked the weight-lifting room door.

We walked Joey upstairs, and Joey asked me to get his glasses, as they had fallen off. I went back to the weight-lifting room to get his glasses, and then Oscar Anderson and I left the YMCA.

Four years after the assault, we took the deposition of Michael Carter. His knowledge of the YMCA, as a result of his prior involvement as an employee, made his actions on the day of the assault suspect. Why this man, in particular, did not report to Paul Ford that there was an argument going on in the weight-lifting room is beyond my ability to understand. Had he done this, surely Nick would not be in the condition that he is today.

When his deposition was taken, our lawyer, Richard Frank, asked him if he had ever been employed on either a full-time or part-time basis by the YMCA.

"Yes, I was," he answered. "I was working with them as a student worker, and I believe that was '75. I was an employee of the youth department and that entailed administrating, helping to supervise the youth as they came in, and I was also helping with the security of the building."

He stated that at one point he had a shirt that designated him as being a staff member.

When questioned further about security of the building, Carter responded that it was his responsibility to see that no one entered anywhere they should not have been and to "see that things were just smooth, running smoothly." When asked if it was his responsibility to keep order on the premises, he answered that he was a "person that was employed to simply see that the rules were being followed, proper behavior, that type of conduct." When questioned about the areas of the YMCA he covered in his supervision, he stated that the weight room was one of those areas.

Nick cannot tell his side of this story, but he certainly demonstrated that he did not believe in the way the YMCA chose to run its weight-lifting room—and he was right!

Finally, on August 10, 1977, the Waterbury detectives traveled to New York to get Dr. O'Donnell's statement. He had left town immediately after the assault. (He was the Dr. O'Donnell who paged us at the hospital but was not available when we answered the page.) His statement reviewed the previous witness statements about the incident, but his deposition revealed a new scenario about the YMCA weight-lifting club. In it he was asked by Mr. Frank whether or not he was under the impression that Tramontano was the person in charge of the weight room or in some kind of supervisory capacity for the Y as far as the weight room was concerned.

"Yes, I was," he answered.

"And you heard him admit that he put up the signs?"

"Yes, he admitted that."

"And would these signs stay up for a period of time or days or weeks or months?"

"Well, they certainly would be up more than days. Yes, they would be up for weeks. We would go in and see them a couple of weeks."

"Did you ever see Mr. Tramontano eject nonmembers from the weight room or the Bar Bell Club?"

"Yes."

"What was the general attitude among the members of the weight room towards each other? What did they say and how did they act towards each other?"

"There was an attitude that pervaded in the Y, in the weight room. It was almost a muscle-type attitude. There was a macho-type attitude, a who-can-beat-up-who attitude. There were discussions about fist fights in bars and outside the weight room and outside dances. And if that is what you are referring to, that was definitely there. It was. There were discussions about who was tougher than whom and who was stronger, and talk about various individuals taking karate lessons. That attitude was there, there is no question about that."

Dr. O'Donnell was asked again, "When you described this macho or muscle attitude, the words that you used, what do you mean by that?"

"That's why I hesitated to answer the question, because I didn't think I would be able to clarify myself. I think just being all men, that we know the attitude that sometimes there is amongst us as we are growing up about who is tougher than whom and who can beat up whom. And this is the same attitude that was there, only instead of being the way it was when we were kids, when we were in high school or whatever, and talk about wrestling and competitive sports and everything, it existed there with some of the older people. And it was an attitude as to who could beat the shit out of whom. That's what it was. It was as to who was tougher than whom, who is the type of person you want to watch out for, that type of thing, that was there."

We had a hard time believing that this atmosphere existed in a Young Men's Christian Association. But it answered our original question, "How could a thing like this happen in a YMCA?"

We were just beginning to understand why Nick literally lost the life he had known and was now a prisoner of the actions and conduct committed against him in the YMCA on June 25, 1977, by Tramontano, but also by the neglect of the executive officers and board of directors of the YMCA who permitted this atmosphere to exist. This crime and neglect should never have happened!

However, all this explanation did not result in our understanding why the five witnesses did nothing to stop these events from ending in the monstrous way they did. Why didn't any of the men in that room back Nick up in his contention that those crazy, bizarre, handwritten signs on the walls of the YMCA room were not just inappropriate, but outrageous?

Further, as far as I am concerned, none of the men in that room had the decency to admit to Nick, to the police, or to us, that *Nick was right in his quarrel* that those signs *were* wrong and that the YMCA staff had no control over Tramontano. Had their sense of propriety really been dulled that much? And what of the management of the YMCA? Why did they permit such signs on the walls of their building? This was not graffiti on the walls of a ghetto building. It was the YMCA. How could they call themselves a Young Men's Christian Association and allow such an atmosphere to grow and thrive on their premises?

A whole year had passed and "the People" had done nothing to Tramontano. He was still free to walk around town, to eat, to work, to play, even to see.

We were losing faith in the judicial system and its ability to punish Tramontano. The "criminal justice" head on the dragon we were fighting was becoming larger and more difficult to battle.

14

The Rehabilitation Hospital

John and I left Kimberly Hall with Nick on May 23, 1978, for Gaylord Hospital. Our goodbyes to the staff were full of mixed emotions. We hoped that we would not be seeing them again as professionals, but they had become our new, intimate friends for over eight months, and we would miss them. Little did we know that this trip would prove how much Nick's life would be used in service for others who would come after him.

Gaylord is located in the former farming community of Wallingford. The site was originally selected for tuberculosis patients who could enjoy the fresh air and the serenity of the peaceful location as they were treated for their illness. Beautiful countryside surrounds the complex, which consists of several buildings, including one main hospital facility. It is approached cautiously by tree-lined, two-lane winding roads. This seems to signify the tone of rehabilitation at Gaylord: Nothing will be done in a hurry, because this kind of physical improvement is not going to be accomplished in a day.

We arrived at Gaylord full of anticipation and expectation. Nick was greeted with warmth and kindness and ushered into a lovely private room. After Nick was comfortably settled in his bed and we had stored his meager belongings in his closet, the admission process began in earnest. A technician came to take the inevitable blood sample, forms were filled in with answers to interminable questions, and medication needs were determined and ordered, as no facility may forward these to another. Nurses, aides, and therapists streamed in and out of the room right up until dinner time. A young, good-looking woman, Dr. Gloria Singleton, came in to examine Nick.

Nick handled all this exceedingly well. All three of us were in a festive mood, and it seemed appropriate to make dinner a little special on this first evening in his new environment. We helped Nick put on his best bathrobe and get into the most comfortable chair in the room. We put slippers on his feet and awaited the arrival of a dinner tray.

Unfortunately, the floor nurse came into Nick's room before the meal did, and she was startled to see Nick sitting up in the chair. She quickly became upset that he was out of bed and ordered us to put him back in bed immediately. Her explanation was that the doctor had not left instructions that he could sit up.

We tried to explain to her that Nick always sat in a chair to eat his supper; that it was better for him to eat in a sitting position; that not only did we do this at Kimberly Hall, but we were used to taking Nick home on weekends with full responsibility for his safety. However, no amount of pleading from us, or signaled indications from Nick, did any good. She ordered us to return him to bed immediately and left the room in a huff.

We removed his robe and slippers, and, over his gestured protestations, forced him into bed. We had just pulled the covers up when he began to seize, and it soon became a whole-body grand mal seizure. We rang for the nurse and several came when they realized what had happened.

The doctor's report noted: "On the day of admission the patient had what appeared to be a generalized seizure which was described to me as shaking of the lower and upper extremities. There was apparently no loss of consciousness and the patient was able to nod his head appropriately throughout the entire event. He remained on seizure precaution throughout his hospitalization, although he had no other seizures or seizure-like activity."

I believe Nick suffered the trauma of this seizure because of the nurse's attitude. It's well known that emotional frustration can trigger a seizure, and she provided all of us with plenty of that. Her lack of compassion in refusing to check with the doctor before ordering Nick into bed was unforgivable. Not only did she insist on the rule being followed, but she was insolent in the manner in which she did it. She made no attempt to stay in the room to help us relocate Nick in his bed and did not summon anyone to assist us. If it was so dangerous for us to have taken him out of bed, surely it was equally as dangerous for us to put him back.

This episode completely spoiled the anticipation we had of spending a joyful evening with Nick and filled our leaving him with anxiety as to how he would be treated. Nevertheless, we eventually had to go home.

The days that followed began with lonely, stressful treks to Gaylord daily to check on Nick's progress. We were encouraged to come and sit in on therapy sessions, which John, Mary, and I did frequently. He was tested by physical therapists, a speech pathologist, and an occupational therapist.

The physical therapist attempted to get Nick to crawl, and he was able to do so for short distances. Watching your twenty-six-year-old son struggle in an attempt to crawl a distance of three or four feet is a humbling experience. It crushes the soul. Even tears are inadequate to hide the awful sight. Children must learn to crawl before they walk. But, oh, how degrading is the struggle to learn it anew when you are a grown man!

The spasticity and contractures in Nick's body severely restricted any attempts he made at coordinating muscles to move in an appropriate way. Even the simplest of tasks, such as picking up a pen or an eating utensil with his fingers, were impossible.

An equally dismal review was given by the speech pathologist who decided, "Due to this patient's severe level of involvement, adequate assessment could not be accomplished. It is very unlikely, given this information, that additional treatment would be successful at this time."

Nick still had drainage from both the gastrostomy and tracheotomy sites, and these were treated with sterile dressings and antibiotics. His chest x-rays revealed poor inspiratory effort but were otherwise unremarkable. His laboratory findings were within normal range and EKG within normal limits.

The physical examination revealed that his "eyes were continually moving; pupils reacted only minimally to light; fundoscopic examination showed optic atrophy." Further, "he was incontinent of urine. Extremities showed decrease in muscle bulk and increased muscle tone with spasticity in the right upper and lower extremities."

After the neurological examination, the doctor noted, "The patient appeared to comprehend what was said to him. He was able to follow simple commands. He was unable to speak but he communicated by nodding his head appropriately. Sensation appeared to be intact to pinprick and vibration."

On May 30, 1978, one week after admission to Gaylord, Nick was started on muscle relaxants, Dantrium and Valium. These were in addition to the Dilantin he was taking for seizure control.

For the first time since his injury, Nick began to exhibit signs of despondency. He became listless, disinterested in anything, and essentially uncommunicative. We were getting worried about a new problem, one we had long dreaded: depression. When Nick realized what his injuries were, how could there be any other reaction? These tests and therapy sessions highlighted even the minute handicaps.

There was another factor involved, however. It was the medical staff and their inadequate knowledge and training in treating a brain-injury patient. This was visibly demonstrated when I attended an afternoon therapy session.

Approximately ten wheelchair patients were placed in a circle, and each one was given a basket to hold that was large enough to catch a ball about the size of a volley ball. The therapist stood in the middle of the circle and threw the ball to each patient to catch in his or her basket. The patient would then attempt to get the ball out of the basket and throw it back to the therapist. As she went around the circle, I sat in a chair on the sidelines and wondered how she would handle the situation with Nick. Surely she knew he was blind. But when it

The Rehabilitation Hospital

came his turn, she made no change in her routine. She threw the ball straight at a blind man! Of course, he couldn't catch it or even attempt to get it out of the basket.

I ached to scream at her but could not bring myself to do so. Placing these patients in position for this exercise, doing it, and getting them back to their rooms required an hour of therapy time. It didn't need to be interrupted by a hysterical outburst from me. The exercise was a good one for developing coordination in sighted persons, but utterly unrealistic for Nick. When the session was finished, I went to the therapist and asked, "Don't you know that Nick is blind?"

"Yes," she said, "but I don't want to make him feel different."

I heaved a sigh and walked away. Incompetent medical personnel were treating my son and getting paid for their ineffective efforts.

In another episode, related to John by the physical therapist, they had attempted to decrease the spasticity in Nick's right leg by anesthetizing it with an ice bath so that they could work on the leg without his feeling so much pain. I don't know how well they prepared Nick for this therapy before trying, but it was reported that the therapist narrowly escaped injury when his leg was dipped into an ice bath. He swung at her—hard. It was a good thing he couldn't see her.

Nick's lethargy suggested he was becoming more depressed as each day passed, and the new medications were adding mightily to his listlessness and inability to do anything. However, the bright spot in this whole trip came from a young nursing aide. She knew Nick was feeling depressed and empathized with his injuries. He was a handsome young man, and she could easily see what he was missing in life.

I watched as she sat by his bed one Sunday afternoon talking to him.

"Boy, Nick, you must feel like this place is the pits."

He slowly nodded his head in agreement.

"You sure have been dealt a mean blow. I mean, to be so handicapped you can't walk out of here and you can't say what you feel about all of this. It must be a lousy feeling, Nick." On and on she went, saying all the things Nick would say if he could speak. Before she was through, Nick was nodding in agreement and moved his left hand to touch hers.

A more beautiful, more effective counseling session couldn't have been imagined. It did wonders for Nick when it happened, though he would quickly forget it. She had touched him in a way that no one else had. I would remember that scene a long time and use what it had taught me: Nick could be reached on a psychological level. Nevertheless, Nick's depression continued. After two weeks, the family was called for a conference. As usual, John and I were there with Mary. We wanted to hear what the team had to say about Nick.

The team gave their negative reports and asked us about our goals for Nick and whether our home was properly constructed for a wheelchair patient. I thought, "They actually expect me to take Nick home and care for him when they have demonstrated time and again that they couldn't manage his care."

Dr. Singleton explained Gaylord's policy. "Patients are expected to show some rehabilitation progress every ten days. The average length of stay is three months. We know your son cannot perform at this pace, but we are agreeable to keeping him another two weeks. After that, we will have to arrange for his discharge."

As I saw it, their discharge goal was our home. However, John, Mary, and I were fully aware of what their reports would show, and we had agreed before going into the meeting that we were terribly alarmed at Nick's depressed mental state. Moreover, he was so heavily medicated that he had regressed from the progress he had made at Kimberly Hall. We told Dr. Singleton, "We want him discharged immediately, back to Kimberly Hall."

She stiffened visibly and made one more attempt to get us to change our minds. Her tone made it clear that we were ungrateful for what they had tried to do for Nick. She seemed stunned that we were rejecting their offer of two more weeks. Upon our insistence, however, she agreed to the discharge, noting in her report, "A family conference was held with the Del Buono family and it was their decision to transfer the patient back to Kimberly Hall Nursing Home the next day. The Gaylord staff had initially requested an additional two weeks of therapy."

We firmly believed that the staff at Gaylord was using Nick as an experimental patient. We wanted no more of it. We happily picked Nick up the next morning for the return trip to Kimberly Hall.

This was June 10, 1978. In 1980, Gaylord Hospital opened a Traumatic Brain Injury Unit in its facility for the first time. It would be 1983 before I would hear a neuropsychologist on their staff, Dr. Stephen Sarfaty, declare in an open meeting that it was Nick, and other patients like him, who convinced them that they did not know enough about how to care for the brain-injured people coming through their facility, and that these patients required special care and different kinds of treatment and therapies from other rehabilitation patients.

15

Return to Kimberly Hall

Though we were glad to have Nick back at Kimberly Hall, we were devastated that the attempt at rehabilitation had failed. Nick's physical and emotional condition was a surprise and concern to the nurses who had cared for him so long. The new medications made him constantly sleepy and listless, so his responses were poor or nonexistent. Four days after his return, the doctor stopped the order for Valium, and by September the Dantrium was stopped. As a result, Nick's attitude improved and he became more cooperative.

During the day Nick seemed content to sit in a gerichair in his room quietly listening to the radio for short periods of time. At night, however, he was unable to sleep in a normal eight-hour pattern. The night nurse frequently noted that he appeared to sleep in long naps, or short naps. He developed a restless nighttime pattern of completely turning himself around in the hospital bed. His head would frequently be found at the foot, or he would be turned sideways with his legs over the rail in spite of the fact that he was restrained with a vest.

We would later learn that this was caused by inadequate depression of motor movement during REM sleep. It was another indication that knowledge and therapies were not available to us or the staff as Nick reached a level of consciousness where he needed people who understood what he was going through. He was trying to communicate his thoughts and feelings in the only way he had to do it. Today, medical personnel recognize these patterns as part of the brain injury the patient has suffered, and they understand and treat them.

Nick would spend his days either sitting in his bedside chair or in a wheelchair, always restrained. In a nursing home, "restrained" means wearing a vestlike garment with ties that can be attached to the back of a chair or to a bedrail. The use of restraints is supposed to be for the safety of the patient, but it is also demeaning to the person and as close to torture as one can come, since the individual so restrained cannot freely move day or night while tied in this condition.

Nick could push himself forward or backward in either the gerichair or his wheelchair, and frequently pushed himself into other patients' rooms. If he was left alone in his room in the armchair alongside his bed, which had no wheels, he would begin to push himself about in that too. All of this was accomplished very slowly, but he was as persistent and determined a person as he was before his injury.

Nick was becoming more able and helpful in performing some routine chores such as washing himself with a mitt or attempting to brush his teeth, but he still required assistance with these tasks and he never completed any of them by himself.

An especially significant incident occurred shortly after Nick's return to Kimberly Hall. I was in Connie Nelson's office discussing some matters with her, and Nick's blindness was mentioned in front of one of the orderlies who was a special favorite of Nick's. Billy had been assisting Nick in and out of bed for months. When I mentioned that he was blind, Billy paled. "You mean Nick is blind? I didn't know that!" he stammered. This dismayed and disturbed me, so on July 25, 1978, I decided to write a booklet especially for the aides and orderlies. In it I reminded them that:

> NICK CAN HEAR—ANYTHING YOU SAY IN HIS PRESENCE.
> NICK CAN THINK—HE KNOWS WHAT IS GOING ON AROUND HIM AND RESPONDS APPROPRIATELY.

NICK CAN ANSWER—MOST ANY QUESTION WORDED IN SUCH A WAY THAT HE CAN NOD HIS HEAD APPROPRIATELY.

NICK HAS MEMORY—HE CAN RECALL THE PAST AND HE CAN BE TAUGHT SOMETHING AND REMEMBER IT.

NICK CANNOT SEE.

NICK CANNOT TALK—HE'S TRYING TO LEARN AND HAS SAID A FEW WORDS AND MADE SOME SOUNDS.

NICK'S RIGHT SIDE IS CRIPPLED TO A GREAT EXTENT—MORE AND MORE IT IS COMING BACK BUT IT IS VERY PAINFUL TO HIM TO BEND HIS KNEE OR HIS ELBOW.

NICK IS INCONTINENT—HE'S TRYING TO LEARN TO USE THE BATHROOM.

NICK CANNOT GET IN OR OUT OF BED WITHOUT HELP.

NICK CANNOT GET IN OR OUT OF A CHAIR WITHOUT HELP—THERE ARE WAYS TO MAKE IT EASIER ON YOU AND ALLOW HIM TO DO MORE OF IT HIMSELF, THOUGH.

NICK CANNOT EAT WITHOUT HELP—HE NEEDS HELP GETTING THE FOOD IN A SPOON OR ON A FORK AND THEN HE CAN GET IT TO HIS MOUTH HIMSELF WITH THE LEFT HAND.

NICK CANNOT DO ANYTHING COMPLETELY BY HIMSELF EXCEPT BREATHE.

THEREFORE, WE ARE ALL NICK'S LIFELINE. WITHOUT US, HE CANNOT SURVIVE. WITH US, THERE IS MUCH THAT HE CAN DO FOR HIMSELF.

MANY THANKS TO YOU FOR TRYING.

This was followed by nineteen pages of Nick's medical and personal history and the manner in which his injuries had occurred. It turned out to be a big help to the staff, and most of the aides and orderlies did read it. Because of my fears that some would not, I wrote the following and put it over his bed so all who worked with him would have to know at least this much about his condition:

NICK IS BLIND—BUT HE CAN SEE STRAIGHT INTO YOUR HEART EVERY TIME YOU ARE NEAR HIM.

NICK CANNOT TALK—BUT HE WILL TELL YOU A STORY ABOUT YOURSELF EVERY TIME YOU DO SOMETHING FOR HIM.

NICK CANNOT WALK—BUT HE WILL TAKE A STROLL THROUGH YOUR LIFE

Acknowledged a Man

YOU WILL NEVER FORGET.
NICK IS ONE INCREDIBLE FELLOW—YOU WILL BE GLAD YOU MET HIM.

I AM
NICK'S MOM.

This stayed over Nick's bed for the next five years. I know it helped many in their efforts to care for him and to learn quickly the important facts they had to know in order to give him the kind of care he needed. Many of them told me so.

Everything connected with brain injury takes a long time to accomplish. There are hazards that must be faced in making any progress, and these can be terrible when there is improper help and lack of knowledge about the injury itself.

Nick was displaying some of the classic behaviors in the stages patients with brain injury go through when they are groping their way out of coma into a new and frightening world that they, most of all, do not understand.

Nick was on the frontier of the new and exploding world of survivors of serious brain injury. He suffered because of the lack of medical knowledge available, and because what was known was so poorly disseminated among medical people. Nick simply had to take his lumps for being out front, leading the way. And literally speaking, he did.

Today there are rehabilitation units in most major hospitals that treat brain-injury persons, and the medical staffs are more cognizant of what these people need and have more understanding of their condition. But those who are not considered eligible for such rehabilitation are still warehoused in nursing homes whose staffs are as unable to deal with brain-injury patients as they were when Nick was injured. Medical decisions regarding rehabilitation services are most often made in favor of those who show the most promise of being able to utilize all the therapies offered. Long-term care services are still extremely poor for the seriously injured.

Frequently Nick was able to sit on the toilet for bowel movements and would indicate the need for this by pointing behind himself.

However, it would take him a long time to finish, and there were problems with either staying with him or leaving him alone for these long periods of time. One time he slipped off the toilet and hurt himself by hitting his head on the wall. He sustained lacerations that required a butterfly closure.

To let Nick exercise any kind of control over his life and environment meant more terrible risks if he could not be observed constantly. Moving about in his gerichair or wheelchair was even more hazardous than sitting on the toilet. Sometimes he tipped the chair over and fell to the floor. On one occasion it was another patient who notified the nurse that he was in this condition.

Were we told of these falls? No, none of them. When I finally read them in the nurses' notes, which we obtained for the court case, I was overcome with grief. I wept and wept at the cruelty of it all, and the pain and suffering Nick had endured in silence. His condition cried out for better treatment, for more help. But where was it to come from?

Seizures were a constant problem too. Today, I realize that some of them were brought on by his wondering what had happened to him and wanting to know where he was. On one occasion the nurse's notes stated that he was responsive and frightened immediately after a seizure episode. These notes indicated that he was always awake and aware during the seizure, and most of them lasted seven or eight minutes. I try to imagine the terror he must have felt but am always unable to do it.

On another occasion Nick had a seizure at 11:35 in the morning; I picked him up at 1:45 in the afternoon to take him home for a visit. I was not told of the seizure before I left with him. I had learned, though, that the most important thing I could do for Nick during one of these seizures was to stroke him and make him as calm as possible. Generally, he did not want anyone touching him and would try to push them away, especially if they were trying to put a bite stick in his mouth. However, he allowed me to talk to him gently and use caressing touches to relieve the tension in his body caused by the seizure.

It is truly a wonder that Nick survived all the seizures he endured. At that time, no EEG or CT scan was ordered for him. The seizures were treated as a normal consequence of brain injury, and even his medications were not evaluated and prescribed by a neurologist but by the attending physician at Kimberly Hall.

The traumatic, penetrating injury that Nick had was the kind most likely to produce epileptic seizures because the protective layers of his brain were invaded by foreign objects, such as skin or hair, and this subjected the central nervous system to infection.

A generalized seizure, as were most of the ones reported in the nurses' notes, is the most severe type of seizure because it involves the whole nervous system. Unceasing generalized seizures, status epilepticus, were a potential life-threatening complication.

There was no way for us to make Nick's life better, because in one way or another we were expending our entire lives in his behalf. He was home with us every weekend so that he could be given the special attention he needed, and we were frequently in attendance with him at the nursing home during weekdays.

During the time we were with him, he was never restrained with the vest tied to his chair. Upon arriving, our first act was to remove this restraint. When he was at home with us, Nick was not restrained, and he never had a fall or a seizure.

I believe these seizures were the beginning of a phenomenon in Nick's life in which he would later claim to see angels and devils. The medical notes reveal apprehension and fear that we were later to discover accompanied the beginning of seizure activity. At the time, I did not know the anxiety he felt was due to this phenomenon and possibly the cause of the seizure, nor did anyone else. Nick was unable to communicate this information to us.

The fact that he was conscious during all these seizures was also a rare occurrence. Some neurologists might say it is impossible. Having been with Nick through many seizure episodes, I know for a fact that it can and did happen, and the nurse's notes verify it.

Further, most medical professionals will instruct that no one touch the seizing person once they are in a position to be left alone. The usual treatment is to let the seizure run its course, and if this lasts too long, Valium may be introduced intravenously to stop the seizure activity. Even young infants are left in their cribs during these episodes untouched. Nick responds beautifully to soothing words and caressing touches to relieve the tension of the seizure, and I believe it helps stop the seizing activity.

Through all this, the environment at Kimberly Hall remained pleasant. The staff cooperated in every way they knew how, considering the heavy amount of care Nick required. But there was no place for him outside a nursing home.

Nick was learning to live a new life. He was listening to talking books for short periods. He was making efforts to vocalize, but these were poor. His day nurse, Mary D'Agata, whom he had grown to love, charted that he was very strong willed and that he would like someone to sit and chat all day.

He was most unhappy about being restrained, and this was also charted. He had moods of sadness, frustration, and unhappiness, although he would also smile, listen, and try to communicate. He got colds and ran temperatures but would get over them with medication. Life as a brain-injured person was becoming "normal" for him.

An incident especially pleasing to Mary D'Agata and Connie Nelson occurred on December 17, 1978. Mary noted that Nick seemed to know exactly where he was and where he wanted to go. He insisted on pushing himself to the Director of Nurses' office with a problem for her. He was able to communicate by signs and gesturing very well.

Mary related this incident to me and thought it wonderful that Nick could manage this episode so well. I still recall her smile as she told me about it. I'm not sure just what his complaint was, but they all understood what he wanted and were so pleased that he could get his point across. The nature of the complaint became secondary. To his credit alone, Nick had developed his own gestural language without benefit of therapists.

On December 1, 1978, Mary D'Agata wrote a summary of the time Nick had spent at Kimberly Hall since his return from Gaylord.

Shortly thereafter, she left to further her education. Her comments spoke insightfully of Nick's condition:

> Having taken care of Nick for over a year it is difficult to be sure our observations are objective when it comes to his comprehension and intellectual levels. At times the wording of our question needs to be changed for Nick to understand but this is much less of a problem now. Nick's memory is good in any area that has been asked about. With pertinent and leading questions it is possible to carry on quite a "conversation" with Nick. He communicates with nodding, shrugging shoulders and signaling with hands.
>
> Lately Nick has taken to smiling quite readily especially with some sarcastic remark, or silly thing that may happen to one of the staff. He is able to smile also, with effort, on command. This has only happened during the past month. Before, only a pleasant look to indicate happiness.

Nick had two homes now filled with people who loved him: one at Kimberly Hall on weekdays and another at home with us on weekends. For John and me, however, a three-headed dragon was devouring our lives: Nick's *medical needs* were incessant; the *criminal case* dragged along as Joseph Tramontano was still unpunished; and the *civil lawsuit* with the YMCA for the brain injury Nick suffered was unfinished.

All the dragon's heads were huge and active, but we were still fighting, with all our time, our energy, and our financial resources, to overcome this monster in our lives.

16
Advocating for Justice

A society cannot call itself civilized if it does not punish criminals who commit vicious crimes against its citizens. When the punishment is delayed for months, and even years, the victims rightfully cry out for vengeance, and the culture loses its values.

Joseph Tramontano had certainly deprived Nick of his right to life, liberty, and the pursuit of happiness. Yet almost a year and a half after his assault on Nick, he was still free to do all the things Nick could not do. As a result, my family and I hated and loathed not just him, but the system under which we had to live.

As is so often the case, the criminal justice system began its long, slow process of dealing leniently with this crime. The episode in court at the bail reduction triggered the first of what would be a long list of letters trying to get justice administered.

The first letter was dated August 5, 1977, and was addressed to State's Attorney Francis McDonald and Prosecutor Arthur McDonald. Its five pages explained the extent of Nick's injuries and objected to the bail reduction.

Joseph Tramontano was presented in court on August 23, 1977, to enter his plea to the charges against him. John, Mary, and I were in the courtroom when he pleaded not guilty to assault in the first degree and elected to have a jury trial. I wrote to the state's attorney that day requesting to know the trial date so that we could be present.

Not until May 29, 1978, did I again write a letter regarding the criminal case. Nine months had passed, and though I had complained to the state's attorney's office about the appearance of the attorney general's law firm as defense counsel in this case, I had not received a satisfactory response.

Therefore, I addressed my next letter to Attorney General Carl Ajello and sent copies to his law partners, attorneys Clifford D. Hoyle and John Sponheimer, as well as to Governor Ella Grasso, Commissioner of Social Services Edward W. Maher, and State's Attorney Francis McDonald. My letter, in part, said:

> I am the mother of John Nicholas Del Buono. Your law firm in Ansonia, Ajello, Sponheimer & Hoyle, has filed an appearance in the criminal case of State of Connecticut vs. Joseph Tramontano, Waterbury Superior Court, for the defendant. As you know, this case involves assault in the first degree which carries a minimum of ten years in State's Prison. My son is the victim. Although Attorney Sponheimer is the attorney who appeared in court for the defendant, Joseph Tramontano, on the day that bond was reduced from $50,000 to $10,000, we have been told that you were seen in the court house at 7 Kendrick Avenue, Waterbury. It is difficult for me to believe that you had nothing to do with the Tramontano case and the bond being reduced, especially since it is my understanding that Joseph Tramontano is a relative of your wife and the prosecutor strenuously objected to the bond being reduced in view of the serious nature of the crime. Since you are also the Attorney General for the State of Connecticut, this does seem a very peculiar situation. In fact, the State of Connecticut is the only state in the Union where an attorney general, or his law firm, could legally and ethically appear in a criminal case for the defendant.
>
> If that were not enough to restrain your law firm from appearing in this case for the defendant, the following should be. As we have advised you…because of the horrible, overwhelming, torturous injuries to our son…the medical bills are well over $50,000 at the present time and there is no end in sight for the rest of his life. It is impossible for us to carry this kind of medical costs and our son had no insurance or property to offset this. As a result, he has had to go on Title XIX of the State Welfare Department, which fact you know. Since you are also the Attorney General for the State of Connecticut and are charged with the responsibility of seeing to it that the Welfare Department collects what monies it can to reimburse itself for expenditures in behalf of our son, will you collect

these monies from your law firm's client, Joseph Tramontano?

You are in a peculiarly vulnerable position to know whether or not he has any assets which should be known to the State of Connecticut Welfare Department, and to us, so that we can sue and collect in behalf of our son and thereby repay the Welfare Department. In fact, Joseph Tramontano's father died recently and an estate has been opened in the Ansonia Probate Court by a creditor of the father's estate, not by his family, though he did own property at 42 Meadow Street, Ansonia, in survivorship with his wife. This property was put up as security on the $10,000 bond which has allowed your law firm's client to be free for nine months since he viciously attacked our son. The other member of your law firm, Attorney Hoyle, is also the Probate Judge of Ansonia, and should be in a position to ascertain the assets in the estate, including any inheritance for Joseph Tramontano; or, will he disqualify himself as the judge in the estate in view of all of the above facts?

As you can see, Mr. Ajello, I am very suspicious that somehow, somewhere, some political pressure will be exerted in the case of State of Connecticut vs. Joseph Tramontano. I have a right not to wonder whether or not it will be. The only way I can is for Joseph Tramontano to employ other counsel than the law firm of Ajello, Sponheimer & Hoyle to defend him in this criminal matter. I have made the State's Attorney, Francis McDonald, aware of my feelings in this regard. By means of this letter, I am making Governor Ella Grasso aware of my feelings.

Can you now see the vicious circle that we are faced with, Mr. Ajello? You, who should be on our side helping us to recover the monies paid out by the Welfare Department in behalf of our son for medical services, are defending the very person who caused these injuries in a criminal action. By means of this letter, I am requesting that your law firm withdraw from defending the case of Joseph Tramontano in Superior Court at Waterbury.

Mr. Ajello replied the next day, March 30, 1978, in this manner:

Dear Madame:

This is in response to your letter of March 29, 1978.

Under the circumstances of the tragic injuries to your son, I shall ignore the offensive nature of your course of action and your letter to me. This will be at least a partial reply.

I certainly do not condone Mr. Tramontano's actions nor would I attempt to excuse or justify them. The facts of the entire incident speak for themselves.

As you point out, I am free to represent any client in a criminal matter in the State and so are my partners free to do so. It is not true that this is only possible in Connecticut, but that fact is not important. Mr. Tramontano's father was a relative of my wife and he has been a client and acquaintance for many years. It was natural and normal for me to speak to him at the Courthouse lockup and so I did that, at his mother's request.

I later told State Attorney McDonald that I would have Mr. Tramontano find other counsel. This is not because I am not legally and normally entitled to represent his legal rights and interest. It is because of the kind of pressures you are attempting to bring, would in my view, prevent his being given even normal consideration by the prosecuting authorities so long as I, or my firm, are part of his case. So you see the effective pressures in this matter are directly opposite those you allege.

Unfortunately, I cannot respond to the bulk of your other accusations and insinuations. You have engaged competent counsel with whom I have tried to be cooperative to the extent possible. He will ascertain all of the proper legal steps to be taken and I'm sure that each of us will meet his responsibilities.

Finally, let me say that if you had something to tell me, it is quite appropriate for you to do so. But for your letter to be so widely distributed in an attempt to intimidate me personally, is most unfair. It will not aid in the plight of your son, nor will it have any positive effect at all.

I trust that this will conclude our communication.

Governor Ella Grasso was not so prompt in her reply but when she did answer on April 12, 1978, it was a classic:

Dear Mrs. Del Buono:
Thank you for sending me a copy of your letter to Attorney General Carl R. Ajello.

It is my understanding that Mr. Ajello has responded to the concerns you expressed in your letter.
With best wishes,
Cordially, Ella Grasso
Governor

We had learned that Tramontano was due to receive an inheritance from his father's estate in the approximate amount of $15,000. We thought about suing him personally and trying to collect at least this sum, but when we read the financial affidavit Tramontano filed in his divorce case on September 22, 1977, in which he listed a $10,000 debt to attorney Clifford Hoyle, we refrained from doing so. Since Hoyle was the probate judge in Ansonia, we felt we had little chance of collecting any money from him.

By May 3, 1978, the Ajello firm was still representing Tramontano in the criminal matter, so I sent a copy of Carl Ajello's letter to me to Governor Grasso. Her response on June 12, 1978, was another masterpiece of brevity:

> Thank you for your further correspondence concerning Attorney General Carl R. Ajello. I appreciate your keeping me informed as this matter progresses.
> With best wishes,
> Cordially, Ella Grasso
> Governor

When Carl Ajello appeared on her ticket for reelection the next term, I could only surmise that his conduct did not bother her sense of propriety for those in public office.

It is of interest to note that in 1982, the last year that Mr. Ajello served as attorney general, the law was changed in Connecticut. Public Act 82-365 Section 3-124 states, "The Attorney General shall devote full time to the duties of the office." In the future no attorney general could maintain a private law practice, as did Mr. Ajello.

The Ajello law firm finally did get out of the case when attorney John Papandrea took over for the defense and Tramontano changed his plea from not guilty to nolo contendere, or "no contest." This change in his plea meant that he was admitting guilt for the crime with which he was charged and was giving up his right to a trial by jury. However, we could not use his nolo contendere plea in the civil suit against him and the YMCA.

Most important, though, it meant that Tramontano would finally be punished for the crime he committed against Nick by being sentenced to a term in prison.

17

A Finding of Guilt

On October 1, 1978, John, Mary, Sally, Debbie, and I were in court when Joseph Tramontano appeared before the judge to enter a new plea of no contest, seventeen and one-half months after Nick was assaulted.

The judge began a long dialogue with attorneys John Papandrea and Francis McDonald and Tramontano. He questioned Tramontano over and over about whether he understood what his nolo contendere plea meant. The judge wanted to know if Tramontano knew the legal effect of his new plea was the same as a plea of guilty, and Tramontano answered that he was aware of that. The judge persisted by asking Tramontano if he knew he had a right to a speedy trial by jury and the assistance of a lawyer at all stages of the proceedings against him and that he was giving up these rights by his guilty plea. Tramontano answered that he knew that too. The judge continued by making Tramontano admit that he was waiving all of these rights.

Tramontano stood before the court with his back to us as the long and tedious dialogue continued. The judge asked him, "So you have now been made aware of the fact that the maximum penalty is twenty years or ten thousand dollars or both; is that correct?"

"Yes, I do," Tramontano answered.

"And the assault in the first degree under subsection three states: that a person is guilty of assault in the first degree when under circumstances evincing an extreme indifference to human life, you recklessly engage in conduct which creates a risk of death to another person and thereby causes serious physical injury to such person."

"Yes," Tramontano answered.

The judge was nailing the coffin shut.

"It says that you are charged with acting recklessly. And, the definition of recklessly is that the person acts recklessly with respect to a result or to a circumstance he is aware of and consciously disregards a substantial and unjustifiable risk that such result will occur or that such circumstance exists. The risk must be of such a nature and degree that disregarding it constitutes a growing deviation from the standard of conduct that a reasonable person would observe in the situation. So, you wish to plead nolo contendere to conduct evincing an extreme indifference to human life, you engaged recklessly in conduct which caused a risk of death to another person, is that so?"

"Yes, sir," Tramontano said.

Mr. McDonald then explained to the judge the nature of Nick's injuries and that at the time of sentencing he would tell the court that this was a very serious crime and they would ask for a serious penalty.

It was then Mr. Papandrea's turn to speak to the judge, and he told the court that Tramontano had been made fully aware of what the new plea in this case meant.

Upon hearing this, the judge changed the plea and noted that the defendant had waived his constitutional rights. He accepted the guilty plea, saying, "The plea is entered to the charge with a full understanding of the offense involved and that it's entered freely and voluntarily."

Mr. McDonald stated to the judge that a presentence report would be required, and the court set the date for sentencing for November 6 when the presentence report would be available.

We sat spellbound through this entire proceeding. It was hard to believe it was finally happening. It was emotionally draining to be in the same room with this man and look at him, even though his back was to us most of the time. On one occasion, he almost let his temper flare, but his attorney got him quickly under control.

When all this occurred, we were not allowed to speak to the court. This was before the era of victims' rights. Now, victims, and their families, have an opportunity to speak to the judge and make him aware of the effects of the crime to the victim and themselves. Efforts are now being made to persuade Congress to make this a constitutional right. We would have been thrilled to have this opportunity available to us, but, once again, Nick's life was being used for those who would come after him.

When it was all over, we left the courthouse feeling limp and emotionally exhausted. We went to a restaurant to vent our anger and to rejoice that this episode in our ongoing odyssey would soon be closed with the sentencing of Tramontano on November 6.

On October 19, 1978, the senior probation officer, James McGrath, wrote to us:

> Dear Mr. & Mrs. Delbuono:
> I am preparing a presentence report for Waterbury Superior Court on Joseph Tramontano. The report has a section entitled "Victim's Attitude" in which the victim is allowed to comment on the offense. In cases where the victim is unable to comment the immediate family's comments are welcomed.
>
> Please contact me at your earliest convenience at the above telephone number.

We responded to this request, both in writing and by interview. In our letter we reviewed Nick's condition so that it could be read by the judge. The concluding paragraph of our letter stated our feelings:

> We ask one thing for certain in this case: That the Judge who handles this matter know the condition of our son and that Joseph Tramontano did this wilfully and maliciously when our son was unarmed and unable to defend himself. Further, he has spent the last 16 months trying to avoid punishment for his crime by every means possible. Our recommendation is that he receive the maximum punishment possible.

John and I both signed the letter.

During the interview, we told Mr. McGrath all that we knew, including information about Tramontano's arrest record and possible psychiatric treatment. He had reported paying $25 per week for psychiatric treatment and $10 per week for medication on his financial affidavit in his divorce case dated May 6, 1971.

Mr. McGrath told us that much of what he had found out from us and others could not be used in his report because it could not be corroborated with the use of names. He left us with the distinct impression that people would not allow their names to be used in the report because they knew that Tramontano's lawyers would read it, and they also knew that Tramontano would soon be out of prison and they didn't want to have to deal with him later on.

We were the only interested parties who would not be given access to the presentence report.

18

The Sentencing of Joseph Tramontano

Sentencing finally occurred on November 27, 1978, 520 days after the crime was committed, with five witnesses present in the room to see it happen. It had been delayed from November 6 so that Joseph Tramontano could spend another Thanksgiving with his family. This was a particularly galling piece of news for us because Nick also spent Thanksgiving with his family confined to a wheelchair, diapered and having to be fed.

At the sentencing, most of our family was in court when the prosecutor, Francis McDonald, began his dissertation of the events that led to all of us being in court that day. He did not recommend a particular sentence to the judge but did state that it was a serious offense and should be punished with a serious penalty.

Then it was Tramantano's attorney's turn to talk. Mr. Papandrea told the judge that this was a situation that in retrospect should never have happened. He stated that in his conversations with Tramontano he felt that he had done nothing that, in any way, should have led to this incident.

Mr. Papandrea displayed a certificate of appreciation given to Tramontano by the YMCA. Then he began a long discussion about what a wonderful man Tramontano was by showing letters of commendation to the judge from Dr. Anthony Sterling, a specialist in orthopedic and sports medicine; the chief of police, Edward A. Turgeon, for the city of Ansonia; the police commissioner of Ansonia, Howard F. Tinney; one from attorney Clifford Hoyle, the probate judge in Ansonia; and another from the mayor of Ansonia.

Mr. Papandrea told the judge that the chief of police had recommended Tramontano for a state police appointment in 1974 and that Tramontano had taken the state police examination. He showed the judge the results of the examination and the letter of acknowledgment from the state police.

Then he delved into Tramontano's military record. "I think it's important that the court be aware of this because he did serve his country with distinction," he said. Then Mr. Papandrea stated to the court that Tramontano was a peaceable man: "He has not had the reputation of anyone going to look for a fight. Outside of the domestic difficulties that he has had, he has not had the kind of behavior that would ever give rise to the kind of incident that we are faced with here this morning."

Then Mr. Papandrea insulted every member of Nick's family in the courtroom that day by saying to the judge, "What we are asking the court to do, however, is to look as closely as it can on what happens to this young man. Is he one who would benefit by being thrown for a very long period of time into prison? What effect would that have? As far as deterrent, your honor, I would be reasonably confident that whatever psychological help, whatever help of any kind or nature that this young man needs can and will hopefully be given to him during the period of incarceration. But, after that reasonable period, your honor, the question is: what deterrent effect would it have? We would submit to you that this is not a violence-prone individual who is out looking for a fight."

Oh, how those words hurt all of us listening to them in the courtroom that day.

After this long dissertation, the court asked Tramontano, "You have heard the statement of your counsel, Mr. Papandrea. Do you have anything you wish to add in addition to what counsel has said in connection with the penalty to be imposed here?"

"No, sir," Tramontano replied.

The judge then stated, "I looked through the report and one of the things that struck me, in reading the report, is the lack of any remorse. Did you want to address yourself to that?"

There was silence from Tramontano. Mr. Papandrea interjected, "He has always expressed remorse to me."

The judge quickly went back to Tramontano and asked, "Do you have anything further to add, Mr. Tramontano?"

"No, sir."

Then came the defining moment we had waited for. Judge Robert A. Wall said, "The sentence of the court in state against Joseph Tramontano is that he be placed in the custody of the commissioner of correction for confinement in the State Correctional Institution at Somers for not less than seven, nor more than fifteen years."

When it was all over, there was a moment of relief, but it soon gave way to feelings of rage because we were not able to address the court in Nick's behalf. We wanted to do for Nick what Mr. Papandrea had done for Tramontano, but we could not. How unfair to the victims the criminal justice system is! The prosecutor's statement on behalf of "the People" was short indeed. Tramontano appealed the sentence to the Sentence Review Committee. We had some satisfaction in that we were able to write to them and express our views regarding this appeal. Our concluding two paragraphs to the Sentence Review Committee summed up our position:

> We do not believe that the sentence in this case should be reduced and have accepted the sentence of the judge of the Superior Court at Waterbury as whatever justice is humanly possible in a matter of this kind. We are tempted to ask for the sentence to be increased to the minimum of ten years instead of the seven that was given, but will refrain from doing so.
>
> We can only hope that this man gets whatever help he needs while in prison where he can do all of the things our son cannot do and that at some point in his life he comes to repent for his brutal act.

John and I both signed the letter.

On May 8, 1979 we received another letter from Mr. McDonald:

> Please find enclosed a copy of the April 17, 1979 decision in which the Sen-

tence Review Division has affirmed Joseph Tramontano's sentence.

Once again, I wish to express my regrets about your son's condition.

Throughout our ordeal with the criminal justice system, Mr. McDonald treated us with kindness, respect, and concern for our welfare and that of our son.

The Sentence Review Committee's decision stated:

By the Division: The defendant, age 34, was found guilty, after a plea of nolo contendere, of Assault in the first degree. He was sentenced to imprisonment for a period of not less than seven nor more than fifteen years.

On June 25, 1977, the defendant and John (Nick) Del Buono angrily disagreed. Before long they were at each other's throats, boxing and wrestling. The defendant armed himself with a baseball bat. He laid it down. Another quarrel erupted; the combatants wrestled. Bystanders separated them. The defendant retrieved the baseball bat, struck Del Buono over the head, then struck him again with the baseball bat and kicked him while Del Buono was prostrate, seriously wounded.

There were claims that Del Buono was the aggressor. But the defendant never ceased in his aggression. He persisted, unwilling to cry enough until he incapacitated Del Buono for the rest of his life.

The sentence is affirmed.

That quick review of what happened by these judges vindicated Nick, for whatever good it does. Of course, I wish Nick had not fought with this brute. Of course, I wish he had walked out of the YMCA building and never entered it again. At times I wish he had done to Tramontano what Tramontano did to him instead. If he had, then he would be the one free from prison today. As it is, *Nick's imprisonment is for life!*

If Tramontano's sentence represented anything like the time he would serve in prison, we could have maintained some faith in the criminal justice system. But the *actual time* that Tramontano spent in the state prison at Somers, Connecticut, was only *three years*. After that, he was transferred to the *YWCA* in New Haven, Connecticut, where he served another *nine months* on a work-release program.

This was outrageous and absurd! And it became more so when we learned that Tramontano was released from prison just a few months before Carl Ajello went out of office as attorney general. Of course we suspected he had pulled strings to get Tramontano out before he left office, though we had no proof of this.

Our criminal justice system has become a farce because of its lack of compassion for victims and in its overprotection of criminals. It causes citizens who want to be law-abiding to be tempted to buy weapons and take the law into their own hands. Only one thing prevented John from doing this: *belief in God!* Without it, there is no reason to restrain oneself. Without it, Joseph Tramontano would be dead.

John told Tramontano's legal assistant to prisoners, "You had better be glad that I am a Christian, because if I were not, Joseph Tramontano would long since have died 'Mafia style' for his horrible beating of my son and the injuries he inflicted upon him and our whole family." For a long time afterward John mumbled "Son-of-a-bitch" over and over again when he was in bed at night.

Later, I had to tell Nick repeatedly who it was that had injured him and try to deal with the question Nick asked in sign language, "Why?" I would tell Nick that Joseph Tramontano had to be crazy to do what he did and that if he did not repent for it, he would probably spend an eternity in hell. The only consolation in all of this is that Nick has learned how to be free in spirit while Tramontano remains a prisoner of the hell of his own immoral behavior. There has never been any indication of repentance from him.

It would take a lot more time for me to be able to say, "I forgive him for what he did." But it finally happened, and I have had a great deal more peace since that time. One should not go on forever being bitter and angry. The bitterness consumes you to the point where you become as paralyzed in spirit as Nick is in body functions. I cannot look into Joseph Tramontano's soul and know why he did this terrible thing. Only God can, and Divine Judgment is His.

Many years later, I got up enough courage to ask Nick, "Can you forgive Joseph Tramontano for what he did to you?"

Nick quickly nodded "Yes" and put his hands together to say, "Let's pray for him."

I told Nick that if he could, I would, and we prayed together!

19

Family Counseling

John had an especially difficult time accepting the fact that Nick was permanently blind. He searched newspapers and magazines for any kind of story that might have a ray of hope for recovery of Nick's eyesight. He saw an article in the newspaper about a breakthrough in eyeglasses that had been made by the VA. He called the VA hospital in Newington and was turned over to a man by the name of Sal D'Amico. They had a long talk about the article and about blindness. Sal could sense on the phone what John was going through and asked him to come to Newington to see him.

Meeting Sal D'Amico made an impression on John and me that we shall never forget. He was a slightly built, thin man with a curve of a smile that was more like grinning than smiling. He had a charming personality; he was very self-assured and quite competent in a situation where that had to be hard to attain. Our meeting with him was an awesome experience. *He was blind himself!* That is why he knew so much about John's feelings. However, blindness was not his only handicap. Both hands were missing, and the stubs of two arms were bare. One arm had been cut so that it had two prongs that acted as large fingers.

While we sat and talked with Sal, he reached into his shirt pocket with these "fingers" and took out a cigarette. He deposited the ashes in a jar of water sitting on his desk. All this was done in a casual fashion, while he sat and talked, questioning us, learning about Nick's injuries and about John and me and our family.

His questions to John were pointed, hitting the raw edges of John's feelings. In such situations, John always turns to humor for the relief of his intense feelings. He did so in this case too, and he and Sal bantered humorously with each other. John warned him about the dangers of smoking cigarettes, and Sal quickly retorted, "It's okay, I'm already in a hospital. You're having a real hard time accepting the fact that your son is blind, aren't you?"

"I just don't want to leave any stone unturned to try to help him, if help is available," John answered.

"But what if there is no help for your son and he has to go through life as a blind person? What will you do then?"

John squirmed in his chair as he replied, "I'm not ready to give in to that. I'll keep looking for every avenue of hope there is."

John was keenly aware that he was talking to a blind person. It was an intense moment.

Sal D'Amico was a social worker with the VA. One of his duties was counseling families of veterans who had been injured. He had been appointed by the secretary of Health, Education and Welfare to the advisory council of the White House Conference on the Handicapped in 1974. This commission worked for more than two years on problems of the handicapped, and they turned in three volumes of reports to President Carter and Congress in 1977, the same year Nick was injured. The result of their work has been the adoption of important legislation for the handicapped and, more importantly, the enforcement of existing federal, state, and local legislation concerning handicap laws.

Sal's work with the VA hospital was primarily with the visually impaired. He was also coordinator of community care and supervisor of nursing home programs for veterans. Further, he counseled families of veterans concerning finances and psychological, family, or marital problems.

With this background, it was no wonder that he immediately saw the need our family had for counseling. He told us that Nick, being a veteran, was entitled to it without charge. But we would all have to make the one-hour trip to Newington for this family help. All members of the family could come, but would they, could they? Counseling sessions would be held during a weekday afternoon. How would everyone manage that kind of schedule? Sal had helped us both so much that first afternoon we were anxious to try to have our family attend.

To our happy surprise, our son-in-law, Tom, arranged to get an afternoon off every other week so that he could join Mary. Joe and his wife would come too. Our daughter, Susan, would get a baby sitter and come, but her husband could not make it because of his job. Sally, Debbie, and Cathy would come with us. This was our entire family, except for Joan, who was in Colorado. Could it be they felt the need for counseling as much as we did?

We began the sessions with Sal and grew to admire and love this man who drew out feelings in each one of us at these meetings. He let our emotions spill out with never a word of reproach to any of us for some of the outrageous things we said. He often goaded us into expressing our deepest thoughts but was never judgmental.

The anger some felt toward Nick for getting himself hurt and turning our lives upside down came out. The worry and concern of others for what all this was doing to their parents were voiced. In-laws, who didn't have the past association and memories of Nick that the immediate family had, now had a forum to plead helplessness and inability to cope with a marriage partner who couldn't seem to get past those memories. Frustration and bitterness among family members was laid bare and talked about openly. The hatred we all felt for Tramontano was very apparent.

Surprisingly, we learned that those in the family who seemed to have the toughest time coping were the ones who were really dealing with their feelings. Those who seemed to have everything under control were repressing theirs. These sessions made us take a good look at each other and what we were trying to deal with.

Sal made it abundantly clear that ours was a catastrophic situation, as it would be for any family. We learned that there was no right way to handle the kinds of emotions such a tragedy brings on. Each of us was free to be ourselves and manage it to the best of our ability to cope. No one was right or wrong. We were all just trying to survive the best way we could.

Mary asked the boldest question of Sal: "I don't know how your accident occurred, but do you feel any bitterness over what has happened to you?" She bluntly told him, "If you won't be offended, I would like to know what caused your injuries."

He answered by discussing it openly and frankly. Sal explained that he had been a demolitions expert in the war. On one occasion he was in a classroom teaching students how to defuse a bomb when he saw one of the students in danger of unintentionally setting off some explosives. Sal acted quickly to try to stop the explosion, but he was not fast enough and was injured. The result was the loss of his sight and the loss of his arms. "It was a terrible ordeal," he stated frankly.

He told us that there was a long period of adjustment before he was able to accept what had happened to him, and that he was not bitter because it had led him into counseling, which very much suited his personality. Moreover, he was actually grateful for this particular career change in his life because he was enjoying being able to help families such as ours.

Sal spoke about the difficulties of blindness. He told us that his mother did not want to accept the fact that he was blind, and so he would kid her along that he could see the light when he only heard her turn on the light switch. His children liked to play being blind by closing their eyes and feeling their way around a room, but after awhile they would grow tired of the game and open their eyes. "Being blind," he said, "is when you grow tired of the game but you can't open your eyes."

I would remember this thought many times as I tried to put myself in Nick's position, and when we tried to teach our young grandchildren what it is like for Nick to be blind. Sal also told us, "Blindness is not something you can just accept and go on about your life as a blind person. Being blind is something you must accept over and over again, every single day of your life."

It was decided that Nick should come to the last conference with the family. We all wondered how this would come off. Sal would be trying to lead the session with Nick, who was also blind and could not speak! How would Sal manage this? We almost felt the attempt would be ludicrous, but Sal seemed to be quite at ease with the idea, and we were too embarrassed to disagree.

When we arrived for the session, Sal had two young women in the room with him. They were students in college, training to do social work. He wanted their impartial observations of Nick and our family. They would be his eyes while he managed the meeting.

The session went very well. Nick got to answer some of the pointed questions Sal had aimed at us. "Being injured and handicapped is the pits, isn't it, Nick?" Sal asked.

Nick's response was an affirmative nod of the head and his familiar military salute. He and Sal "talked" this way about blindness and the family. We all had an opportunity to thank Nick for the counseling he had made possible for us by his military service, and we watched as he saluted again in a gesture of "That's okay."

Debbie had a chance to scream at him for getting hurt and ruining all their beautiful plans. Then she ran from the room crying. Nick handled that better than most of us did. We were astounded that she would confront him like that, but he sat in contemplative silence as everyone in the room tried to find words to express their feelings. Sal finally asked Nick, "How do you feel about what Debbie said?"

Nick gestured, "It's okay."

I believe Sal was somewhat surprised with his associates' report on how well Nick looked. His skin tone was good since all the bruises had healed, his hair had grown out, and he had gained weight. However, Sal's questions about me to the two young women revealed a concern I had not thought of. Was I taking care of myself, was my hair done properly, did I care about my appearance? My voice sounded okay, but he warned that this kind of catastrophe could result in a mother going to a mental hospital.

I told Sal about the time I experienced feelings of hatred for a young man I didn't even know when I saw him swimming in a pool one day. Nick had been a good swimmer, and I hated this stranger for being able to do what Nick couldn't. Another time I was driving along the streets of New Haven and had these feelings rush in on me when I saw a young man quickly tripping up the stairs in front of Woolsey Hall. Something about the way he did it reminded me of Nick, and Nick would never be able to do that again.

I know now that I will always have moments of these kinds of feelings. They are temporary rushes of emotion that I cannot help. But now they quickly subside when the wise, accepting part of my brain starts operating and I remember the wonderful son that I do have.

The counseling sessions came to an end with an open invitation from Sal for any of us to return at any time. His invitation would be accepted, as some of us did return. Sal D'Amico had affected all of us in a very positive way.

We had to take Nick back to Kimberly Hall, but we all felt good and wanted to celebrate first. We decided to stop at Valle's Restaurant in Hartford for dinner. We had taken Nick there before because it was wheelchair accessible. Nick could "read" the menu by listening to us tell him what was on it and indicating the selection he wanted to eat. He would raise his hand or nod in an affirmative manner when we mentioned something he liked. His preference was usually steak, and he ordered it on this occasion.

As Nick was eating, a piece of meat became lodged in his throat, and he began to choke. John and I jumped up and jerked him out of the chair, and Mary quickly applied the Heimlich maneuver to him. The piece of meat came flying up! I was frozen with fright. I felt limp and couldn't eat another bite. The realization that he could have died right there on the spot overwhelmed me. Without question, Mary had saved his life.

All of us were shaken, and I would not give him any more steak, though he wanted it. Once the incident was over, Nick felt perfectly okay and wanted to continue his dinner. It was as if he had already forgotten what had happened. But we had not, and our feelings of celebration came to a quick halt with the reality we had just witnessed.

Family Counseling

Our mood of elation was broken, and we were far more somber when we left the restaurant. We had just experienced one more ride on the brain-injury roller coaster, and I knew then we would never be able to find an exit.

Though the family counseling sessions had helped all of us, our emotions would remain on this unwanted ride forever. No amount of counseling would change that, but we understood more about what had happened to us, and perhaps we would be better equipped to handle our feelings.

All of us needed to try to adapt and learn how to live with a brain-injured family member. It was important that we accept Nick in this new life of his. Yet how could each of us go on with our lives and still find the time to give Nick the attention he required in his slow-motion world?

A few of us would be willing to straddle this dragon and fight it, but most would not.

20

Hunting for a Trial Lawyer

Though we were spending most of our time with Nick, John and I had to pay attention to another head on our dragon, the civil lawsuit. We needed to hire a prominent negligence attorney to try Nick's case.

John had handled negligence cases all his legal career and prepared this one for trial. But because Nick was his son, he could not try the case before a jury. Therefore, John called attorney William Davis in Hartford. He turned down the case on the telephone when John told him that it involved a fight. Mr. Davis had just concluded a long trial, which he had lost. He commented that he might be turning down a million-dollar opportunity, but that John had caught him at just the wrong time.

It was then decided that I should make an appointment with another prominent trial lawyer, Theodore Koskoff. He was president of the American Trial Lawyers' Association, and his office was in Bridgeport, Connecticut. I traveled there alone for the appointed conference and brought with me pictures that had been taken of Nick in the hospital.

The office was located in a dingy building in Bridgeport. I was somewhat dismayed as I took the elevator upstairs. Nevertheless, after a brief time in the waiting room, I was escorted into a spacious room, with very modern, Hollywood-like furnishings. It was very impressive, as was Mr. Koskoff sitting behind what I would have termed "the director's desk."

I told him that I was Nick's mother and that I had been appointed conservatrix of his person and estate on July 13, 1978. Mr. Koskoff listened patiently and then began to call in his team one by one. First, attorney Richard Beider, whom I had seen on the elevator; then another gentleman; and finally, a young woman whom he introduced as a "nurse" on his staff. He said she was part of the team, and that one of her duties was to decipher medical records.

Suddenly, all the questions became medical ones. Was Nick monitored in the emergency room? How soon was he taken to ICU? Did the neurosurgeon leave the hospital before he went into a coma? Did he leave before the first operation? Was there any alcohol on his breath in the emergency room? What was his reputation in the community? Did I have the transcript of Nick's medical records from the hospital?

I could see the turn that the conference was taking: medical malpractice, not negligence. I was numbed by the stinging questions that were flying through the room.

Nick hadn't been monitored in the emergency room! The doctor did leave the hospital before Nick went into a coma and before the first operation! He had to be called back to the hospital. It had seemed like an eternity before Nick was admitted to ICU, and the scene at the hospital before we were allowed to see Nick was weird. We had not smelled alcohol on Dr. Sturman's breath that afternoon, but John did detect it when he returned to the hospital in the evening. He was going through a divorce, and alcohol was rumored to be a problem. His reputation, insofar as we knew, was as an excellent neurosurgeon with poor doctor-patient relations.

Two vital issues never came out at the meeting with Mr. Koskoff, and I could not bring myself to voice them. One was that Dr. Sturman should have given us a choice about whether to send Nick to Hartford Hospital for an immediate CT scan of his brain. This would have revealed the serious clotting that was not attended to for three weeks.

The other was that the long delay between the first and second brain operations may have caused severe and permanent brain damage, some of which might have been avoided.

I explained to Mr. Koskoff that I did not have Nick's medical records but that I would get them. As we talked, the name of a neurosurgeon was mentioned who might be used as an expert witness. His name was Dr. William Collins of Yale-New Haven Hospital. The team spoke eloquently about his reputation, and they commented that his integrity was beyond question. They said he would call the shots just as he saw them and would testify in court if he truly felt there had been a case of malpractice. On the other hand, he would be upfront with the lawyers if he felt there was none. They touted him as one of the five best neurosurgeons in the world with impeccable qualifications that would easily qualify him to testify as an expert.

The last recommendation was the one I was most interested in hearing. They would have Dr. Collins examine Nick's medical records for malpractice, but I wanted him to examine Nick for possible rehabilitation treatment for his injuries.

I was escorted to the door by the nurse on his staff with the admonition to get Nick's medical records to them as soon as possible. I was in a stupor while riding the elevator down to the main floor.

In the car on the way home, I cried and cried. Had we been so traumatized that we had unknowingly allowed malpractice to happen to Nick on top of the assault he had suffered? Were we to blame for letting it happen? What had been the matter with us in that emergency room? Should we have demanded that Nick be taken by ambulance to Hartford for a CT scan? What kind of parents were we to let all these unanswered questions just hang in the air?

When I returned to John's office, I was in a state of panic. John and I talked for a long, long time. He too had handled malpractice cases, and he was not impressed with it as a legal possibility in Nick's case. "Trying to sort out the damage done by the baseball bat as against any that might have been done due to malpractice is too much to consider," John explained. This made sense to me and calmed my nerves. Thank God, not only for the lawyer that I married but for the man that lawyer is. We never sent the medical records to Mr. Koskoff and did not contact his office again.

Nevertheless, the conference with Mr. Koskoff had revealed the name of the neurosurgeon we wanted to examine Nick. We believed he had made significant progress since his admission at Gaylord and hoped, once more, that Nick might be a candidate for another try at rehabilitation. With the glowing recommendation from Koskoff's team in our minds, we believed Dr. Collins was the only one to evaluate Nick for this possibility.

After having been turned down by Mr. Davis and the malpractice episode in Mr. Koskoff's office, John contacted a New York lawyer, Lee Goldsmith, but he also turned the case down. Attorney Fred Heller, who was going to do a film of "A Day in the Life of Nick Del Buono," recommended another New York lawyer, Richard Frank, to us. He had successfully represented Connie Francis in her lawsuit against the Howard Johnson motel chain when she was brutally raped in one of its rooms.

When we went to see Mr. Frank in his New York office, he said that one of the reasons he was willing to take the case was that the father of the victim had prepared it. He knew there would be extraordinary effort used to seek the evidence needed for trial. Further, he had sued the YMCA previously and knew a great deal about the operation of its facilities. He was not impressed with the Y's professionalism. He agreed to take Nick's case and filed his appearance in the Waterbury Court.

We have always been pleased that we chose Richard Frank and that he chose us. Hunting for a prominent trial lawyer was a difficult task indeed.

21

Permanent Injuries

The realization came slowly, over many months, that Nick was a thinking, remembering human being trapped inside a horribly crippled body, and this knowledge led us to desperately seek ways to help release him from his prison. I was constantly reminded of Alexander Dumas' story, *The Man In The Iron Mask*—and decided that Nick was much worse off than he.

Discovering the abilities Nick still possessed was like mining for gold, a slow, tedious process. His handicaps were so numerous they hid his strengths. The doctors had predicted he would be like a small child and have the mind and emotions of one, that his memory would be gone, that the part of his brain that stored information would not be functioning. As we spent more and more time with Nick, we found that some of these predictions were simply not true.

Nick could spell simple words with about four letters in them. By using games of multiple choice, he could pick out the right spelling by a nod of the head. In the same manner, he could discern simple parts of speech, like nouns and verbs in a sentence. He could correctly identify opposites and similarities. Playing these games occupied a lot of our time when we were with him. We all believed that he was progressing sufficiently to warrant another try at rehabilitation.

The long-awaited trip to Yale-New Haven Hospital to have Dr.

Collins examine Nick for possible admission to a VA rehabilitation hospital had been carefully planned. I had talked with a staff person at the hospital and was assured that I could stay with Nick at night. I was told a cot would be set up in his room so that I could sleep next to him.

A conference with the staff at Kimberly Hall preceded the trip. Connie Nelson, Mary D'Agata, and the physical therapist all joined me in a discussion of Nick's future. Everyone agreed that the nursing home was no longer the appropriate place for him, and that a VA hospital would probably be a better setting, since he would be with other young men. There was an especially good one in Massachusetts for rehabilitation of spinal cord patients. We all hoped Dr. Collins would send him there.

When we arrived at this world-renowned institution in New Haven, we felt as if we had been transported back to the 18th century! We wheeled Nick down dark corridors with high ceilings in an old part of the institution where the neurology ward was located. There was nothing about the atmosphere to remind one of a modern hospital.

We were shown into a small room with three beds in it, two of them already occupied by male patients. It was difficult to maneuver Nick's wheelchair into the tiny space next to the empty bed. There certainly was no room for the promised cot! When I questioned one of the staff persons about it, she seemed not to know what I was talking about. It quickly became clear that if Nick was to get this long-awaited evaluation from one of the five best neurosurgeons in the world, at this world-famous hospital, then I was going to have to forsake the promises made to me in favor of reality.

I was petrified to leave Nick alone in the room. Both the men in the other beds were also brain-injured persons, and I had not had an opportunity to talk with them. Also, Nick was in strange territory again. He held onto me tightly and would not let go. I had to keep in voice contact with him at all times for him to have any peace of mind.

The fright that I felt from the thought of leaving Nick alone was indescribable. I couldn't do it, until it became extremely uncomfortable trying to sleep in his wheelchair. About 3:00 AM, when all the patients in the room were sound asleep, I left to go for a walk. I entered the lounge and saw a comfortable couch that looked very inviting. No one was in the room, so I decided to lie down on it and stretch my legs. The sensation was heavenly, and I quickly drifted off into a deep sleep I hadn't intended. About an hour later, I woke up with a start. I was in a state of alarm as I rushed back to Nick's room.

Nick was halfway out of bed, with his left foot on the floor! He was trying to get up because the bed was wet. There was no nurse in sight, so I pulled, and Nick pushed, until he was finally back in his bed. I changed the sheet and whispered to him for a very long time before he went off to sleep again. This time I stayed close by, sitting in his chair and holding his hand.

The days that followed were filled with tests, evaluations, and a great deal of observation. I was watched while I fed Nick, and the staff monitored John and me as we walked with Nick up and down the hall in what seems to me now to be a pitiful fashion. At the time, we were quite proud of what he could do. To us, it was a miracle that he could stand on his left foot and hobble on the right one, with one of us on each side, holding him up. To the medical personnel, we must have looked like two unrealistic parents, off in a dream world of their own, helping a mummy walk.

Nick's eyesight was tested again, as was his ability to remember and think. He could remember who the president of the United States was, but he couldn't tell what town he was in. He thought it was a hospital in Waterbury, not New Haven, and that seemed significant to them.

When Nick had to be taken anywhere, I implored the nurse to let me go with him. His crude form of communication was a mammoth barrier in this hurried hospital atmosphere. I had learned that the planning was poor when he had to be tested on any of their machines. An EEG and CT scan were both ordered.

When Nick arrived at the room for the EEG test, I was told to wait down the hall in a waiting room until it was completed. The

Acknowledged a Man

wheelchair attendant who had accompanied us had already left. Nick looked pretty normal sitting in that chair. I was reluctant to leave and begged the technician to just let me show her how to transfer Nick from the chair to the very high table he would be lying on for the EEG test. I told her he was blind. She unwillingly agreed to my suggestion.

I proceeded to go through the slow, complicated routine of standing Nick up, helping him take a step or two, explaining to him where the table was that he was going to have to lie down on, and what he was going to have to do to get on it. The EEG technician became more alarmed with every move we made and every word I said, obviously concerned about our safety and the hospital's responsibility.

I succeeded in getting him on the narrow table, which had no straps with which to anchor him. If I left the room, the technician would have to operate the machinery outside the room looking through a glass window. With Nick alone on that narrow table, one move either way and he would be on the floor! I told her that for safety's sake I felt I must stay with him.

The technician went to the phone and called the neurology ward. She told the person on the other end of the phone that they had better never schedule another patient like Nick for an EEG unless they brought him to her on a stretcher, strapped down. She said she would do the EEG test because I was there to help, but they had better never place her, nor a patient, in that kind of peril again.

All this was said in front of Nick as though he couldn't hear. Nick really didn't want to get on that table. He did it for me. I wanted him there because I hoped the crude little machine called "EEG" would register something that would show he was improving so he could be sent to another rehabilitation hospital.

A similar scene took place when the CT scan was to be done. However, this time the staff was quick to recognize that I knew how to handle Nick and allowed me the time I needed to transfer him to their table. They were curious when we communicated with each other and used me as their interpreter with him throughout the session.

All of us, temporarily, become like Nick is permanently when we enter a hospital. Although our eyes are open, we are really as sightless as Nick, because we have to blindly trust that these people know what they are doing. We are helpless in their care. We have one great difference from Nick, though. We can agree or object. He cannot.

The evaluation was completed, and the time came when Dr. Collins scheduled a meeting with John and me. He had already talked to me once, and I knew the news was not good about Nick's eyesight. I also knew how hurt John would be when he heard it. I cautioned Dr. Collins about John's optimism, and he promised to answer any questions John had as fully and as honestly as he could.

He asked how we were handling this financially. I explained that Nick's medical bills were being paid by Title XIX, but that did not take into account what it was costing us. "Frankly, we have been overwhelmed by all of this, including the financial burden," I said.

It's true that Nick's medical bills were being paid by Title XIX, but John's law practice had dwindled to its lowest point since he had opened practice on his own. He was struggling to keep food on our table and pay the necessary bills while he worked day and night on Nick's lawsuit with the YMCA. We had to pay all the costs of instituting this kind of lawsuit and the attendant expenses involved in doing it. These came to over $27,000 before the case was finished. But that was not the biggest expense. This lawsuit cost John five and a half years from his law practice and then another five years while he built it back up again. It is a wonder he was able to sustain himself in private practice and maintain a home with three teenage daughters to raise. But he did it. His professional and personal sacrifice in behalf of his son was heroic.

Also we were forced to give up the business of publishing books that we had started. I had hoped for a career in writing and Mary and Nick wanted a share in the publishing company as well. All these careers were either put on hold or ended forever.

In the conference the next day with John and me, Dr. Collins explained that he and his team had thoroughly reviewed Nick's records. He had called St. Mary's Hospital for many of them. He told us that Nick's injuries were very severe. He said the brain damage was done in the first five or ten minutes while he lay on the YMCA floor.

He began his dissertation on Nick's injuries by explaining to us that although Nick had light perception coming through one tunnel of vision in one eye, it was of no practical use to him. He could not distinguish very large letters or numbers when they were held up for him to see. Further, he did not believe the cells of Nick's brain that stored memory (such as what a window or door is) were functional. He said that even if Nick could see these things, he would not remember what they were and would have to be taught this all over again.

"Your son is not a candidate for any rehabilitation hospital, anywhere in the world," he bluntly stated. "I routinely do examinations for admissions to the VA hospital in Massachusetts, and it will do no good to send his records to them because they will not admit him. Your son's cognitive deficits are severe. His intellectual level has been decreased to that of a small child at best," he explained. Then he added the worst blow of all, *"If there is anything worse than death, this is it."*

He chided us by saying, *"Rehabilitation efforts would be cruel to your son and would only serve to prove to you what he cannot do. His injuries are permanent.* He will probably encounter regression, rather than progress. Your goal for Nick should be to make him as comfortable as possible for the rest of his life."

With a prognosis like this, there are few questions to ask. We had been stunned many times in the past two years, but nothing equal to this! There was such a finality to it. We walked out of his office in a daze.

The staff had Nick on a stretcher, ready for discharge immediately after the conference was over. No explanations were made to him. His hopes had been high too. I had seen the effort he had made during the days of testing, and I knew this meant a lot to him.

Nick's discharge records had been placed on the stretcher beside him. An aide wheeled him down to the car as I stumbled along beside them. My mind was numb, unable to protest. As we got inside the car, I was in a state of shock. John had driven to New Haven in a separate car because he had to return to the office immediately after the conference with Dr. Collins was over.

I was alone with Nick, trying to find our way off the hospital grounds and onto the streets of New Haven. Through my tears, I looked for signs indicating directions to I-91. Nick was sitting alongside me in our Thunderbird, pulling on my arm. I wasn't really conscious; I was operating on a kind of remote control, as if someone else were guiding me through this.

As I look back on that scene, I realize how important emotions are and how very, very little the medical profession knows or cares about them. During their training, they seem to carefully and systematically insulate their feelings from their work. Maybe they feel they have to, but I don't agree. Some are made insensitive, emotional cripples by this insulating process. It's done in such a subtle way they don't seem to realize it has handicapped them. Neurosurgeons seem to be especially susceptible to this, and Dr. Collins was apparently detached and desensitized to what he had done.

I found I-91 and we were on our way, with Nick persistently tugging at my arm. I knew what he was asking. "Where are we going?"

I began to try to explain to him, through my tears, "We're going back to Kimberly Hall."

"Why?"

If you have ever seen someone raise the muscles in one shoulder and arm with the palm of the hand opened in a gesture of exclamation, you know how he asked me "why" and how I understood him.

"You are not yet ready for a rehabilitation hospital as we had hoped. We will have to continue the exercises we are doing a while longer," I tried to explain.

I couldn't bear to tell him the prognosis John and I had just heard. He kept pulling at my arm, gesturing that he did not want to go back to Kimberly Hall, he wanted to go home.

I was almost glad Nick could not see at that moment. My eyes were so filled with tears that I could hardly see to drive. I'm sure angels guided us on that trip, saving us from harm. Every moment of the ride was unsettling and dangerous.

Connie Nelson phoned while we were at Yale-New Haven Hospital and explained that they were moving Nick from his private room into a room with two beds. He would have a roommate. At the time of her call, I placidly accepted this and thought nothing of it. Actually, I had expected it for some time. I didn't even mention it to Nick. What a mistake!

When we arrived at Kimberly Hall, I wheeled him into his new room. A gentleman was sitting in a chair in one corner of the room. I had seen his name on the door, so I introduced Nick to him. Nick immediately went into a whole-body grand mal seizure sitting in the wheelchair. I grabbed him so he wouldn't fall and screamed for help. Someone came and immediately rushed from the room for more help, leaving me alone to try to hold Nick in the chair. It took four people to move him from the chair to the bed. The seizure began to subside soon after he was placed in his bed. It had been all I could do to keep him from falling out of the chair. I was limp from the ordeal, and my back hurt.

They prepared Nick for nighttime and gave him medication. Finally, we were alone in his part of the room. The other gentleman was still sitting in the corner of the room, far from us, so I pulled the curtain around Nick and me. We held each other and cried, me with tears and him without any. He just moaned. I said out loud what we were both feeling. I didn't try to hold back the tears for his sake, as I had done so many times before, and I didn't sugarcoat the situation for him either.

"This is just about the lousiest deal that ever happened to anyone," I said. "Hell can't be worse than this. I feel like screaming and making everyone sit up and take notice. I hate this situation more than I ever hated anything. Sometimes I'd like to just literally die. I hate people who can go about their lives as though none of this is happening."

On and on I went. I didn't care anymore. Nick was nodding "yes" throughout this tirade, and we cried over and over, him just moaning, me with tears streaming down my face. We hugged each other many times, and he finally went off to a blessed sleep. At that moment I was a ruined, beaten, exhausted human being.

I hated the thought of leaving Nick there alone in a room with a man I didn't know more than I ever hated anything in my life. He watched us but never said a word. No emotion, just stoicism. I didn't know what was going on in his mind about what he had just seen and heard. I didn't even know what was wrong with him, why he was in this nursing home.

It would be an hour's drive home, and I had to get started. Nick was asleep and probably would not remember any of this tomorrow. *I hoped he wouldn't with all of my being.* It was the only solace there was to brain injury. Had I not known and trusted the nursing staff at Kimberly Hall, especially Nancy Gay, the nurse who would be on duty that night, I could not have left. The realization that this place was Nick's home really hit me.

Just before Easter that year, I had made arrangements for Nick to come home for three days and two nights. I had become very sure that I could take care of him even though he required total care. John knew I couldn't, but he also knew the agony I was in with him in a nursing home.

We prepared a bedroom next to ours and rented a hospital bed. We put a string of bells on the side rails of the bed for him to ring when he needed us. We picked Nick up early on a Friday morning, and I took on the job of being a therapist, nurse, aide, laundress, cook, and cleaning lady. All these jobs were done by different people in the nursing home, and new people came on duty every eight hours. Now I was doing all this on a twenty-four-hour-a-day schedule with only John to help, and our daughters intermittently.

The nursing home would not give me enough diapers for the weekend, so I had to rent some. Nick used two at a time when he was up and four while he was in bed. These had to be washed each day. My supply of sheets was limited, and these had to be put through the washer too.

Feeding Nick took a long time to do properly; a half hour to forty-five minutes was usual. John was helping me with the feedings and laundry while I tried to cook and bathe Nick. We exercised him, read to him, and spent every moment of our time with him because he required it. At night he would wake up and shake the railing with the bells on it. He was always wet. I would get up and wash him and completely change his bed. This happened three to four times each night.

On one of those occasions, he indicated that he did not want me to leave his room. I finally figured out that he wanted to get out of bed. I explained that it was the middle of the night, but he insisted. So I helped him into a standing position, and he was quite content. I asked, "Is that all you wanted, just to get out of bed and stand up for awhile?"

He nodded, "Yes."

I held him tight and cried silently so he wouldn't know. I couldn't help thinking how many nights he must have wanted this simple little treat and could not express his wish to have it. "Make his life comfortable," Dr. Collins had said. "How could we, Dr. Collins, without help?" There were no facilities to treat a patient like Nick, and none would be provided for us if he came home.

After these nighttime bed-wetting sessions, I could not get back to sleep easily. By Sunday evening I was in bed myself, so John had to take Nick back to Kimberly Hall without me. I stayed in bed for two days afterward. Besides exhaustion, an old back problem had flared up. I had to admit to myself, to John, and to everyone in the family how foolish I had been to think I could take care of Nick at home. So Kimberly Hall had to be Nick's home.

It was June 1979. Two years had passed since this ordeal had begun. The family had to be told the devastating news that Nick's injuries were permanent. It would take so much hope out of all of our lives. Joan had made a surprise trip home from Colorado while Nick was in Yale-New Haven Hospital. It must have been like shock treatment for her to have come home at this particular time and hear this news.

Sally had recovered from a very poor junior year in high school to graduate with honors in 1978. Debbie had just graduated from high school as an honor student too. Neither of them had made plans to go to college. Both were working, and we felt that a year away from pressure would be good for them as well as us. Also, we were not financially able to send them to college at this time. Cathy still had a year to go before completing her high school education. Mary and Susan were mothering their families and helping us with Nick in every spare moment. Joe was working to support his family.

Hopes were shattered when we gave them the news from Dr. Collins and his team. A gloom settled over all of us. Each one had to deal with this in his or her own way. I could not shake the melancholy that had crept into my spirit. It seemed to be consuming me. My recourse was to sit down at my typewriter and pour out my thoughts on paper. It seemed to be the only way of getting rid of my morose feelings.

> It is June 29, 1979. My 25-year-old son, Nick, died in unbelievable agony and pain on the floor of the weight-lifting room at the YMCA in Waterbury, Connecticut, on Saturday afternoon, June 25, 1977. It is now more than two years since his death.
>
> He was beaten about the head several times with a baseball bat wielded by an angry, frustrated man. It was all over within minutes. A vibrant, witty, charming, interesting, handsome young man died in a pool of his own blood on that YMCA floor. It has taken me all of these two years to realize fully that the young man who was my son really died on that floor in that room.
>
> But his was an unusual death. It was so rare, in fact, that I can be forgiven for taking so long to come to the reality of it. There was no wake with friends and relatives coming by to pay their last respects to him and offer condolences to his family. There was no casket covered with beautiful flowers in tribute to a beautiful life. The person that was my son died on that blood-drenched floor, but the body in which he was encased did not die! It lives on! And in the two years that have followed there has slowly emerged a new creature, a different kind of man, but a real person. This new person still looks like my son. He has the same childhood memories of the young boy to whom I was a mother. But this new person seems unable to remember what happened yesterday—or even a half hour ago. Yet, this new person, whom we still call by our son's name, seems from another world.

On and on I went, page after page, putting my thoughts and emotions on paper. I completely emptied myself of all the feelings that were draining the life from me. It was my catharsis after having been confronted with the words *"permanent injuries."*

Nick's nurse, Mary D'Agata, had her own problem dealing with the terrible prognosis of Dr. Collins. She too wrote down her feelings about Nick.

To Nick—Two Years Later

Brain jellied by a baseball bat
There he sits,
Eyes vibrantly alive
But unseeing
He tramps through my heart
Quiet, but demanding
Love; his unspoken but freely given.

Changes wrought by circumstance,
A young man's life
Full, now empty
But for the love, the caring
His very presence demands.

The cacophony unbearable,
Insane confusion enveloping:
Could one choose—deaf or blind.
Death or life
Unfulfilled?

Cruel God, where is the purpose?
Will he live
To understand?
That fulfillment lies in others'
Spirits growing day by day;
Enriched by his example
Of fortitude, love, forgiveness.

—Mary D'Agata,
Nick's Nurse at Kimberly Hall

The permanent injuries Nick had to live with were turning out to be the largest head of our dragon, the one that we could not kill. This battle would go on for the rest of his life and ours. Nick had suffered traumatic blows to the head that had ruined his life, and our lives changed with his. None of us would ever be the same, but *we were only beginning to really believe it.*

22

Suing the YMCA

The YMCA organization reaches into the heart of every community, where its volunteer boards operate its Associations. Many prominent persons in each city or town become involved with the local YMCA because they like to be associated with such a long-standing, reputable charity. They like the honor and prestige of being listed on the boards of this organization, and it also gives them a chance to meet other well-connected citizens in their communities.

However, the members of these boards are responsible for the operation of local YMCAs and the programs they offer to the public. The Constitution and By-Laws of the National Council make them very responsible. The members of these boards cannot take advantage of the honor without the obligation of providing proper programs to the public they serve.

We knew that YMCAs were in existence in communities all over the United States. As our children grew up, each one of them attended either the YMCA or the YWCA. All eight had learned to swim in one of these facilities. I certainly believed that both organizations had national standards for the operation of their local associations and the programs they offered to our children. The YMCA and YWCA were a part of our lives. I trusted them and taught my children to trust them too, based on this belief. I considered our children to be safe in either facility.

Now we were in the incredible position of having to sue the YMCA because we believed that YMCA officials were responsible for the injuries Nick sustained because of their negligent supervision of Joseph Tramontano. Our belief was not enough: we had to prove this in a court of law.

To prove our case, we were going to have to sue first and gather the evidence we needed from inside the YMCA organization by forcing it to turn over documents and materials pertinent to our case. John spent an entire month drafting the complaint, and I typed it in its entirety. Documents necessary to attach the Waterbury YMCA building were prepared, and a $3 million attachment on the property was obtained from Judge Margaret Driscoll. The case of *Del Buono vs. YMCA* was on its way.

The first piece of evidence came from Nick, however. It was his membership card, which said he was a senior member of the YMCA. On the back of the card it said:

> The Waterbury YMCA is a part of a world wide fellowship of youths and adults of all races and creeds, united by the common purposes of helping each other to become adequate and healthy persons motivated by the teachings of Jesus and the desire to build a world community based on Christian principles. This card is issued with the understanding that membership is not transferable; may be forfeited for violation of rules; must be shown when requested. Membership is continuous unless YMCA is notified to the contrary. Please notify the membership office of any change of address.
>
> Carry this card with you as your introduction to your fellows in a worldwide brotherhood.
>
> The Waterbury YMCA is a member organization of the United Council and Fund of Greater Waterbury, Inc.

There was a place for the member's signature on the bottom of the card, where Nick had signed it, and John Mercier signed on the front for the YMCA.

One of the Y's own publications asked the question for which we needed an answer: "What is a YMCA?" It said that YMCAs are locally organized, incorporated, and operated entities, each directed and managed by its own volunteer board, committees, and staff. A YMCA's board dominates policies, formulates budgets, holds title to property, employs staff, and is responsible for policy making.

We received two very important sources of help outside the YMCA organization, though, which put us on the right track right away. The first source was a former client of John's who brought him a flyer from the YMCA entitled "You Can't Weight to Join." It told this most unbelievable story:

> Our YMCA Bar Bell Club is designed for those who enjoy weight training and wish to take responsibility for their own workout programs.
>
> First, be sure and talk with Y Director Bruce MacFarlane. Demonstrate your willingness to learn on all pieces of apparatus. If you're in high school, you're welcome to use the club during the hours listed on the schedule.
>
> The room is only available to club members because of our desire to avoid injuries, loss of equipment and problems developing when persons not properly oriented with weight-lifting take part.
>
> When you arrive, you're the boss. Supervise each other to avoid dangerous situations. Teach beginners how to use the equipment. Make sure the room is left orderly. If you are alone, lock the door when you leave.
>
> Members of the Club pay a $12 annual fee to cover Y's additional expenses for keys, equipment, repairs and purchase of new materials.
>
> We can't weight to have you join us.
>
> —Greater Waterbury YMCA, 754-2181.

The legal implications of this flyer were staggering. It was hard to believe that the YMCA had put out such a document, but here it was, right in our hands. Members of the "Club" were given keys to the room! They were told to teach beginners how to use the equipment! They were supposed to supervise each other to avoid dangerous situations! These words had significant legal meaning. They were too fantastic to believe!

When you give someone the keys to your home or your car and tell them what to do and how to behave, that person becomes your agent.

Of course, none of the men in the room that day would admit they were supposed to provide supervision in the Bar Bell Club room. Each, in turn, would say, "I was just a member of the YMCA." None of them, with the exception of Michael Carter, had been told that he was responsible for supervision, nor felt any obligation to perform it.

By court order, John obtained the right to inspect the YMCA Bar Bell Club room, which was located in a sub-basement. Members had to be admitted into the physical facilities of the building at a place on the first floor called the Athletic Services Desk where the YMCA card would be turned in, and the member would then be admitted through an electronic door operated by the person on duty at this desk. The weight lifters would then travel downstairs through a maze of corridors to reach their Bar Bell Club room.

The weight-lifting room was a small one; ten people working out would have been extremely crowded. On June 25, 1977, it was entered through a locked door unless someone was already there working out. It had no extension phone to the desk upstairs, nor was there an intercom. Both of these would have been very inexpensive pieces of equipment.

On the fateful day, Nick turned in his card at the desk and was admitted the way a member should have been. Tramontano, on the other hand, was permitted entrance into the physical area of the YMCA through the electronic door twice (as if he were a member of the staff) without ever having shown a membership card. The second time he was carrying a baseball bat, which he had procured from his car parked on the street outside the YMCA building. At this time his shirt had blood on it from the nosebleed he got in the mat room.

By interrogatories and disclosure motions, John obtained documents that told part of the story about how this Bar Bell Club came into existence. It was the brain child of Tramontano, who was a serious weight lifter. He was unhappy with conditions at the YMCA for weight training. He was a volunteer staff person and suggested that the YMCA provide a place where the best equipment could be moved into a location for serious lifters.

According to minutes kept by the Health and Physical Education Committee, Tramontano was present on September 12, 1974, when the idea was presented to this committee. It was agreed that members of this "Club" would be given keys to the room and that they would pay one dollar a month for the key and use of this room. As preposterous as it sounds, it was agreed that the club members were to supervise the room when it was open.

Just four days later, on September 16, 1974, this idea was presented to the board of directors at their meeting. A lengthy discussion was held, and it was decided to adopt the program as an "exclusive club concept" in order to "solve the problem of the misuse and abuse of the weight room." Ten members of the board of directors of the Waterbury YMCA actually approved this Bar Bell Club idea by saying that "qualified members only will be accepted." Seven members had the good sense to oppose it.

I wondered how the publisher of the *Waterbury Republican-American* newspaper, William Pape II, voted on this matter. He was chairman of the YMCA board of directors. I sincerely hope he was opposed. His newspaper had never once mentioned in all of its articles concerning this assault that Tramontano had been an instructor in the Bar Bell Club program or that he was instrumental in starting it for the YMCA.

On March 14, 1975, staff meeting minutes list Tramontano's name as one of the Bar Bell Club instructors.

Tramontano and this club were discussed by John Mercier in his recorded interview with Charles Martin, adjuster for the Travelers Insurance Company. Mr. Mercier stated that "at one time Joe Tramontano had been a volunteer for the YMCA, had been instrumental in developing the whole Bar Bell Club."

Mr. Mercier told Mr. Martin that the reason for the fee was for "safety, supervision, and to have a little reserve for equipment." He said, "Bruce MacFarlane, our program executive, reviews applicants to the Bar Bell Club, making sure they understand the safety aspects of it, explain the fact that it is only open to the Bar Bell Club members, so that it has its own built-in supervision, and then each member, after they pay the $12 fee, receives a key to the room, so that it's not generally open to either our regular membership or the public."

Mr. Martin asked Mr. Mercier if on the day that this happened with Del Buono there was anyone actually in charge in the room who would have been a supervisor. Mr. Mercier responded, "No, all the

Bar Bell Club members, you know, really act in that kind of supervisory capacity, kind of police their own club, so to speak. We do have a professional staff person on duty during all the times our physical education department is open, which includes periodic tours of the facility as a monitor to what's going on."

At his deposition, John asked Mr. MacFarlane, "How many members formed the Bar Bell Club at the time when it first started?"

"Total of fifteen, maybe," he replied.

"Who gave the keys out?"

"Joseph Tramontano, when we initially started."

"Was he ever given T-shirts from the YMCA with the word 'Instructor' on them?"

"Yes."

"And was he a member of the volunteer staff?"

"Yes."

By 1977, Mr. MacFarlane acknowledged that there were approximately a hundred members of the Bar Bell Club! All one hundred of these people had the right to use this small room any time the YMCA was open. According to John Mercier, all one hundred were supposed to act in a supervisory capacity.

And this was supposed to be a professional YMCA program? In my opinion, this Bar Bell Club was run in such an unprofessional manner that it made *everything* the YMCA staff did suspect in our minds. Young boys running a club in a hut in the woods could have done a better job!

23

A Previous Assault at the YMCA

The assault on Nick by Joseph Tramontano was so tightly interwoven with the YMCA that we could not separate the two. His name constantly came up in the documents we received from the YMCA, and it quickly became evident that the Y had been consistently having problems with his behavior while in its building. Yet it did not act to keep him out of its facilities permanently due to his conduct. Two questions will always haunt us. How and why? How could a thing like this happen in a YMCA? Why didn't the staff and board of directors of the Waterbury YMCA refuse to allow Joseph Tramontano admission in its YMCA due to his behavior?

Attorney Robert L. Chase, a member of the YMCA board of directors, gave a statement to Mr. Martin on condition that the Travelers Insurance Company could not use it to deny insurance coverage to the YMCA. In it he stated he had witnessed an incident in which Joseph Tramontano punched another YMCA participant on the basketball court before Nick was injured.

Mr. Chase said that he was jogging on the track and witnessed a basketball game in progress on the gymnasium floor. He observed that Tramontano was one of the participants in the game and that during play, other individuals made attempts to enter the game, and one was more eager than the others. Tramontano refused to allow him into the game. Tramantano and the other person exchanged words, and Tramontano struck the young man on his face with a closed fist.

Mr. Chase was asked if he was involved in the disciplinary action that followed the incident. "No," he answered. Yet his name appears as one of those present when it was unanimously approved that Tramontano be suspended for two weeks.

The date when this punching incident took place became the subject of controversy when Tramontano's deposition was taken. Tramontano stated that the incident the YMCA officials claimed occurred on April 29, 1976, actually happened in February or March 1977. Tramontano testified: "I told you, counselor, I only did this for the simple reason that no one is going to make a God-damn liar out of me, I don't care who it is. I'm not a liar. Anyone who knows me, I am not a liar. That's a lie. That's utter nonsense, that date."

Attorney Frank asked him, "After the two-week suspension, you resumed your normal membership in the Y doing what you had done before?"

"Yes, I was," Tramontano answered. "When I came back it was in April of '77. So my membership would be good to April of '78, and I had this incident with Del Buono in June of '77, June 25th."

Mr. Frank read from a letter the YMCA had given us regarding the suspension, and Tramontano answered, "That didn't happen in June of '76, that happened in the wintertime when I whacked the kid on the court. I asked him twice, two times, he called me a mother fucker, and I went over to him and whacked him in the face. I slapped him."

Mr. Frank questioned, "You are saying that happened in '77, in the winter of '77?"

"February or March, in there, one of the months. I'm not sure which month that was. It was '77," Tramontano replied.

When Mr. Frank showed Tramontano the letter addressed to him regarding his suspension, he said:

> That is definitely my signature, but as far as I'm concerned, I never seen this before, this date, April or whatever....No, that date is not right. This letter is correct about as far as what happened in the incident, right. But, as far as me, I never got one of these in the mail or handed to me. I had a verbal conversa-

tion with Mr. Mercier. He called me to his office explaining this to me....I was never given one of these. What they are saying here was told to me in person, you know, by Mr. Mercier. That's definitely my signature. I am not going to deny that. How it got there, I don't know. I don't ever remember signing this. This is not my handwriting where it says "I have read the above letter." Whoever wrote that filled that in, that is not my handwriting.

I am just going to say the only reason, like I say, I talked more than I wanted to is because no one is going to make a God-damn liar out of me. I am not a liar, I never lied in the criminal. [sic] I don't have no reason to lie. For what reason? I mean, if you want to give me a million dollars, gee, they tell me money works wonders. If you wanted to give me a million dollars—I am bitter here—gee, I might get amnesia if you shot me that kind of money. You got a poor man. You are looking at a pauper. I come out of prison, and you act like I am getting something here or something there. The next thing, you want to get my God-damn clothes for Christ's sakes. And I am bitter, and I want you to know that I am bitter.

From this deposition, we were getting to know the kind of man who had so viciously assaulted our son. And we were getting to know the YMCA that acknowledged this man as an instructor in weight lifting and permitted him to run the Bar Bell Club program. It was not a pretty picture.

John Mercier talked about the "punching" incident in another recorded interview with Charles Martin. He said that this incident had occurred about a year to a year and a half ago. He reported to Mr. Martin that Tramontano had been provoked and swung at another gentleman on the court and hit him pretty good on the jaw. He stated that the YMCA suspended him and revoked his complimentary privileges at that time.

When John took Mr. Mercier's deposition, he asked him: "Mr. Mercier, did you have any conversation with the individual that Mr. Tramontano was supposed to have struck on April 29, 1976?"

"I did not," Mercier responded.

John was never able to determine the name of this individual, so he could not interview him to get his side of the story. No incident report was filed in the YMCA regarding it, nor were there any minutes of board meetings in which it was discussed. This was another instance in which it was hard for us to believe the YMCA personnel were telling the truth.

The last, and strangest, official papers from the YMCA with regard to Tramontano appeared on Y stationery dated June 18, 1976:

> IMPORTANT NOTICE TO: All Lockerroom Personnel
> FROM: Bruce MacFarlane Re: Joseph Tramontano.
> Joseph Tramontano will not be admitted into the facilities by use of any kind of pass, or reason. This is effective immediately. Also may not be issued a membership.

At his deposition, Tramontano said of this notice, "This here was backed up. This copy here is utter nonsense. Not only have I never seen it, but how could that be so when I was an active member at the time? That's utter nonsense. I gather from this, in other words, I didn't belong to the Y at that time. I was not allowed to join the Y or I wasn't part of the Y any more at that particular date, June 18, 1976? This wasn't up in all the locker rooms or wherever they had it."

The controversy over the dates of these documents was a very important issue in our case against the YMCA. What if Tramontano was telling the truth in his deposition? What if the incident reported by YMCA officials to have happened on April 29, 1976, actually happened in 1977? What if the June 18, 1976, "Notice" was issued on June 18, 1977, just one week before Nick was assaulted? Someone was lying under oath. Was it Tramontano, or was it the YMCA officials?

At Mr. Mercier's deposition, he was asked about Tramontano's membership in the YMCA after the alleged suspension in 1976. He stated that Tramontano had joined the YMCA Leisure Time Association because he was unemployed at that time and presented an unemployment card to prove it.

Yet, at Tramontano's deposition, he said, "All I remember is the complimentary. They told me they ran out and they weren't giving any more out. There were no more instructors. Everybody had to pay. That was what I was told by Mr. MacFarlane himself, the funky [sic] of the Y, the errand boy or whatever. That's what I called him."

Mr. Frank asked Tramontano if at the time when the incident with Del Buono occurred he was a volunteer instructor in the Bar Bell Club.

"I was an instructor. They accepted my services," he said. Mr. Frank asked him about a T-shirt with the word "Instructor" on it and whether he wore it at the YMCA.

Tramontano answered, "Counsel, what do you want me to tell you? I wiped my ass with the T-shirt. Did I wear the T-shirt? Come on, Jesus Christ."

Mr. Frank persisted in his questioning. "Did you wear that when you worked out in the Bar Bell Club and the weight room at the Y prior to June 25th, 1977, the day of the incident?"

"I don't know. You are a well-educated man, and that is an asinine question, to ask me if I wear a T-shirt. I used it on the flagpole in front of the Y and wave it. Jesus Christ. I don't believe that you asked me that question like that. That's like asking me if I buy new pants, am I going to wear them. I wore the shirts."

From this deposition we learned that Joseph Tramontano was a crude, brutal sort of person who would not be welcomed in the company of more civilized people. So why did the YMCA staff and board of directors allow him to run their Bar Bell Club in their YMCA? Were they really that desperate for volunteer help?

Bruce MacFarlane had a lot to say about the Bar Bell Club and Tramontano when John took his deposition. John asked him if he had had a chance to observe Tramontano over a period of years from 1969 to 1977.

"Yes," he answered.

John then asked if he had formed an opinion about his temper and character. Mr. MacFarlane answered, "He was a hot-headed Italian. He was loud, argumentative, boisterous...members of the Bar Bell Club had complained to him [MacFarlane] about his fiery temper."

Mr. MacFarlane said that Paul Ford "knew the guy." He further stated that Tramontano "had a personality that was very, very loud, a very strong type of personality that came across which was irritating to many people." He said that Tramontano would "express himself if he disagreed with a person's opinion and made it clear that he disagreed."

John asked Mr. MacFarlane, "Referring to Joseph Tramontano's assault on the boy in the gymnasium and the suspension, what action, if any, was taken by Waterbury YMCA to notify members of the Bar Bell Club that Joseph Tramontano had been suspended and that he was no longer on the volunteer staff?"

"None that I know of," MacFarlane answered.

When John persisted in this line of questioning, Mr. MacFarlane said, "Word travels fast." That was his only comment on how other members might know of the suspension.

When John asked if anyone on the YMCA staff had notified members of the Bar Bell Club that Tramontano's authority on behalf of the Y to supervise, teach, and clean was no longer in force, Mr. MacFarlane answered, "There was nothing."

John asked him who had taken Tramontano's place in the Bar Bell Club and he answered, "No one."

"Were any additional precautions taken to supervise Joseph Tramontano so he wouldn't hurt anybody else after he had been reinstated?"

"No."

"Do you remember interviewing John Nicholas Del Buono for membership in the Bar Bell Club?" John asked.

"No, sir."

"Had anybody complained to you about the signs that Joseph Tramontano put on the wall of the Bar Bell Club?"

"I had gotten complaints about signs on the wall."

"Did you ever tell Joe Tramontano not to put the signs up?"

"I don't remember."

"For the year prior to June 25th, 1977, did the Waterbury YMCA represent to the general public that its health facilities were adequately and properly supervised by a staff of competent employees?"

"Yes," Mr. MacFarlane answered.

After testimony like that, is it any wonder that we had trouble accepting at face value the documents submitted to us under court order by the YMCA? The witnesses in the room that Saturday afternoon agreed that the only time any staff persons came around was when they were showing a prospective member the room. The ugly signs on the Bar Bell Club room walls had been up for a long time.

A Previous Assault at the YMCA

No one on the YMCA staff had the courage to take them down. It seemed to me the YMCA staff had abandoned the Bar Bell Club program, and it had become Tramontano's private club to run as he saw fit.

By 1977, the YMCA was no longer posting a list of "Instructors" for the Bar Bell Club with times for them to be on duty. Nevertheless, Joseph Tramontano thought he was one, and that any time he was in the room he was on duty. No one on the staff of the YMCA took charge of the room after they claimed Joseph Tramontano had been stripped of his "volunteer staff" status. Admittedly, his behavior was not "exemplary," yet he was allowed back into the Bar Bell Club program, where the YMCA staff expected him, as well as all the others, to "supervise each other to avoid dangerous situations."

The staff obviously didn't like Joseph Tramontano. He was causing a lot of trouble for them. Members were complaining to the staff about him. Yet they would not act to get rid of him or see to it that he was closely supervised while in the building. Why? Did they believe he would do to them what he did to Nick sometime when they were outside the YMCA?

I think this showed clearly in the Incident Report that Paul Ford filed after Nick was assaulted. Ford wrote, "I told her [Judy Heitman] to call Tom [Paternostro] and tell him that if they saw Joey in the building to do nothing—not to speak to him—that he was armed—very dangerous."

Ford also gave a recorded interview to Charles Martin on June 29, 1977. It was far more revealing than anything he had said before. He was asked if he knew anything about Tramontano.

"I know at times he has caused problems here. At times, he has a very hot temper, he's gotten upset with people, he's threatened people. He was very meticulous about the weight room. He would get upset with the guys if the plates weren't put away, if the floor wasn't swept at the end of the day. Sometimes it would be just talking. Other times he would be screaming and yelling, threatening to close the room and not let anybody in, which he really had no control over, no power to do."

When Paul Ford was asked how the Bar Bell Club was supervised, he said, "It's supervised by the members themselves."

The Hartford Courant published an article on July 27, 1977, in which their reporter, J. Herbert Smith, interviewed John Del Buono and John Mercier. "'The YMCA portrays an image of professionalism that lulls people into a false sense of security,' said Atty. Del Buono. 'But that image just wasn't real. I think that is what hurt my son,' he said. 'To the best of our knowledge Tramontano was in charge of the [barbell] room.'…But YMCA Director John Mercier said Monday Tramontano never has worked for the YMCA and is simply one of the members of the Barbell Club."

With controversial and damaging testimony like this, we believed we could prove our case against the Waterbury YMCA. However, there was one last witness we needed.

24

An Expert Witness in Recreational Facilities

To proceed to trial, we needed an expert in recreational facilities to testify regarding the manner in which weight lifting should be supervised in any facility where this type of program is offered.

We went to North Haven to talk with the owner of a health spa who had been vice-president of European Health Spas for many years and who traveled across the country inspecting these spas for safety regularly.

His facility was located on the ground floor. When we walked in, there was an attendant behind a glass enclosure. He could easily observe everything that was going on in the room where several men were working out on weight-lifting equipment.

The owner explained that without supervision in an atmosphere where weight lifters trained, there would be constant fights to prove who was "king of the hill." He emphasized that the atmosphere had to be regulated so that any raising of a voice would be immediately stopped. He had signs on the wall (professionally printed ones) stating, "No profanity allowed." He said that the "macho" training that these men indulged themselves in would psychologically prevent them from walking away from a fight. Therefore, it was up to management to see to it that a fight could not begin, let alone go on for an hour.

I had often wondered why Nick didn't just walk away from that whole sordid scene until this interview. The same reasoning applied to the other Bar Bell Club members as to why they did not leave that day.

Nick was at the YMCA doing his weight training program when Joseph Tramontano came in. He admittedly came there "just to bullshit." Nick kept going back to his training program between confrontations with Tramontano. He said that he didn't want to fight Tramontano.

Tramontano went there dressed in "civilian clothes," as he put it. He had no intention of lifting weights. When he started ordering Nick around, Nick began, at that moment, to do the job that the YMCA employees would not do. He tore down the signs that should not have been up. He began to put Tramontano in his place (which the YMCA staff should have long since done). Nick took on Tramontano when Mercier, MacFarlane, and Ford would not. It was hard to believe that Ford was put in charge of a building where he would have to supervise Tramontano. I believe Ford was scared to death of Tramontano, and his superiors knew this, or should have known it.

Nick and Tramontano had never laid eyes on each other before that Saturday afternoon. Nick had joined the YMCA only six weeks before. All the others in the room had been members of the Bar Bell Club for a long time, and knew Tramontano well. Nick did not. Tramontano was a ticking time bomb. Nick didn't know it, but the YMCA employees did. It seems to me their statements and depositions prove it. They allowed Tramontano to continue to come into their weight-lifting room until he exploded, and the explosion took place on Nick's head when Tramontano hit him with his baseball bat.

Nick's dues had been paid a year in advance. If he had submitted to Tramontano's behavior that day, he would have acquiesced to being subjected to the un-Christian atmosphere in that sub-basement Bar Bell Club every time he wanted to lift weights in the "professional" Waterbury YMCA. It is sad to say that all the other "men" in that room had already agreed to being treated in this manner inside the YMCA building.

Never, before the day that we interviewed this expert in recre-

An Expert Witness in Recreational Facilities

ational facilities, had I so loathed what I believed the YMCA management had done to Nick. As brutal as he was, Tramontano was a pitiful creature screaming for help himself. The YMCA was run by some of the most prominent and respected citizens in the community, all of whom should have known better.

The YMCA executive director was a psychology major. The chairman of its board of directors was the publisher of the local newspaper. The chairman of its Health and Physical Education Committee was an attorney. Both the publisher and the attorney were members of the YMCA board of directors. Why all these people permitted Tramontano to maintain a membership in the Waterbury YMCA and particularly in its Bar Bell Club program is beyond my comprehension.

At the end of our interview, the expert in recreational facilities declined to be a witness in our case when he was told that Tramontano and the YMCA were involved. We had the distinct impression that he knew Tramontano and probably the Waterbury YMCA.

We finally secured the services of a recreational expert from the Midwest, Dr. Alan Caskey. He had a doctorate in recreation and had testified in court at least twenty-five times. He had previously testified in cases for and against the YMCA.

His written report stated that safety in recreation was taught nationally, so there was no difference in the standards from state to state. He said that the Waterbury YMCA had taken the position, expressed in its literature about the Bar Bell Club program, that any one of the Bar Bell Club members was as qualified to supervise this program as any one on the staff.

He went on to explain that only certain types of recreational activities could be reasonably spot-checked, such as card games and that sort of passive play. But even in these, arguments could develop, so frequent spot checks were necessary. He maintained that active recreational programs required more than spot checks and that once an hour would not only be inadequate but would be totally unacceptable for a weight-lifting program.

Dr. Caskey said that if a facility had experienced trouble before, it should charge more for fees and tighten the security. As for the Bar Bell Club members supervising themselves, it was his position that they would have had to go through a training program to learn the requirements of supervision, and this only if they had consented to do so.

He explained that after Tramontano had displayed aggressive behavior on the basketball court, the YMCA director should have interviewed him to determine whether or not he had a criminal record and if he had ever had any psychiatric treatment. Above all, he should have insisted that Tramontano have counseling before being allowed back into the facilities. After having displayed violent behavior on the basketball court, Tramontano should never have been allowed into the Bar Bell Club program, where he was expected to act in a supervisory capacity under the system devised by the Waterbury YMCA.

It was a relief to learn how this program at the YMCA should have been run, but it was also a very deep hurt for me to become aware of just how negligent the YMCA officials had been in operating the Bar Bell Club. It is the reason Nick lost the life he knew and has to struggle through the hell of brain injury for the rest of his life.

25

The National YMCA

John was so certain that the local YMCA was the agent of the National YMCA that the first pleading he filed in court pertaining to the National YMCA was a Request to Admit that the national organization had the right to control the actions of the Waterbury YMCA and that it actually did so.

Attorney Jeremy Zimmerman of the prestigious law firm of Wiggin & Dana in New Haven had filed his appearance on behalf of the National YMCA, but he failed to follow the rules of the court and respond to the request within thirty days. Beyond this time, these were to be considered admitted facts in the case.

However, once Mr. Zimmerman discovered that he had not replied to this pleading, he quickly filed a Request to File Late Responses and stated that his failure to do so was due to oversight. Though John strenuously objected on the grounds he had proof of these facts from the National YMCA and had submitted them in court, the judge permitted Mr. Zimmerman to file the late responses, which were, of course, denials. We were going to have to prove this fact at the time of trial.

From documents produced through Motions for Disclosure, we quickly learned that we had sued a giant international corporation. Not only was it huge in size and income, but its worldwide influences went into the nooks and crannies of every single town in which its associations operated. This charitable institution was one of the largest and most respected "sacred cows" ever to exist.

One of its publications claimed that in 1977 there were nearly 700,000 volunteer leaders and more than 6,000 professional directors. This made up what the National YMCA called its lay-staff partnership, which directs, operates, and manages more than 1,800 YMCAs in the United States, with a membership exceeding 9 million and assets totalling $800 million.

We also learned that internationally, YMCA movements existed in eighty-eight countries, united into a global network of some 12,000 YMCA Centers through the World Alliance of YMCAs, with headquarters in Geneva, Switzerland.

Statistical data for 1976 revealed revenue of $369.9 million. From program fees the YMCA collected $116.9 million, and membership dues amounted to $104.4 million. Contributions were $62.8 million with allocations from the United Way totaling $52 million.

In the twenty years since Nick was injured in the Waterbury YMCA, the movement has grown tremendously. As of December 31, 1996, there were 2,100 YMCAs in the United States, with a membership of over 14 million. In 1989, buildings and land belonging to YMCAs in the United States were valued at $2.3 billion. In 1996, membership dues accounted for $717.5 million of revenue, and program fees brought in $400,500. Contributions, including from the United Way, were $321.4 million.

The executive director is David Mercer, and the National Council of YMCAs describes itself as an umbrella for local YMCA organizations. The National Council still maintains that it cannot make a local YMCA do anything, though there are still six to eight requirements that a local YMCA must meet in order to call itself a YMCA, including proper use of the logo (trademark); support by sending a certain amount of its revenue to the national organization each year; and having its CEO meet qualifications required by the national organization.

One particularly revealing document we received in our court case was called, "Recognition of Achievement and Certificate of Eligibility for National Health and Physical Education Program, Young Men's Christian Associations of the United States." It listed six requirements that the Waterbury YMCA was supposed to have met to receive this recognition certificate, which appeared to have been designed to be framed and prominently displayed.

We also received a document concerning instructions for petition to the National YMCA from a local YMCA in order to receive this certificate. It stated that the certificate should be looked upon as a mark of distinction, and that where possible, newspaper pictures should be taken. It suggested coverage of the award by radio and TV programs and said the certificate should be moved from office to office so that it would be highly visible. Further, every YMCA needed this document for its members to be allowed to participate in interassociation sports events and competitions.

This certificate seemed to us to be proof that the National YMCA not only controlled the programming in the local YMCA, but that the national organization "certified" this programming. What could all the argument be about?

One phrase in the certificate bothered us. It said: "This is to certify that the Greater Waterbury Young Men's Christian Association has examined its qualifications." Everything in this document suggested pride in accomplishment. But who did the testing? Surely it wasn't the Waterbury YMCA personnel testing themselves! Yet all the Waterbury YMCA had to do to obtain this valuable certificate was to examine itself and send a check for $10 made payable to the region/state. Obviously the Waterbury YMCA rated itself "Good," "Very Good," and "Excellent" in all the categories listed. In fact, it was instructed to do so on the Evaluation page, which said, "Policy Statements, to be acceptable, should rate 'good' or 'better' upon this scale."

Why would any YMCA say otherwise about itself? Kendell Shailer and John Mercier, who signed for the Waterbury YMCA, certainly rated themselves well. All they had to do after that was pay $10, and the prized certificate was signed and sent to them by the National YMCA. How absolutely convenient! We could do away with a whole department in state government if citizens were allowed to "test" themselves for a driver's license. And how about lawyers? Doctors? Nurses? Teachers? Wouldn't it be great if all any of them had to do was to certify themselves as qualified?

What the National YMCA was doing was absurd. As farmers say, it was a classic case of the fox guarding the henhouse. There wasn't one single visit or inspection from anyone outside the local YMCA making an independent evaluation of whether or not a YMCA should receive this certificate, which was signed by their national dignitaries.

When John talked with Mr. Zimmerman on the telephone one day and referred to the certificate and what it said about the local YMCA having examined "its qualifications," Mr. Zimmerman replied that it must be a misprint. Even counsel for the National YMCA could not believe it.

In 1977, the national organization exacted 3 percent financing from the local YMCAs, including the Waterbury YMCA. Therefore, part of Nick's dues was sent to the National Board. We learned from another publication that "joining fees which are required over and above regular membership dues, i.e., not in the nature of a freely given contribution" were subject to assessment by the National Board. So Nick's Bar Bell Club dues were clearly in this category, since he was required to pay them to belong to the Bar Bell Club over and above his YMCA membership.

This publication set forth rule after rule by which a YMCA would have to operate to be "recognized" by the National YMCA as a member YMCA. It stated that the National YMCA's authority was derived from the By-Laws of the National Council and that, in part, its responsibilities were to approve the list of associations entitled to membership in the National Council. This membership could be suspended or revoked if the National Board decided to do so.

The second source of evidence for our case came from outside the YMCA in an article published in the *Naugatuck Daily News*. It reported the settlement of a case in Vincennes, Indiana, against the National YMCA and a local YMCA. A young girl, about five years old, had nearly drowned in a swimming pool at the Vincennes YMCA. She too was seriously brain-injured.

John wrote to the court clerk for copies of all the pleadings in the case and from these learned the names of the lawyers involved in it. Depositions of several key executive officials of the National YMCA had been taken shortly after Nick was injured. These depositions would, therefore, be admissible in our case.

However, the depositions had been removed from the court file in the Indiana clerk's office, so John contacted one of the lawyers and obtained them from him. The information gained from these documents turned out to be a treasure chest of knowledge.

From the depositions we learned that in 1977, Violet Pauline Henry was the executive of the Organization Development Group of the National Board. Her supervisor was the executive director, Dr. Robert Harlan. She admitted in her deposition "that there would be nothing in the official records at the National Board headquarters which would indicate the reason for the suspension of a local YMCA by the committee on Member Associations of the National Board." She revealed that members of the Committee are provided with the details of the reasons for an association being considered for flagging or suspension and that they make their decisions at that meeting. The committee does not state the reasons it uses for flagging or suspending a local YMCA, and the National Board is not informed as to why an association has been flagged or suspended. And she declared that no member of the National Board has the right to inquire as to the reason for a suspension or flagging, and it is the practice of the committee not to share this information.

So the Committee on Member Associations was a very powerful one, and its deliberations could certainly be placed in the "secret" category. Further, its decisions were followed through, since "flaggings" and "suspensions" did occur. This committee had the authority to establish rules and procedures for local YMCAs and to grant exemptions. It wanted uniformity throughout the regions in the application of the criteria for membership, the imposition and enforcement of sanctions for noncompliance, and procedures to bring flagged or suspended associations into compliance as members in good standing of the National Council. Yet it vehemently denied control over local YMCAs.

Besides having eight qualifications for membership in the National YMCA, the committee had added one for newly admitted associations:

> In the event of failure to maintain such membership it shall relinquish the use of the name "Young Men's Christian Association", the letters "YMCA", the letter "Y", and the symbols and trade-marks used or registered on behalf of the National Council and National Board of YMCAs.

The Committee on Member Associations used the word *must* in writing the requirements it wanted from local YMCAs in their annual reports: "Annual reports for each year must be filed with the National Council office by each member Association. The reports shall cover all matters relating to the criteria for National Council membership." Further the committee stated, "the Chief Employed officer in an Association is expected to meet the requirement for Roster listing as a Senior Director or Director." To top it off, this committee reserved the right to request a certified audit or other satisfactory information from a local YMCA.

Dealing with the National Council was tough business for any local YMCA. The local YMCA would either meet the council's demands or have the services of the National Council stopped, which meant employees would be tempted away and the local United Way would be notified in an effort to dry up contribution funding.

We believed this constituted an agency relationship between the local YMCA and the National YMCA. It was John's contention that any organization which could exercise this kind of control over any aspect of the local associations had the right to control anything it wanted to. He believed the council didn't have the right to exact a percentage of Nick's membership dues and then deny it had any control over what went on in the very programs for which he paid these dues.

The issue of control of local YMCAs by the national organization was hotly denied in the Vincennes, Indiana, case. Attorney Thomas Hicks questioned the executive director, Dr. Robert Harlan, by setting up a hypothetical situation in which a YMCA in southern Alabama suddenly declared that it would not accept any blacks inside its building and put a sign right up in the front yard saying, "No Blacks Allowed." He wanted to know what would happen to that YMCA

The National YMCA

from Dr. Harlan's standpoint as national director.

Dr. Harlan answered that the local YMCA would have to complete a report at the end of the year and that if it would not or could not sign, then the matter would be taken up with the regional committee on member associations, and the committee would undoubtedly recommend that this YMCA be flagged. That process would go on for a year. If the local YMCA persisted, then it would be suspended as a member of the National Council until it changed its policy.

Mr. Hicks changed the hypothetical situation by asking what would happen if that YMCA signed the necessary certificate at the end of the year saying it would not discriminate, but the national president of the NAACP walked into his office and sat down and said, "Dr. Harlan, they are a bunch of liars down there in Wallace, Alabama. They signed your certificate for you, but they are not letting blacks in. Now what happens?"

Dr. Harlan took the position that "we would have to explain to this person that that is a matter for that YMCA to deal with. We don't have the authority to take any action."

Mr. Hicks continued with his hypothetical YMCA. "Let's assume that we have this fictitious YMCA in Wallace, Alabama, and someone comes in your office and says, 'Doctor, they are drowning on an average one kid a week because [even though] they have bona fide rules and practices.' Would you do anything about it?"

"There is nothing we can do," Dr. Harlan answered.

In the Vincennes YMCA case, the deposition of Dr. Lloyd Arnold, national director for health and physical education, was taken. Questions were asked of him by attorney Hansford Mann regarding his job and any control exercised by the National YMCA over the programs in local YMCAs.

He testified that he had obtained a seat on the Olympic Committee as a result of his position with the YMCA and that his duties for the YMCA were to serve as a resource to local associations to give them the kind of support systems they needed to carry out their functions.

Mr. Mann asked him if anyone with the National YMCA made inspections of local chapters.

"I'm not aware of any such person," he answered.

Dr. Arnold testified that so far as aquatics were concerned, local YMCAs "can do it any way they want to."

Mr. Mann pressed on. "If they want to, they can just have nobody taking care of the safety of the YMCA at all in the pool?"

"Yes," Dr. Arnold answered.

"If we have a swimming program at the YMCA and nobody is employed there to watch, save lives, no lifesavers, kids can go in there anytime of day without anyone watching them, go alone or with somebody whether they can swim or can't swim; and you as head of the program for the National Council of YMCAs wouldn't do anything about it if that state of affairs came to your attention?"

"If you mean local YMCAs, that's true. We have no authority."

"You wouldn't try to do anything about it?"

"No," Dr. Arnold replied.

"Would the National be interested enough to even conduct an investigation into complaints made against the local?"

"Probably not. I can't think of any case where they would."

"Has your department, Health and Physical Education, ever been interested enough to even conduct an investigation into the complaints made against the local?"

"Probably not. I can't think of any case where they would."

"Do you have the right to ask a question of an executive director?"

"Oh, of course."

"Do you in fact do so?"

"I can't think of any time I have."

It is difficult to believe that this man was going all over the United States giving speeches on behalf of YMCAs; that he was on the Olympic Committee because of his position; and that conditions like these could exist at the highest level of this gigantic "charitable" organization that receives millions of dollars in contributions each year just from the United Way. The United Way campaign goes into every shop and factory it can to glean money from workers to support this kind of "charitable" function.

Violet Pauline Henry was equally informative in her deposition about the National YMCA when Mr. Hicks questioned her.

"Let's go back to a couple more hypotheticals," he suggested. "Let's assume that your personnel director gets a letter from Sam Smith in Indianapolis, Indiana, who was a lay private citizen. He says, 'My boy was approached for homosexual activities by George Jones, who is a director of the local YMCA. And I can't get any satisfaction on the local level. And I want to know what you're going to do with it.' What happens?"

"I would write back to the person who wrote it, indicating that kind of issue related to a professional employee of a local association is one over which we have no jurisdiction. And I'm in no position to respond to his complaint."

"And he says, 'Lady, I have been to the local board, and they tell me they don't believe it. I can prove it.'"

"There would be nothing I could do."

"What if—and here again, I go to an extreme—what if the National knew that a local board had been totally infiltrated and was being run by homosexuals? Would it do anything about it? And that those homosexuals were in turn employing other directors who were homosexuals? And they were in turn making advances to both boys, girls, etc. What would National do about that?"

"I can't think of anything that National would do," was her reply.

The head of the Office of Communications for the National YMCA was Joseph A. Pisarro. He was deposed in the Vincennes YMCA case, and Mr. Mann questioned him about the advertising produced by the National YMCA.

"When you produce spot announcements for the use of your local YMCAs, is it your intention to convey the impression that the classes at the YMCA will be conducted in a safe manner?"

"Yes, yes."

"And that people who are teaching the classes are experts in their field, not only in teaching swimming but in water safety?"

"I would say yes."

"When you make spot announcements for use by local YMCAs concerning any athletic endeavor, do you attempt to convey the impression that people at the Y are experts in the fields of endeavor which are the subject matter of the ad?"

"Yes, we do attempt to convey the impression that the people working in the area of fitness in YMCAs around the country are fitness experts, yes."

The YMCA advertised its organization as "one of the finest of Human Care Organizations." John and I and our family will spend the rest of our lives caring for Nick as a result of its lack of human care. What these people, on the highest levels of the National Board, were saying in these depositions justified beyond a shadow of a doubt our feelings of resentment and indignation toward the National YMCA.

We were on notice that the officials of this organization would turn themselves inside out to keep from admitting an agency relationship with the local YMCAs. The battle would be uphill all the way, but we had an ace we planned to play in this mind game the National YMCA was playing on the issue of control.

26

Those Precious Trademarks "YMCA" and "Y"

The ace we had in our lawsuit that the other lawyers had missed was the YMCA and Y trademarks and the trademark law regarding them. Finally, there were laws that the YMCA could not deny unless they wanted to lose their precious "marks." John acquired every piece of evidence available from the trademark office in Washington, D.C., concerning the National YMCA and its use of trademarks in marketing the services provided by local YMCAs.

What he learned was that the National Board of YMCAs had registered more than twenty trademarks with the United States Patent Office, which it used in various ways to market the services provided by local YMCAs. However, the marks that were of keenest interest to the National Board and to us were the two with which all of its services are so prominently advertised: "YMCA" and "Y." These were registered for "indicating membership in the applicant's association." Furthermore, the applications to the commissioner of patents contained some rather startling differences between the use of the name "YMCA" and the use of the mark "Y."

In the application for the YMCA mark, the organization stated that it had adopted and was exercising legitimate control over the use of this mark, and that it was for the purpose of creating a worldwide fellowship of men and boys united by a common loyalty to Jesus Christ for the purpose of developing Christian personality and building a Christian society.

The "Y" trademark application made no reference whatsoever to the "YMCA" purpose. Was the organization trying to change the identity of "YMCA" to "Y"? We thought so. The significance of this, I believe, is that it no longer advocates the Christian principles and beliefs that were its foundation.

The "Christian" designation often seems to give the organization trouble, as it did in the case of *Jean Harder et al v. Town of Ridgefield, et al;* wherein Judge Clark T. Hull ruled that the town of Ridgefield could not give land valued at $50,000 to $100,000 to the YMCA because of the group's "corporate purposes," which were in furtherance of a Christian organization. The general director of the regional Y, Jeremiah M. Balser, testified in this case, and Judge Hull summed up for him, in his Memorandum of Decision, "Mr. Balser's claim that the National Y has no control at all over regional and local Ys and that the affiliation is mainly for the name, good will, and programs, flies in the face of the 'corporate purposes' to be described."

Judge Hull commented on the eternal dilemma with which the YMCA organization is faced in its attempts to be Christian and deny it at the same time—to control and deny control for the expediency of profit:

> It is both obvious and understandable in a changing world that the Regional Y has a split personality. In operation it is decidedly non-religious. It is certainly not pervasively sectarian. Except for a moral overlay and the name, a user of the Regional Y would not know that he was dealing with a Christian organization. Yet in its stated "corporate purposes" and also in its general moral imperative, it is a Christian organization and therein lies the keystone of Constitutional inquiry necessary to decide this case.

Judge Hull commented on the statement of another officer that further split the organization's personality: "In fact, one officer testified that the Regional Young Men's Christian Association does not particularly serve either the young, or men, or Christians."

Judge Hull properly pointed out, however, that "the Regional YMCA and the Ridgefield Family-Y are both controlled by the Constitution and By-Laws of the National Council of Young Men's Christian Associations."

Judge Hull actually used the words "controlled by," which were being so vehemently denied in our case. Then he asked the all-important questions:

> Then why affiliate with the Regional and National YMCAs? The name is somewhat of an anachronism. But the long highly admired history and reputation of the Y brings inestimable moral authority and strength to regional and local Ys. The accumulated respect earned in one hundred fifty-five years of almost unparalleled community service inures to the benefit of any Y. To put it very simply, can one conceive of a viable project, such as this, under the aegis of the "Z"? The Y has deservedly stood for a wholesome life style for its adherents, and associations with it, despite its determinedly moralistic virtues, which may seem outmoded by some, is of great local value.

The trademarks used by this organization, which were owned by the National Board, were of inestimable value to both the national and local YMCAs for the money they could bring in. And neither would try to do business without them because of the long associated goodwill that had been established over 155 years by this "Christian" organization. They were now trading in that good will, to the tune of hundreds of millions of dollars per year.

Yet what the National Board did not want to admit in our case was that it was "exercising legitimate control" over local YMCAs who were using its marks. This important wording in its applications for registration of its marks and the accompanying affidavits sworn to by its officers excited us. After all, our case would be tried by a jury, and the men and women on that jury would have a chance to look at the official documents John had obtained from the U.S. Patent Office, bound with royal blue ribbons and bearing the red seal of the patent office on them. He would take full advantage of the dilemma they had created.

In his deposition, Dr. Harlan was questioned about the use of these marks. He stated that "it's for their use any way they see fit." What a dangerous statement for him to make and then deny control! I don't think the patent office would look favorably on such a remark from the national director of the YMCA.

Dr. Harlan was questioned about the inclusion of an additional provision in the constitution stating, "In the event of failure to maintain such membership it [a local YMCA] shall relinquish the use of the name 'Young Men's Christian Association,' the letters 'YMCA,' the letter 'Y,' and the symbols and trademarks used or registered on behalf of the National Council and the National Board of YMCA." He answered that he had input into the inclusion of this paragraph and that "it was felt that a YMCA that did not meet the eight qualifications for…official listing as members of the National Council, that there ought to be some community evidence to the fact that that YMCA does not meet those qualifications, and this appeared to the Committee on Member Associations to be the most tangible evidence of that."

So the marks were an immediate identification of National Board control, and when an association failed to measure up to the qualifications it imposed, the association would be stripped of those marks and the valuable goodwill they represented in bringing in patrons with money to spend.

Did the National Board ever sue anyone regarding the unauthorized use of these trademarks? Yes, they did! Only the National Board could sue, since it was the only rightful owner of the marks. In the case of lawsuits for infringement on its marks, the National Board was not only quick to exercise some control over the local association, but also quick to act as its plaintiff.

The Beloit YMCA Boy Choir and Parent Association was sued by the National Board in U.S. District Court, Western District of Wisconsin. They asked the court to enjoin and restrain this group from "using in connection with their activities the mark 'YMCA' and/or any symbol bearing the letters 'YMCA' such as but not limited to plaintiff's 'YMCA' triangle mark."

In the case of trademark infringement, the National Board did not want anyone using its marks except its "affiliates," because this might confuse the public into thinking that they were "under the supervision of the plaintiff" (National Board).

Was this the same National Board that claimed through its top executives that it would never do one single thing to "interfere" with a local YMCA, let alone "supervise" the local group? Was this the same National Board telling the courts that it didn't want the public to be confused or deceived when the "YMCA" mark was used by a group over whom it had "no control"?

James F. Bunting, who was the executive director of the National Board in March 1968, when the Beloit case was initiated, gave an affidavit in support of the National Board's motion for temporary injunction. In this affidavit to the court, Mr. Bunting said:

> The National Board of YMCAs, since its organization, has...conducted and *supervised* extensive religious, social, educational and physical activities directed toward the furtherance of said purpose all of which has been, and now is, attended by great expense to the National Board of Young Men's Christian Associations and has become favorably known throughout the United States and other countries of the world for its said activities [italics added].

In our own case, we asked the National YMCA to admit the following (which it did):

> That since March 21, 1968, up to and including June 25, 1977, the National Board of Young Men's Christian Associations was continuously actively and extensively engaged in the same purpose and activities as stated by James F. Bunting in his Affidavit dated March 21, 1968.

Did the National Board ever sue any of its associations that failed to maintain themselves in good standing with the Committee on Member Associations? The Meriden, Connecticut, YMCA was involved in just such a lawsuit.

The marks owned by the National Board are called "service marks" and "collective service marks." The trademark law defining these marks is found in the *U.S. Code*. The important wording that affected our case was that they had to be used by persons "exercising legitimate control over the use of the marks."

We knew that we would be able to get these marks introduced into evidence because John had authenticated the copies in accordance with the Code. This was the federal law upon which we would depend to show that the National YMCA, as owner of these marks, had to exercise legitimate control over the use of the marks by the local YMCAs or they would lose them. What we needed now was case law with which to enhance our position. We found it in abundance, but it was very clear in the case of *Kipling v. G.P. Putnam's Sons,* 120 F. 631,635 (2d Cir.), wherein it declared:

> A trademark owner may extend the territory in which he has the right to exclusive use of his trademark either by expanding his own operations or by introducing his trademark and creating a demand for his goods in new territory through licenses subject to his control. The licensee thereby acquires only the right to a limited use of the trademark, and the control, right and title to the product remain in the licensor. Correlative to the right of an owner to license his trademark to others is his affirmative duty to himself and to the public to exercise control and restraint upon his licensees to prevent losing his property rights thereunder.

In the case of *City of Hartford,* supra 395, the law further stated:

> "Naked licensing," that is to say, licensing without the exercise of supervision by the licensor, on the other hand, may constitute an abandonment. The reason for the distinction is that the risk that the public will be deceived is minimized and the purpose of the law is effectuated when the licensor exercises supervision and control over the operations of his business.

There was one very interesting case involving trademarks with the Charleston, South Carolina, YWCA. The pertinent part of it was the judge's conclusion. He used the federal court to protect the trademarks owned by the National Board because without the court's protection, it could not control and direct the operations for which the trademark made it responsible.

We felt that this case put the National YMCA in a real dilemma. It wanted to protect its trademarks, but it denied any control whatsoever over its local affiliates. The National Council simply could not have it both ways, and we believed the judge in the South Carolina case proved our point.

The three-and-one-half years spent with Mr. Zimmerman representing the National YMCA were in sharp contrast to those spent with Mr. Danaher, who represented the Waterbury YMCA. Mr. Zimmerman caused us an unceasing amount of frustration. His apparent lack of ability to admit realities really hurt us.

This was undoubtedly brought on by the contortions that the National YMCA went through to deny that it had the power to control the activities of local YMCAs. Therefore, we believe Mr. Zimmerman was forced to take unreasonable positions and stand on them steadfastly.

At no time was there ever an attempt to try to negotiate a settlement. It was an out-and-out endurance contest, as well as a legal one. Did we have the money to last until trial? The fortitude? Could we manage a trial of this magnitude?

The YMCA did not know what kind of man it had gotten into a fight with this time. Either it would go down, or he would. Nick's father was not about to give up.

When all the pleadings were closed and our case was ready for the trial list, Mr. Zimmerman insisted on filing a motion for summary judgment that would let the National YMCA out of the case completely. Considering the abundance of evidence that we had, which we forced him to admit in court time and time again through requests for admission, this was an expensive, useless gesture.

Mr. Frank successfully defended us in this motion, and Mr. Zimmerman lost it. The judge had to rule that there was enough evidence on this subject to let a jury decide the issue. But defense law firms make a very fine living off such pleadings, regardless of the outcome. Unlike plaintiffs' lawyers, who take these kinds of cases on a contingency fee basis (they get paid only if they win or a settlement is made), attorneys for the defense get paid for every hour of work they spend on a case by the insurance company that hires them. I'm sure that the case of Del Buono vs. YMCA paid for a great deal of the very expensive overhead for the prestigious law firm of Wiggin & Dana.

I believe the National YMCA and its defense law firm grossly underestimated our determination and management skills in taking our son's case to court.

27

Leaving Kimberly Hall

Daily living at Kimberly Hall became different for Nick after the dismal medical reports from Dr. Collins. The staff knew there wasn't going to be a transfer to a veterans' hospital where Nick might be with some young men his own age. They had to face the same facts as the family: there simply was no place for Nick to be cared for on a long-term basis.

Kimberly Hall was primarily a nursing home for the elderly, but it had become home for twenty-seven-year-old Nick Del Buono, a young man with all the multiple handicaps that severe brain injury brings. Kimberly Hall did not have the rehabilitation techniques to help him try to overcome as many of these handicaps as he could, nor the facility to provide a permanent living situation.

The staff had applied all their nursing skills in Nick's behalf to bring him this far. Now he needed much more skill than they were capable of giving. All their efforts to help him come out of coma and get ready for rehabilitation seemed for naught.

Nick spent his days vested and restrained in a wheelchair. He propelled himself about his room and the hallways in as boring and monotonous a fashion as could be imagined. His nights were no better, except for periods of intermittent, blessed sleep. When he awoke, he was a prisoner strapped in his bed and then in a chair.

Acknowledged a Man

Nick hated these restraints and indicated over and over he didn't want them. Regulations from the Department of Public Health now prohibit these in nursing homes:

> Before a resident is restrained, the facility must demonstrate the presence of a specific medical symptom that would require the use of restraints, and how the use of restraints would treat the cause of the symptom and assist *the resident in reaching his or her highest level of physical and psychosocial well-being.* Appropriate exercise, therapeutic interventions such as orthotic devices, pillows, pads, or lap trays often assist in achieving proper body position, balance and alignment, without the potential negative effects associated with restraint use....Potential negative outcomes include incontinence, decreased range of motion, and decreased ability to ambulate, symptoms of withdrawal or depression or reduced social contact.

Once again, Nick was suffering for others who would see these changes come about in the future, but he had to endure the restraints all the time he stayed in convalescent homes.

The nurses' notes were full of indications of how repetitious and monotonous Nick's days had become. He pushed himself about the facility with his feet, aimlessly. He roamed the corridors and wandered off the unit. He was found in the janitor's room, slowly pulling and shoving with his feet, but he was not hurt. He did not like being confined and annoyed his roommate. He frequently tilted his wheelchair and pushed himself about regardless of the brakes on the chair. But the notes also said that he responded appropriately to requests and seemed to understand conversations and directions. He liked to be talked to.

At 3:20 PM on July 29, 1979, the nurses' notes showed that Nick had another grand mal seizure.

> Leaning toward right side. Appears to be experiencing grand mal seizure—starting predominantly on the right side and then involving entire body, lasting approx. 4-5 min. Frothing at mouth freely from right side—uttering sounds throughout episode—Eyes open—focused upwards into space. Rigidity of entire body following tremors. Into bed. Alert upon cessation of rigidity of body. Responding with head nodding to yes and no questioning.

I would recall the words *"Eyes open—focused upwards into space"* many times in the years ahead. Nick could not express himself at this time, but later, when he could, he related experiences like these as seeing angels and devils and heaven and hell. Unfortunately, we were unable to interpret what he meant by this.

The concerns of one member of the staff regarding Nick's condition showed in her notes. "Uncooperative at 9:00 a.m. Refused to take meds. When questioned by nurse as to what was the matter, nodded head affirmative to statement 'Are you angry?' 'Have you given up?' 'Do you want us to give up?' Answer, negative nod."

Accidents and falls were a constant problem too. On December 21, 1979, the day after his twenty-eighth birthday, Nick was "found in room with finger (3rd rt hand) pinched in w/c. Indentation noted in two areas on finger. Ice packs to area. Dr. Lucas notified. Brought out in hallway where close supervision could be given. Tylenol tabs given for discomfort. Able to move finger."

When I learned of this accident, my insides felt as if they would explode out of me. There are no tears that can wash away this kind of anguish. I covered the spokes of Nick's wheelchair with plastic so that he could not catch a finger in them again. Two days later, on December 23, the notes say that Nick's "rt hand, across knuckles appears swollen. Supervisor notified. Family requests that x-ray be taken."

When I got upset with things like this, I became known as an uncooperative parent. On one occasion when I came to take Nick home, I was immediately told by the nurse at the desk that Nick was belligerent and uncooperative. I flashed a response to her, which she recorded: "Mother in to take home at 11 a.m. Very upset and states staff does not care about her son. He needs to be walked several times a day. 'He does everything I tell him.' Reassured staff was walking and doing all possible for her son. R knee area healing well."

We were doing all we could to relieve the terrible situation Nick was in at the nursing home. The records are full of notes that Nick was "out with family," and that "family was in to visit." But there was never an expression of thanks for all the extra help we provided. Nick was content and happy during the hours we had him at home, but someone was always in constant attendance. At no time did we have a behavior problem with Nick at home, unless you would label as a problem his ceaseless motioning to us to take him back home every time we started to return to the nursing home. I do not believe such behavior is anything but an expression of normal emotion. Yet, at the nursing home, they would note that he

"Appears to be destructive at times

"Revolves w/c until rubber wheel becomes dislodged

"Patient put in straight chair while w/c being repaired —very angry and very restless. Put back to w/c. Able to make self understood.

"Pushes locked w/c around corridor. Ramming into walls and knocked roommate's night stand over breaking after shave lotion."

It is true that Nick did all these things and more. He would completely rearrange the furniture in the room by blindly pushing himself about. He would literally push anything to one side that got in the way of his moving his wheelchair. He ruined the metal baseboard heating unit. He tore wallpaper from the wall with his chair. The room had to be redone with a plastic wallboard. If he got his closet or a drawer open, he could remove all the clothing and let it fall on the floor. These actions were not malicious and were probably done without his full awareness. His motivation was to move himself about and do something!

He wanted to be out in the hall where there were people he could listen to. Yet this was dangerous too, because he was blind and could not see where he was going. He could hurt elderly patients who were unable to get out of his way. He simply did not belong in this atmosphere. Neither we nor the nursing home were to blame for the situation in which we both found ourselves. Nevertheless, it caused us to be pitted against one another.

Rules at the nursing home were changed so that no wheelchair patients were allowed in the corridors unless they were moving from one room to another. This rule affected many patients adversely, not just Nick. I became gloomy every time I visited, so much so that the assistant director of nurses, Caroline Stender, called me into her office one day and bluntly asked, "What is the matter?"

I was so full of pent-up emotion that I cried right on the spot. "It's hard to criticize people who have been so good," I said, "but I can't stand watching Nick, and all the other patients, suffer because of this rule that they must remain in their rooms at all times."

She asked me to speak to the director of nurses and the administrator about my displeasure over these new rules, so I did. I was very upset, and their notes recorded it:

> Mother in to see D.O.N. and administrator. Extremely agitated and angry. States she has put in a call to Dr. Lucas—wants him to order private duty aides for "Nickey"—mother states "the state will pay for anything necessary for his care. I will not have him left in his room alone. He must have someone with him all the time. If he can't have a private duty aide then he should sit at the nurses' station in the hall." Mrs. Del Buono also stated "KHS was an excellent nursing home now it's a hole because Nickey is not allowed to sit in corridor all the time." Charge nurse reported also that Mrs. Del Buono requested to take all PT's meds home today in case it becomes "icy" tonight and she is unable to bring him back.

It is true that Title XIX paid for all necessary medical care for Nick, but officials at the Department of Income Maintenance who administered the Medicaid program for the federal government drew the line at hiring private aides to be with a patient. Our request was refused, but the further irony of it was that they would not allow us to hire aides either. The rationale was that if we did that, we could pay for all his care, and we were told that if we hired aides he would be cut off the Title XIX program.

No latitude was given for the fact that they did not have any facilities to take care of long-term brain-injury persons like Nick. He was not an elderly patient in a nursing home but a young man who needed extra attention because of his injuries. The battles over the lack of care for brain-injury patients were just beginning, and Nick was one of the survivors who took his licks for being a leader.

The administrator explained that he had been forced by the state to repay persons who had provided aides for institutionalized patients who were on the Medicaid program. In other words, the state mandated that any service given to a Title XIX patient must be paid entirely by the nursing home. No one could subsidize the care given to such a patient. But no consideration was given to the fact that Nick's family spent endless hours "subsidizing" the care given by the nursing home until all our energies were drained out of us.

All I could exclaim was, "It's a catch 22." We couldn't hire aides to help Nick, the nursing home didn't provide enough help, and the state had no place available where Nick could get the kind of services he needed. We couldn't take him home without help, and we could not supply financial aid to him.

Nick was now a new victim, of medical neglect, a neglect that, in my opinion, bordered on being criminal.

Our only hope for relief of Nick's situation was the lawsuit. We needed a film to show the jury what a day in Nick's life was like. There were many problems to overcome in getting such a film. The nursing home had to give its consent for the cameras and crew to enter the building to do the filming. We had to make sure it would be done in such a way that a judge would allow the jury to see it. Consents had to be obtained from all the people who would appear in the film. And we were going to have to pay for it.

One by one, we overcame the obstacles. The nursing home reluctantly agreed. Mary D'Agata would appear in the film as Nick's nurse, and one of the aides consented to be in the film. The physical therapist refused to have anything to do with it. The speech pathologist would sign the consent only if it was agreed the film would be used for teaching purposes only.

There were very strict rules governing the admission in court of such films, and this is why we obtained the services of attorney Fred Heller. Guy Ortoleva of Geomatrix agreed to do the filming.

The day before the filming was to be done, we received a call from the nursing home advising us not to come. We were told the whole facility was quarantined due to an outbreak of the flu, so we could not even visit Nick. I later learned that in addition to the flu quarantine, Nick had fallen and bruised himself badly. Sunlamps were used to cover up the bruises as quickly as possible, and when we were allowed into the nursing home again, Nick had no visible abrasions.

The film was rescheduled for March 11, 1980, and everyone arrived at the home early that morning. Not one scene in the film was rehearsed. Everything was done as an actual "Day in the Life of John

Nicholas Del Buono." There was a poignant scene which could not be used in the film that would be shown in court. Nick was alone in his room, moving about in his wheelchair. The radio was on, and Frank Sinatra began to sing the song, "That's Life." Reviewing the film afterward, everyone was stunned as Nick, alone in his room, slowly pushed his chair as Sinatra sang the familiar lyrics. The words described his life perfectly.

Watching it made me acutely aware of what Nick had been through and how he was going to have to live his life. It would take everything he possessed in motivation and skill to "get back in the race," and it was doubtful he ever would. When the filming was over, we knew more clearly than ever that the situation had to change, yet there was no easy solution.

The atmosphere at Kimberly Hall grew worse. Caring for Nick was a real problem for the staff, even though we provided many hours each week of relief for them by either taking care of him while we were there or taking him home. But no amount of help was enough to relieve the tension this scenario created.

On one visit, I learned that Nick had had two grand mal seizures the night before. This alarmed me so much I sought and obtained permission to stay with Nick overnight in his room. I sat next to his bed in the wheelchair. During the evening, I prepared him for bed, pulling the curtain between his bed and that of his roommate.

His roommate was ambulatory but nonconversant. He arose early each morning, and was seldom in the room unless he was lying on his bed. His one really bad habit was that he never urinated directly into the toilet and thus there was always a residue of urine on the bathroom floor, causing an odor in both the bathroom and bedroom.

The nighttime hours passed without incident, and Nick was awake at an early hour. I fed him breakfast and bathed and dressed him. The stench of urine was strong, and we needed to get out of there for a while. (On other occasions, Nick just had to bear this odor.) His roommate had long since left the room. Nick would not go to the TV room, and the only other place for us was the large vestibule, where there were a number of other patients and comfortable chairs. I placed Nick's wheelchair in an out-of-the-way corner and was reading to him when someone came to tell me that I was wanted in the administrator's office. I could not leave Nick alone, so I took him with me.

As soon as we were in his office, the administrator told me that I had violated the patient rights of Nick's roommate and the home's rules by spending the night with Nick. I was aghast at his accusations. I explained that permission had been given by the night supervisor and that I doubted seriously if his roommate even knew I was there. I'm sure the administrator didn't believe me regarding the permission I had obtained, because he sent someone to check on what I had said. It had obviously been charted, and he grudgingly acknowledged the fact that I had not violated their rule or a patient's rights.

I told him the circumstances of the seizures as the reason I wanted to stay overnight. He then told me that the male nurse on duty the previous night was considering a lawsuit against me for questioning his professionalism. The whole scene now turned hostile on both sides. I told the administrator, "Your male nurse must have been the reason for the seizures, considering the stupid way I am now being treated."

Nick was sitting in his chair, raising his hand at every point in agreement with me. I stood up to go and ended the conference by telling the administrator, "Your nurse is an ass and this whole conversation has been utterly asinine." I left his office with Nick signaling his approval all the way.

Once outside the office, though, I was shaking with rage. I had been up all night with Nick. I had slept in my clothes and would have loved a shower at that moment. That was not possible, so I wheeled Nick to the telephone and called home. I was exceedingly tired, but I couldn't leave Nick there. John was as appalled by this turn of events as I. He agreed that if I brought Nick home that day, he would drive him back in the evening.

I felt strongly that this kind of encounter was the administration's way of getting rid of an unwanted patient when they could not legally ask us to place him in another nursing home.

We kept trying to find ways to speed the lawsuit along, to provide more coverage for Nick by family members, and to place him in a nursing home in Waterbury. None of these options met with success. Nick became ill with a cold and was given antibiotics. He was becoming passive and lethargic, which made us suspect that someone was giving him even more drugs than those for seizures.

Mary was becoming more alarmed every day over his deteriorating condition. On one visit, when Debbie accompanied her, they both left with real fear in their hearts that Nick would die unless we could get him closer to home.

As soon as Mary returned to Watertown, she called a nursing home a few blocks from her house. She learned that a bed was available for a male patient. Such beds were very hard to come by, and it was even harder to get an administrator to accept a brain-injured young man. She was also told that if we moved Nick to this nursing home, we would have to get our own attending physician for him. This might not be easy.

It may seem odd that we jumped on the chance to move Nick to a nursing home without having inspected it, but we were so desperate to get Nick out of the environment he was in that any alternative close to home was acceptable to us, because we could provide many hours of care for him.

Susan asked a doctor friend of hers if he would recommend someone who would be Nick's attending physician at the nursing home and he suggested Dr. Richard N. Taylor, Jr. We called him and found that he would be willing to take Nick on as a patient in the nursing home. The administrator told us that the doctor would have to agree to come to the home at least once every month to examine Nick, be on call for any emergency visits, attend him any time Nick was in the hospital, and communicate with the staff by telephone whenever they called. Dr. Taylor agreed to these terms. Nick could be moved! He would be in Watertown, just a few blocks from Mary and about twenty minutes from our home.

We were extremely relieved and notified Connie Nelson to prepare the necessary papers for Nick's transfer to the Watertown Convalarium. We went to Kimberly Hall for the last time on January 13,

1981. Leaving Connie Nelson was difficult. She had been a very good friend to Nick but was now bound by the rules of the place of her employment, and those rules did not allow her to be as helpful as she had been in the past.

We drove down the long, beautiful driveway for the last time with a lethargic son who was still very ill with a cold. We had no illusions that life would be better at the new facility, but at least we would be closer and could provide a great deal more help for Nick than we could at Kimberly Hall. And Nick needed all the help we could give him because, once more, we believed his life was in jeopardy.

28

The Convalarium

The Convalarium was a dramatic change from Kimberly Hall. It was quite small for a nursing home, with only thirty-five beds on two wings. The whole facility was about the size of one of the six wings at Kimberly Hall South. It was perched on top of a small hill and, from the road, could have been mistaken for a large house. The conference with the administrator, Dick Quatrano, was short. His office was in a tiny room off the foyer, with only one chair for visitors. The left arm of it was touching his desk, and I had to sit sideways in the chair in order to face him. He let me talk as much as I wanted without interruption, and his door was always open. He had an attentive, blank stare that never changed. I considered it to be his up-front mask. You never knew what he was thinking.

His message was simple. The nursing home would provide routine nursing care for patients, but they would not attempt to be family to them. We were welcome to spend as much time with Nick as we wanted.

He did not take me on a tour of his facility, for good reason. Each wing contained bedrooms and toilet facilities. In the center was a foyer with the one and only nurses' station in it. Just behind this station was a large room that was used for the dining room, the television room, and the recreation room for all patients. When any one of these activities was going on in this room, the other two ceased.

The only semiprivate area in the facility was a very small room referred to by the nurses as the "meditation room," whatever that was supposed to mean. The only place to sit in this room was in two loveseat chairs facing each other in a space so narrow that when two people sat opposite, their knees would touch. There were a lot of potted plants in the room, a very small bookcase, a pay telephone on the wall, and a bathroom with a toilet and sink. Only one wheelchair could be accommodated in the room at a time.

This turned out to be the place where Nick was supposed to do physical therapy. There was no other space in which to do it except the corridors. The room that had been designed for therapy was used for storage of gerichairs. The "meditation room" was directly across the hall from the nurses' station in one direction, and Dick Quatrano's office in another. It certainly could not have been considered very "private," as no phone calls could be made from the Convalarium without the staff hearing at least one side of the conversation.

Beyond the "dining-TV-recreation" room was an area referred to as "the terrace." It was the size of an ordinary home patio with a badly cracked concrete floor, a broken picnic table and bench, and one chair that was safe to sit on. There was no sidewalk around the facility and no yard for patients to be able to walk out of doors. The area in front of the facility was sometimes used by persons to sit in the sun, but there was an immediate, steep driveway that presented hazards for wheelchair patients. Cars picking people up would drive right up to the front door to avoid this danger.

The bedrooms were just large enough for each patient to have a night stand on one side of the bed and a chair on the other. Small closets were built into the wall, and there was one sink in the room for two patients. The "bathroom" contained a single commode that was used by patients in adjoining rooms, so four people shared a toilet. It was impossible to fit a wheelchair into such a small space, so Nick usually used one of the bathrooms in the hall where the showers were located.

This was just the sort of place I vowed Nick would never go to, but I had been reduced to being glad that he was there so we could spend more time with him. I'm quite sure incarcerated prisoners like Joseph Tramontano have more room than Nick did at the Convalarium.

Connie Nelson had sent an Inter-Agency Patient Referral Report. In it she wrote:

> Nick is 29 year old blind non-verbal—understands everything that is said to him & will follow simple instructions—He has a hearty appetite & is fed a 1500 calorie diet—Has gained 12 lbs in one yr. Visitors must be watched—they bring in extra food. Nick spends days fully dressed in w/c with jacket vest. Ambulates with assistance of 2 usually P.T. Was seen by podiatrist 1/8/81. Has start of ingrown toenail—Domboro soaks had for one wk, should be seen by podiatrist this wk. Karaya paste is applied to area around stomach. Family is very attentive—but tend to be unrealistic.

No one at Kimberly Hall had ever complained to us that we brought in extra food or that they were concerned about Nick's weight. If we had to be watched, surely someone should have said something to us. And, of course, there was that old jab again about our being "unrealistic." It seemed the medical community agreed with Dr. Sturman's philosophy: "Just put him in a convalescent home and go on about your life." In other words, leave him to an early death.

The report listed the medications Nick was taking, and Dalmane had been given to him each night at Kimberly Hall, just as we had suspected. These sleeping pills were building up in his system to the point where he was lethargic most of the time. It was one of the reasons we couldn't get any responses from him and why we felt compelled to get him out of Kimberly Hall.

On admission January 13, 1981, Nick weighed 183-1/2 pounds, his skin condition was clear; and his vital signs were within normal limits. He was sick with a cold, though, so we were reluctant to leave him that first night in these new and strange surroundings. We stayed with him as long as we could, and called at 10 o'clock to check on his condition.

In the days that followed, coughing spells were a constant problem. On January 20, he had a coughing spasm that lasted forty minutes. We walked him in the corridor each day, trying to prevent the onset of pneumonia. By January 24 we began to take him home for visits again. On January 30 he vomited a large amount of undigested food and repeated the vomiting of his meal the next day at noon.

Both of Mary's children were now in school. Therefore, she had free hours to spend with Nick each day. We worked out a plan whereby she would stay with him several hours during the daytime and John and I would cover the evening hours. Susan would help in the afternoons whenever she could. Mary was with Nick on January 31 when he vomited his noon meal. At dinnertime his food was pureed. John took me to the Convalarium about 4:30 PM and stayed with us until 5:00. Then John went home while I remained with Nick.

The aide came by with pureed food for Nick, but he was sleeping. Nevertheless, it was dinnertime in the nursing home, so she raised the bed and a very sleepy Nick was fed a spoonful of the puree. He gagged but got some of it down. On the second spoonful he began to seize, and in a matter of seconds began a whole-body grand mal seizure. The nurse was called, and she ran to the phone to notify the doctor.

I had been standing next to Nick's bed and reached down to hold him while he was seizing. There was no letup in the intensity or duration of the seizure activity. The doctor finally ordered that he be taken to the hospital, and an ambulance was called. We waited while Nick's entire body convulsed. I was bent over his bed holding him. This continued for an unconscionably long time, so long that I began trying to calm both our fears by saying the "Hail Mary" prayer. Never was one more urgently said, and it helped. I repeated it many times, but the ambulance did not arrive. It was a full hour between the time Nick began to seize and his arrival at the hospital, still seizing. (Nick was in a condition referred to as status epilepticus—a seizure that won't stop.) He was immediately started on Valium intravenously to control the seizure activity. He was conscious the whole time.

Nick's Dilantin level was at the toxic range, 32.4. It should have been in a therapeutic range of 10 to 20. Blood serum levels were supposed to be checked monthly to determine Nick's level. How it got to be 32.4 is a mystery to me. By February 3, his Dilantin level was still high at 29.0.

I was questioned closely by doctors and interns about his activity preceding the onslaught of seizures. I had to tell them it occurred while he was trying to eat. This seemed to cause more concern about his ability to swallow food than his blood serum level.

On February 5, Dr. Henry Merriman came to Nick's room while I was in attendance with him. He explained that they planned to insert a laryngoscope into Nick's throat area to try to determine the condition of the tissue and his ability to handle swallowing. I was not allowed to stay in the room, so I waited in the hallway. Nevertheless, I knew what was happening, and I cried helplessly as they shoved the tube down Nick's throat.

Dr. Merriman exited the room with a look of doom on his face. He explained that Nick's gag reflex was not working, and that he would have to have the gastrostomy tube reinserted for feedings. I had little ability left to control my emotions and only wanted the doctors to leave so I could cry in private.

On February 6, Nick went to the operating room, where Dr. Philip Gedeon reinserted the gastrostomy tube in Nick's stomach. By the ninth his Dilantin level had descended to 20.6.

On February 11 Nick was discharged back to the Convalarium on a dosage of 300 mg. of Dilantin and 150 mg. of phenobarbital. He was being fed a can of nutritional supplement four times a day by pouring the liquid directly into his stomach through the tube. The gastrostomy opening was covered with gauze, and an abdominal binder held the tube in place.

We quickly learned the procedure for administering tube feedings, because we continued to take Nick home every chance we got. By February 20, Dr. Taylor had authorized us to give Nick lollipops, and we began to hope that the tube feedings would not be permanent.

Nick continued to have slight tremors, especially in the right hand. Also he wanted to move about in his chair every time he was in it. This became as much a problem at the Convalarium as it had been at Kimberly Hall. However, this staff was not about to put up with Nick's disruptions as tolerantly as the people at Kimberly Hall had done. We were in another "catch-22," and new forms of torture were in store for Nick.

When Nick tried to move about in the hallway, they restrained the only foot he could use, the left one, by tying it to the chair. He was returned to his bed by 2:00 or 2:30 in the afternoon and restrained there until the next morning time and time again.

He was noted as being uncooperative at 7:15 in the evening but out of bed shortly thereafter when his parents visited him. They even noted that I took him to the bathroom and his bowels moved and that I brushed his teeth myself when they wanted him in bed and I did not.

The real battle for survival was just beginning. Day after day, the nursing notes showed that Nick was put to bed for a "nap" before the 3 to 11 shift came on duty. This "nap" began to last until the next day, when the aide came in to bathe and dress him. We had been prepared for nursing home life, but nothing as cruel as this.

When the weeks became months and the same routine continued, the tension between family and staff grew worse. We were providing many hours of nursing coverage for Nick, but he was obviously not going to be allowed out of bed in the afternoon unless we got him up.

Not only were the days going to be peaceful without Nick's brain-injury behavior in their hallways, but, from their point of view, nights were going to be restful too. Though I had requested that Dr. Taylor not give Nick sleeping pills without my knowledge, he was called about Nick's increasingly restless nights on April 5, and 15 mg. of Serax was ordered prn (per required need). Apparently his requirement for sleeping pills was constant, as he was given one each night thereafter. Neither Dr. Taylor nor the nursing home staff notified me of what they were doing.

The records after this period show a constant pattern of family in to be with Nick or family taking Nick out for several hours at a time. Furthermore, the charting of our activities became constant and obsessive, as this typical notation indicates.

> Family (sister) visited at 1:45; removed leg restraint; upset about seeing leg restraint. Has been told many times previously by nurse in charge and therapist about necessity of this; Family are becoming uncooperative @ times regarding care.
>
> Visited by sister (7:45). Nurse asked her not to get him up because it was

time for his 8:00 p.m. feeding. Sister got patient up and took him to bathroom. Put back to bed at 8:45.

The leg restraint meant that Nick's right leg (which was contracted) was tied to his wheelchair without regard as to whether it was painful to him or not. The staff was too busy to inquire about the severity of the pain. Sometimes the left leg was tied as well to prevent Nick from moving his chair about the hallways.

It may be hard to understand that this happened in a nursing home and that the family was helpless to change it, but it did. It was taken for granted that this was appropriate treatment. If any mother treated her child in the same manner, she would be arrested for abuse by the authorities.

Nick had been at the Convalarium for only seven months when Dick Quatrano was arrested for Medicaid fraud of a most scandalous nature. An article in the *Waterbury Republican-American* newspaper on August 15, 1981, by reporter Ed Butler, stated, "Watertown—State nursing home fraud investigators Friday arrested Richard Quatrano, administrator and part owner of the Watertown Convalarium charging him with misusing $15,577 in Medicaid funds, including leasing x-rated movies."

The Hartford Courant printed another article headlined "Hearing Set for Nursing Home Owner," and more details were revealed.

> Richard Quatrano, 45, of Watertown, was also accused of defrauding the state to pay for his home utility bills, school tuition and medical and dental expenses for family members and to finance Florida vacations.
>
> He was charged with four counts of first degree larceny and one count of second degree larceny and released on a written promise to appear in Hartford Superior Court.
>
> The false information allowed him to receive a higher Medicaid reimbursement rate than he was entitled to, the warrant charged.

The case was reported on television as well as in the newspapers, and John was exiting the Convalarium after a visit with Nick when cameramen and reporters from Channel 3 in Hartford were filming the front of the building to show on their evening news broadcast.

All these accusations caused us more concern than ever over the way Nick would be cared for in this licensed "SNF" (skilled nursing facility). The story was also particularly bitter since we had requested that we be allowed to put an air conditioner in Nick's room and had been refused permission to do so. The rooms were sweltering with heat in the summertime because there was no air conditioning for Dick Quatrano's patients in his nursing home, though he was accused of using their funds to put one in his home.

By September, the tension between family and staff had deteriorated to civil hostility, though we both kept polite attitudes as an outward appearance. My frustration over the fact that the Convalarium was licensed as a skilled nursing facility and the staff's apparent reluctance to get a thirty-year-old man out of bed on the 3 to 11 shift finally boiled over.

I confronted Dick Quatrano about the problem and he said, "You can always move Nick elsewhere."

When I peered directly into his eyes and asked him point blank, "Are you telling me to take Nick elsewhere?" he quickly retreated by saying, "No."

I knew that Nick had rights as a patient in this facility; his bill was being paid. Dick Quatrano received his license based on the fact that he could care for patients like Nick; he had accepted him into his facility, and he could not refuse to care for him without good cause. He did not have a right to ask me to take Nick elsewhere based on my requirement that Nick be out of bed on the 3 to 11 shift.

I told him forcefully, "I strongly object to the fact that Nick is being put to bed in the afternoon for a nap that lasts until the next morning, and I have every intention of going to the State Health Department about the matter." Quatrano was standing behind the nurses' station when I said this to him, and he actually retreated into the corner of the station as if I had pushed him there. I knew I had hit a sensitive nerve.

This confrontation with Dick Quatrano signaled the end of a period in my life. No longer would I hope to be liked by staff or administration of any facility. I would gladly settle for respect and, if not that, then fear of what I would do next.

The Convalarium

I believe the torture that Nick endured by being tied in bed from 2:30 in the afternoon until whatever time he was bathed the next morning, and then being restrained—body and legs—in a gerichair was inhuman in every sense of the word. No person should have to endure this kind of pain and degradation, and no one can stand this treatment, day after day, without either going insane or giving up all will to live. I didn't want Nick to be forced into that kind of agonizing choice, but my resources for rescuing him were extremely limited.

29

TBI: A Newly Recognized Disability

True to my promise to Dick Quatrano, I called the State Department of Health and talked to the chief social worker, Ken Smith. John joined in the conversation and, to our amazement, Mr. Smith welcomed our story! He asked us to repeat it to Deputy Commissioner Kerrigan, and we did. It seems people from all over the state were deluging the health department with complaints about the lack of proper treatment for their loved ones who had suffered a brain injury.

We were invited to speak about Nick and his treatment to a group of people in state health agencies who had formed an Interdepartmental Committee on Traumatic Brain Injury. Ken Smith was chairman of the committee, and representatives from the other agencies included Mental Health, Mental Retardation, Income Maintenance, Developmental Disabilities, and Office of Protection and Advocacy. Gaylord Hospital and an administrator of a nursing home completed the committee, except for persons listed as "Support Group." These were family members, like us, who had sons and daughters with brain injuries.

John and I went to the meeting and told our story. We were invited to become members of the committee and agreed to do so. This was not immediate help for Nick, but it was quite consoling to learn that we were not alone. I made the administrator and staff at the Convalarium aware of our involvement with Ken Smith and his committee. It certainly couldn't hurt Nick for them to know that we were working with the State Health Department on this issue, and perhaps they might be more careful in their treatment of Nick.

One of the goals of the Interdepartmental Committee was to get the governor to appoint a Task Force on traumatic brain injury to study the problems that the people in the state were facing with regard to this newly recognized disability: traumatic brain injury (TBI). The other was to undertake to do a prevalence study to determine the scope of the problem in the state.

About this time we also learned that there was an organization in Massachusetts called the National Head Injury Foundation. I wrote to them. They had only begun their organization in 1980, but they were able to give me the name of a woman in Connecticut to contact, Charlotte Kane. She also had a young son who had been injured. She and some other families in her area were trying to start a new organization which would be known as the Connecticut Traumatic Brain Injury Support Group.

I also talked with the case worker for the Department of Income Maintenance in charge of Nick's case. After listening to my complaints, she told me she was going to break the rules and give me the name of another mother who was having similar problems and who was just as distraught over conditions for her son as I was. Her name was Cynthia De Prodocini from Lakeville. I had another long talk with another mother in the same situation.

These conversations with Charlotte and Cynthia convinced John and me that there was a real need for a statewide parents' group to advocate for the needs of TBI people in addition to the Interdepartmental Committee.

Plans were being made to incorporate a nonprofit organization. We were invited to join with the other families for their organizational conference. In October 1981, John and I made the two-hour trip for the evening meeting in Norwich, and the group passed the necessary votes to incorporate. I agreed to serve on the board of directors for a term of two years, as well as on the executive committee.

By February 27, 1982, John and I had contacted enough families with brain-injured sons and daughters to have a support group meeting in Waterbury at John's office. It was the formation of the Waterbury Support Group, soon to become a satellite of the state organization. Eight families were represented at this first meeting.

I conducted the meeting and went around the table asking each family to tell their story about their brain-injured child. Although each one was an individual story, similarities quickly showed in the lack of care available to properly treat these young people. Their stories were shocking and heart-rending.

None of this was immediate help for Nick, though. Therefore, we made attempts to move Nick to more agreeable surroundings in another nursing home. I visited every new convalescent home in the area. On one of these trips I found a place called River Glen in Southbury. I asked if I might apply to have Nick considered for admission: I requested a tour of the facility and was taken on one. It was a far nicer place than the Convalarium.

I made an appointment for John and Mary to return with me for an interview and tour. They were as impressed as I had been. We were taken to the second floor and introduced to a nurse who would be on duty if Nick was accepted as a patient. We were told that the staff, as well as the physician, would like to have an opportunity to examine Nick to see whether or not they could give him the kind of care he required.

We were also told that the facility was not accepting Connecticut Title XIX (Medicaid) patients because the Department of Income Maintenance would not pay a rate sufficient to properly care for them. We knew that no nursing home in Connecticut was legally permitted to refuse patients based on the fact that Medicaid paid their bills. It was explained, however, that River Glen was one of the New MediCo homes and that this corporation and the state were involved in a lawsuit over this matter. Therefore, pending the outcome of the case, the home was refusing Title XIX patients. I was asked to write a letter to my legislator in support of their position, and to get others to do so as well.

In spite of this policy, the staff still wanted to examine Nick, so we assumed they would make an exception in his case. On the appointed day, John, Mary, and I picked Nick up at the Convalarium and drove with him to Southbury. We were taken to a large room on the second floor where a few people were gathered. In just a short time, more and more staff persons arrived until there were about a dozen. Then another man entered the room, and we were introduced to Dr. Ian Lawson.

We chatted with the staff, answering all their questions. Dr. Lawson proceeded to make a few examination-type gestures toward Nick. They were mostly observatory in nature, and he talked as he watched Nick move his wheelchair about with his left foot. Every word during the interview was spoken in front of Nick: questions about what he could do and could not do, the nature of his injury, his handicaps, and his care plan. Their conclusion was stated in his presence as well. He would need more care than they were capable of giving. He had flunked the "exam"!

Everyone looked at us with pity while congratulating us on what a fine job we were doing with Nick and commenting on what a heroic family we were. They exited the room as quickly as they had entered, and the interview was over.

Nick exhibited signs of being upset and hurt. The look on his face was one of anger, and he kept motioning for us to go. In this instance he was more conscious and alert than were we. The three of us were too stunned to be anything but polite, not really comprehending the enormity of what had just happened. It was all so neat and swift. We had just been given the "bum's rush," but this time it had been disguised as great drama. The only thing missing from the scene was mood music.

Going home in the car, we vowed never to look at another nursing home, but to put all our efforts into fighting for a better life for Nick in every way we knew how. Nick would have to stay at the Convalarium, receiving as much help as we could give, until we could rescue him.

We decided on two avenues of hope. One was to try to bring our lawsuit to trial and win it. The other was to try to help the newly organized support group in its efforts to get off the ground in order to change the system of care for these patients. We hoped that by our efforts other parents in the future would not have to endure what we were living with Nick.

A grant obtained from the Developmental Disabilities Council gave the support group the financial impetus it needed. Nevertheless, the volunteer work involved in starting a nonprofit organization is monumental. I spent a minimum of twenty hours a week on organizational efforts for well over a year. John contributed many hours of his time as well. There were many others doing the same.

Board meetings were held at Gaylord Hospital because of its central location in the state. The support group office was in Norwich. Charlotte became the first executive director. She was supposed to work part-time in the office, but there was no way the duties it required could be handled in a few hours a day.

The office had a toll-free number, and the calls were pouring in as knowledge spread that there was such an organization. Jean Harkins was soon hired as a full-time director, and she made many friends for the TBI cause.

The board members worked in a unison that was a joy to behold during their first year. The monumental number of hours they labored, and the generous manner in which they contributed their time, deserve much praise. The results this group achieved are testimony to their efforts and abilities. The first board must be credited with making the public aware of TBI and what it means to the victim and the family.

One of the outstanding members was a young doctor from Gaylord Hospital, Stephen Sarfaty. He was also on the Interdepartmental Committee, and he worked tirelessly with the committee and the support group to realize their common goal to get the governor to appoint a task force.

Election time for the governor was drawing near, and Governor O'Neill had not yet acted in our behalf. No such task force had been appointed in any other state, but we felt strongly that one was needed in Connecticut. To raise the level of public awareness, a campaign was mounted to get newspapers to print stories about people who had suffered brain injury. Another campaign to put pressure on the governor to appoint the task force was begun. I wrote the governor about this. He replied on August 12, 1982:

> Dear Mrs. Del Buono:
> This is in response to your recent letter concerning the establishment of a Traumatic Brain Injury Task Force.
>
> I am pleased to announce that we are about to undertake that effort. It is my intention to appoint officials of seven state agencies and representatives of the medical community and the families of TBI victims to the Task Force. I will ask the members to study existing services and facilities, possible alternative programs, and the need for financial and other forms of assistance to families of TBI victims. The Task Force will have to focus its work on the need for acute care when injury or illness first strikes, as well as short-term and long-term rehabilitation.
>
> It is clear that TBI victims and their families face tremendous personal and financial challenges and that the existence and coordination of treatment and rehabilitation facilities and programs is essential if these needs are to be met.
> Sincerely,
> William A. O'Neill
> Governor

This was tremendous news, but the official announcement was not forthcoming. We were afraid the election would be held without reaching our cherished goal. We were concerned that we would have to start all over again with a new governor, so I called Governor O'Neill's office to relay the message that I wanted to know when the task force would be announced; I said people in my Waterbury Support Group wanted this information before election day.

On October 17, 1981, just two weeks before the election, the public announcement was made that the task force would be appointed by Governor O'Neill. The board of directors of the support group and the members of the Interdepartmental Committee all felt very good about this, because no matter which way the election went, we would have our task force. Fortunately, Governor O'Neill was reelected.

It was becoming well recognized, however, that brain injury was a big problem nationwide, too. The National Head Injury Foundation had published a very effective brochure entitled "The Silent Epidemic" (see Appendix, BIA) which stated:

> Until the establishment of NHIF in 1980, no single existing federal, state or private agency concerned itself exclusively with the unique problems faced by the head injured and their families. Until NHIF, this "lost population" was silently and shamefully closeted away, and inappropriately placed in psychiatric institutions, schools for the retarded or nursing homes.

In an article entitled "Head Injury: The Problem, the Need" (Programs for the Handicapped, produced by the Department of Education, Office of Special Education and Rehabilitative Services), brain injury is defined this way: "Severe traumatic head injury occurs when there is either direct damage to the brain (e.g. caused by gunshot wounds or bone fragments), through severe concussion, which may cause brain swelling, bruising, or damage through an increase in intracranial fluid pressure."

It also tells how the injury can result in damage far more severe than can be immediately determined: "An impact to the head severe enough to cause brain injury will cause the brain to rebound within the skull wall, leading to damage far from the initial injury location. This effect contrasts with the greater probability of many other diseases of the brain, such as stroke and brain tumor, which are limited to local areas....Each traumatic head injury can therefore be expected to produce a unique set of resulting brain injuries and problems."

This definition and explanation is what sets TBI apart as a unique disability that requires specialized treatment. It is the most prevalent injury in our society today, though often undetected.

Some of the cognitive deficits, emotional disturbances, and personality changes that may occur as the result of TBI are discussed in a paper on closed head injury.* They are: impairment in attention and concentration; fatigability; disturbances in memory; emotional insta-

---

* "Behavioral Consequences of Closed Head Injury" (*Central Nervous System Trauma Research Status Report, 1979,* National Institute of Neurological and Communicative Disorders and Strokes, Arthur L. Benton, Ph.D., D.Sc., Department of Psychology, University of Iowa).

bility and lowered tolerance of frustration and noise; personality alteration in the direction of either depression and withdrawal or disinhibition and euphoria; aphasic defect; basic and higher-level sensory deficits of various types. Some symptoms occur with remarkably high frequency as late effects of head trauma.

The gravity of this injury can be properly understood only if one becomes aware of what the brain really means to each individual. What is the brain? What happens when it is damaged?

Nothing on earth resembles the human brain. It is the most magnificent structure in all the world. The information capacity alone of human memory in the average adult is at least 500 times that of the information stored in the entire Encyclopedia Britannica. It has been suggested that a four-year-old child has more knowledge stored in the brain about the family kitchen than will fit into the biggest computer now available.

Every human function we perform is directed through our marvelous computer, the brain. It is an absolutely awesome machine. But it is not an assembly-line production from IBM. Each person has a brain with unique characteristics peculiar to that individual. The structure of this special part of the body is what makes each of us the unique personality that we are. It is what distinguishes us from one another. Our brain is our world, our own little planet on which we live.

When the brain is injured, it is comparable to a bomb dropping on our planet. It can destroy our whole world completely, merely change it slightly, or make it forever different to the point where we cannot recognize ourselves as the same human being we were before the injury occurred. No other disability can so completely accomplish this result.

When brain injury occurs, a kind of death happens, but not complete death. That is why families are so terribly affected by this injury. They must continually mourn the person they loved, who almost died, but they must care for what is left of that person and help their loved one develop a new personality, a new being with an injured brain.

This brings on the most fantastic psychological problems. The magnificence of the human spirit adjusts to these new challenges, and most families display a courage, a behavior, an endurance that even they did not believe possible. However, unless you are forced to deal with TBI, you will not want to know about it. Even then, some persons are never able to come to terms with it even when it happens to a member of their family. For those who can, they slowly learn that love is the healer.

The families of brain-injured persons desperately need the help of their friends in society to cope with the day-to-day physically exhausting, emotionally draining problems that brain injury brings. Without this help, they grow weak, develop diseases early in life, and sometimes die in the effort. That is why so many have joined together to try to bring their plight to public attention. TBI is a family disability that needs community help.

30

Surviving

The year was 1981, and while we were working on the lawsuit and helping to get the brain injury organization going, we still had the problem of helping Nick survive until things could get better for him. We began to pick him up after work and take him home until time for bed. If we couldn't do that, we stayed at the Convalarium and got him ready for bed there.

We never just "visited" Nick; we took care of him totally. We changed his diapers, gave him skin care, brushed his teeth, washed his hair (his scalp was always dry), made sure his fingernails and toenails were cut, walked him in the corridors, read stories to him, played music, and took him to as many recreational activities at the nursing home as we could.

A kind woman named Tish was the recreational therapist. She and Mary did a great deal together to make Nick's life in the nursing home better. With Mary sitting beside him, he could join in the Bingo games. With the help of Mary and Tish, he succeeded in joining the ceramics class and painted a lovely cream colored vase with mauve swirls on it that he gave me as a surprise gift. He molded another one that he gave to Sally as a wedding present. Nick accomplished this by having the vase placed in his contracted right arm with a paint brush positioned in his left hand. With Mary's assistance, he could get paint on the brush and stroke the side of the vase. Sometimes his right arm would contract too much for him to work on it any longer, and he would have to quit.

Tish and Mary became friends too, because she was kind to Nick in so many ways. Volunteers would come to the home on Fridays to sing for the patients. They would bring baked goods to serve after their program. It would hurt Nick to be present when these were served, since he could not have any. Tish knew that we were feeding Nick, and she would frequently sneak something in his room so that Mary could feed him outside the watchful eyes of the nurses.

Much of what we did for Nick upset the nursing staff, especially that we fed him. There was no way we could agree on his care. If we saw situations that we felt were wrong for Nick, we changed them, often to the chagrin of the staff. They were willing to provide what they believed to be good nursing care, but in Nick's case it was not enough, and we knew it. We were the only ones who could make up the difference, but instead of applauding our efforts and cooperating with us, our actions were taken as an affront to their professionalism. They hadn't the foggiest notion of what to do with a brain-injured person because they had never had any training in the field. Nevertheless, they had to cope with just such a patient, as did we.

A bright spot in Nick's stay at the Convalarium was that speech therapy had to be continued, and we had the opportunity to meet Lisa Golymbieski, a speech pathologist. Mary was present when she first tested Nick. So many of the things that she wanted him to do could be accomplished only by a sighted person with finger dexterity. The testing went badly, but she was patient and kind.

It was her theory that everyone, no matter how injured, must have a means of communication. Sign language was not a possibility because he had no fine finger control on either hand. She knew about a gestural language that had been developed, but it incorporated the use of both arms. Lisa was willing to try to adapt it to the use of the only body function Nick had for this purpose, his left arm.

The doctor had to authorize speech therapy, and when Lisa explained to him what she had in mind, he was of the opinion that Nick could not learn the gestures, and even if he did master some of them, he would not remember to use them. It was a risk of professional time and expense, but Lisa wanted to try, so the doctor agreed to let her begin the experiment.

It was about the crudest form of communication one could imagine, but Nick painstakingly learned a few gestures (about three a week, at first), and he remembered to use them at appropriate times! Over a period of many months, he learned about 150 signs. This was miraculous, considering Nick's prognosis.

These gestures gave Nick a way to express his most basic needs. Lisa was pleased, and we were ecstatic that he could now communicate a little better with us. Lisa offered to hold an in-service conference with the staff to teach them his most basic gestures, but her offer was refused. They picked up the ones most often used by watching Nick with his family and made do with those. They didn't spend much time with him, so it was not as important to them to communicate with him as it was to us.

It may seem a strange statement to make that the staff in a nursing home does not spend much time with the patient, but it is true. Their duties are routine and accomplished quickly. When these are completed, they leave the room. When the patient is nonverbal, there is even less contact.

Nick could now express his thoughts and emotions by use of these gestures. He would sign with them to "say" short sentences and phrases, which released his ability to tell us what he wanted and needed. For instance:

"I love you."
"I love God."
"I want a drink."
"I want to eat."
"I want to go home."
"I want a blanket."
"I want my teeth brushed."
"My stomach [or any other part of his body] hurts."
"I am upset."

"I want my hair combed."
"I want to talk to Dad."
"Turn off the radio."
"Read to me."
"I want a pillow."
"I want to go to the bathroom."
"Please give me a (bath, Kleenex, shirt, etc.)."
"Mary is good to me."
"I don't like the noise."
"Please be quiet."
"I want to see a doctor."
"What time is it?"
"Where am I?"
"What's wrong with my body?"

A vivid memory of Nick's communicating clearly occurred when John brought Nick home to celebrate Christmas with the family. Late Christmas day, when festivities with everyone had settled down a little, Nick began to sign for attention. He began writing a word in midair with his left hand: P-R-E-S-E-N-T. He wasn't ready to let go of the Christmas spirit. He wanted to hang on to it longer, and he wanted a present! And he got some—music and story cassettes for him to listen to and a few new clothes. We had to be careful what we left at the nursing home, as possessions so often disappeared.

Nick became an even more difficult patient when he was able to express himself with gestural communication. He could now let his wants and desires be known and tried very hard to do so all the time. This was not always met with success or understanding.

On most night shifts, an RN by the name of Mary Chapin was on duty. She was outwardly pleasant, robotlike in her duties, and she was firm about not upsetting her routine. From my observations of the way she performed her duties, patients who were a bother were put in their place rather quickly on her shift. She apparently considered Nick's "place" his bed. I did not, and she knew it. On September 11, 1981, the 3 to 11 shift had its usual note, "Remained in bed." However, this particular day contained an additional notation: "Very uncooperative. Leg over side rails. Turned sideways in bed 3x. Bed & PT straightened out. Left leg restrained. Visited by parents. Mother very upset about leg restraint. Parents dressed PT and took him to his sister's @ 7:45. 8:00 PM feeding sent & PT returned at 9:25."

What she did not put in her notes was the real story of how I was told about the leg restraint. As I walked through the front door, followed by John, Mary Chapin shouted across the foyer, "We have a very uncooperative patient in your son. You'll find his left leg tied to the rail when you go in to see him."

I found her manner to be intimidating, accusatory, and yet defensive. I asked her, "What in the world do you mean by tying the only leg he can move to the bed?"

"He is constantly putting his leg over the rails and turning sideways in his bed."

"Do you know that Nick has learned a gestural language with which to communicate his wants and needs?"

"I do know that."

"Well, then, do you suppose that Nick is trying to tell you something? He wants out of bed."

John and I went to Nick's room, and we took him out of the nursing home so that he could spend some peaceful time out of bed in a friendly environment. It was also necessary for me to leave the Convalarium in order to control my exploding anger.

The nurses' notes the next day show how fearful I was at how he was being treated.

"Mother visiting at lunch. Took him out-of-doors for 1/2 hour. Returned to bed at 2:30."

On the 3 to 11 shift, the notes said: "Visited by mother. Up in wheel chair at 5:45 until 7:30. Put to bed by mother after being in bathroom 1/2 hour."

The situation became ludicrous in no time at all. Mary Chapin began to note all manner of things we did that obviously annoyed her. The other nurses added their comments too. I was accused of taking Nick in the "meditation room" and feeding him chocolate pudding.

Nick would be accused of being "belligerent" when he would refuse tube feedings and indicate he wanted to eat. He would put his arm across his abdomen and refuse to allow them to pour the liquid feedings in the tube. When they persisted, he would swing his left arm at them. But they won the battle with assistance from more than one nurse, and the tube feedings were poured into his stomach. I fed him a doughnut and they noted that, too. But their notes also reported that Nick "slept well" after being given food.

The nursing staff was critical of us and constantly frightened that Nick would aspirate. They showed no pleasure that he was handling solid foods and that there was hope he could return to normal eating.

When we learned that Nick could swallow food again, nothing could have kept us from continuing to give him food. We were not ashamed of this or trying to hide it. On the contrary, we were quite proud of his accomplishment and told everyone about it. I walked through the front door many times with a bag from Dunkin' Donuts or McDonald's.

We were, however, always looking for a few precious moments of privacy, because their prying eyes were always watching us. They really believed they had to do this because they were afraid we would kill our son. What they wouldn't admit is that when families are reduced to the level of living that we were, chances are something you don't mind taking. We had been told many times that Nick would die, and I would much rather have seen him choke on a hamburger, just the way he liked it, than on a Serax pill such as the one Mary Chapin gave him each night to put him to sleep. One of the few places of refuge and privacy was on the toilet. We spent an extraordinary amount of time there, as Nick liked to sit and talk. It was the only place free from the nurses and aides and the noises so many of the senile people couldn't help making. On one such occasion, he asked Mary, in sign language, "How old am I?"

"You're twenty-nine," she told him.

By using his left arm to spell the word in the air, Nick answered, "Old."

It was the first time he realized how much time had gone by, and he could not account for it. She relieved the tension by telling him that she was still a year older than he.

The time came when Dr. Taylor left his practice in Connecticut to go to another state. This meant that we had to get another attending physician to take over Nick's case. I went to see Dr. Curtiss Tate, who was in practice with Dr. Taylor, and he agreed to replace Dr. Taylor.

We continued to learn new things about Nick's capabilities. For instance, he was not totally incontinent. He could use the urinal at certain times of the day and could indicate to us when he had to have a bowel movement. If we were there to take him to the bathroom and wait, he was often successful.

We discovered new ways to pivot and walk with Nick that made his care much easier, but when I tried to show the aides what we knew, they were uninterested in learning. They had their own crude way and would not change. Occasionally, an aide would take an interest. When this occurred, it resulted in less work for her and far better treatment for Nick.

The gastrostomy opening became a source of constant irritation to Nick. Gastric juices would leak out onto his skin and cause it to be red and itchy most of the time. The bandages needed changing frequently. This was another reason why he was a difficult patient in a nursing home where the staff had many demands on their time. We changed the dressings when we took him home, so we learned to check them frequently. On October 24, 1981, it was charted: "Mother visiting at 12:30. Returned to bed at 2:30. His mother removed binder and checked dressing and asked nurse in charge to change it. This was done at 2:35."

If I had not checked the dressing, Nick would have lain there all afternoon with wet, stinking gauze pads with gastric juices on them further irritating his skin. On October 26, the notes stated: "Blood noted on 'jonnie.' Bleeding from area around gastrostomy. Took binder and dressing partially off and was scratching skin around opening. Skin very irritated. Bleeding. Cleansed with H2O. A&D ointment applied to area."

By December 1, Nick had a terrible rash on the buttocks area to add to this discomfort. The nurses noted that he was "trying to scratch constantly," that the "rash was spreading around buttocks," and finally, on December 4, 1981, "Rash looks worse. Dr. Tate notified at 7:45. Returned call at 8:15."

I was at the nursing home at 5:30 and spoke to the nurse about the rash. She listened and said they were doing all they could. By 7:45, I could no longer tolerate the agony that Nick was enduring and called the doctor myself. I talked with him at 8:15 and asked that he have a dermatologist look at Nick as soon as possible because Nick was suffering miserably from the rash covering the entire buttocks and groin area.

The dermatologist did come and ordered soaks and cream for his irritated skin. Compassion for the pain Nick was suffering seemed to be more my concern than the staff's. Nick was suffering unbelievable agony, and life for us was being lived at a pace we never imagined we could run.

On December 4, John, Mary, and I took Nick to Dr. Merriman. We wanted to see if the gastrostomy tube could be removed, because we knew Nick could eat and swallow. We helped Nick into the examining chair and were talking with him in our usual gestural manner when Dr. Merriman came in.

He took one look at Nick and another at us. His demeanor communicated his thoughts: we were trying to converse with a helpless, severely brain-injured human being who was not understanding us. Therefore, he was going to have to deal with an unrealistic family who could not be relied on for good judgment. He performed his exam quickly, and we already knew what the outcome would be. We had lost again in our efforts to help Nick out of another terrible predicament due to a doctor's apparent inexperience with brain injury.

On December 9, Mary and I took Nick to see Dr. Gedeon at the Waterbury Hospital emergency room for a prearranged appointment. We wanted him to review the conditions existing on Nick's skin with regard to the gastrostomy tube opening. Something needed to be done to prevent the gastric juices from leaking directly onto his skin.

Dr. Gedeon called a nurse who took care of the hospital patients with gastrostomy tubes, and they recommended that a rubbery stoma pad be applied directly to Nick's skin around the opening. It had a gluelike substance on one side, which stuck to the skin when applied. It was believed that this might prevent the juices from touching his skin. It could be removed with a spray and changed as needed. The nurse instructed us on the procedure and wrote detailed instructions to the staff at the nursing home, with the information that they could call her with any questions.

Nevertheless, the itching and resultant scratching became a serious problem. At times, Nick's left hand would be tied to the bed rail so that he could not scratch either the stomach area or the groin area, both of which had an itchy rash covering them. If there is a more demeaning form of torture, I can't imagine it.

We were doing all we could to try to relieve Nick's situation, but another problem was creeping up on us. The Dilantin in his blood was once again rising to a toxic level, but we were not made aware of how high it was. Nick came home for Christmas, lethargic and pale. Something was obviously very wrong and caused us to worry about him a great deal. On December 27, 1981, on the 7 to 3 shift, it was noted that Nick had experienced generalized jerking motions eleven times.

I was with Nick at the nursing home at about 4:30 that day. He was in bed and wanted very much to get up and go to the bathroom. We rarely ever used the one serving the adjoining room because Nick took so much time, but the other bathroom was down the hall. I decided to let him use the one in his room and got him seated on the toilet when he began to have seizure activity. I called the nurse, and she phoned the doctor immediately. He ordered that Nick be taken to Waterbury Hospital by ambulance.

The ambulance came quickly, and the attendants entered the room where Nick was still seated on the toilet with me holding him. The seizure had become a whole-body grand mal type. The ambulance personnel quickly picked Nick up and put him on the stretcher and wheeled him outside to the ambulance. Once again, I accompanied Nick to the hospital, sirens blaring, while I constantly talked to him in soothing tones, trying to calm his seizing body.

The problem this time was abnormal liver function, related to the use of Dilantin as an antiseizure medication. Nick was admitted to the hospital and remained there until January 9, 1982. It was the full two weeks that the nursing home bed would be paid for by Medicaid. Nursing homes did not have to readmit a Medicaid patient after that length of time.

In the two weeks that Nick stayed in the hospital, the Dilantin was discontinued as a drug. A neurologist, Dr. Roger Bobowick, was called for consultation and monitored Nick through the change in medication to 1000 grams of Tegretol each day and 150 grams of phenobarbital. This was the first time that a neurologist became involved in Nick's medication for seizure control. At the time of discharge, Nick had been seizure-free for one week with normalization of his liver function.

This hospitalization was a relief for us from the nursing home scene, which we badly needed. But Nick was soon discharged, and I accompanied him in the ambulance back to the Convalarium. In a matter of hours, I felt as if we had never left. My stress was becoming so intense that I could no longer continue my nighttime vigils with Nick on a regular basis. Mary needed relief too.

John decided to borrow money by getting a second mortgage on our home. With this money we hired aides to assist in Nick's care at the nursing home and didn't ask anyone's permission to do so. I was becoming exhausted, and John felt there was no alternative but to give us all some relief regardless of the consequences.

The charting of our activities continued to be constant, and the fact that we fed Nick food was now an obsession. On January 17, 1982, Mary Chapin's only note charted for the entire 3 to 11 shift was, "Mother observed feeding Nick a donut this evening in rec room."

On January 25, 1982, Mary Chapin must have planned her strategy carefully, as her notes said that Nick was "visited & examined by Dr. Tate. Note new orders—Dr. Tate had long discussion with Nick's parents. Parents very critical of doctor & nurse care of Nick. Slight tremor noted in hand at 10:00."

Dr. Tate did visit Nick that evening. To say that he examined him is ludicrous. Mary Chapin accompanied the doctor in the room where Nick was seated in his wheelchair near the sink. John was sitting on the bed, and I had just finished shaving Nick. He looked very nice and comfortable.

Dr. Tate entered the room with a wooden tongue depressor in his hand, said a polite hello to us, and quickly inserted the tongue depressor into Nick's mouth. Just as speedily, he withdrew it, and began a dissertation, directed toward John and me, about the dangers of feeding Nick food, stating that he had no gag reflex.

Mary Chapin had conveniently located herself behind me at this point. I listened to Dr. Tate and knew immediately what had happened. The nursing staff wanted orders from the doctor that we could not feed Nick food. Fear and anger welled up inside me. If he ordered us not to feed Nick, we were in real trouble if we did.

I turned toward Mary Chapin and glared at her. Then I asked Dr. Tate, "Did the nursing staff complain to you about the fact that we are feeding Nick?"

"Yes, they have," he replied.

"Well, I am concerned with the quality of Nick's life, not just the quantity of years. I want you to be Nick's doctor and not just the convalescent home doctor."

John interjected, "We know more about Nick than either doctors or nurses, since we are the ones who are constantly with him. Doctors come and doctors go, and so do nurses, but the family is always here."

Then I said, "If you are thinking of ordering us not to feed Nick, you had also better order a lot of psychological counseling to try to explain to this brain-injured man why he is never going to be allowed to eat again,"

"There is a danger of Nick aspirating on food," Dr. Tate explained.

John saved the day for Nick with just two short sentences. "Dr. Tate," he said, "all your discussions are cerebral. Have you ever seen Nick eat?"

"No, I have not."

"You get a can of pudding out of his closet and feed it to Nick," John said to me.

Nick heard all this discussion and was just as upset as we were.

With a shaking hand, I put the spoonsful of pudding into Nick's mouth. He took each one, swallowed it, and waited for the next. He had no trouble swallowing as he ate. Dr. Tate watched as Nick ate the whole can.

"If you are willing to take the risks accompanied with feeding him, I will leave instructions that you can do so, but not the nursing staff."

"Are you willing to take the risks?" I asked Nick.

He quickly shook his head "Yes."

John and I instantly agreed that we were willing too. We had finally won a battle with the staff with Dr. Tate's help.

We began to keep our own diary of Nick's daily activities, and this was a new source of irritation to the staff. Since we had hired aides to be on duty with Nick, I wanted to know when I went to see him what had been happening. On one occasion an aide was called into the office of the agency from which I had hired her and told not to chart the fact that Nick was wet when she arrived or that his call button was disconnected from his bed. When I heard of this, I was dumbfounded and angry. Obviously, they had been reading my diary without my permission and had called the agency. Of course I never used that agency again.

I put a note on the front of the diary that said, "This is my Personal Diary about Nick. I keep it in the privacy of his room. Anyone wishing to read it or write in it please do me the courtesy of asking my permission. It is personal to me alone." My request was not honored, as the physical therapist not only read it but made a note in it about getting Nick a Braille watch! As should have been obvious, there was no way on earth he could have used a Braille watch.

Surviving was becoming a very hard thing to do for all of us.

31

What's Wrong with My Body?

As Nick became more aware of himself and his surroundings, he wanted more attention and more answers from all of us. He became restless at night, especially, and would turn himself completely around in bed trying to relate to someone the fact that he wanted to get up, or looking for someone to talk to him about the things that were on his mind.

He had become alert enough to know something was terribly wrong with his body, and he could now communicate that to us. He wanted to know what had happened and why. The problem was that he suffered from short-term memory loss, and he couldn't remember the answers I gave him, so the story had to be repeated over and over to him.

It was very difficult to tell Nick how he had been injured, but he needed answers to his questions, and it was important that they be truthful ones. As I told him about the assault and his injuries, I learned that he was not falling to pieces, he was not having seizures or even getting upset with the answers, as I was fearful he might. Instead, he was eager to hear more and more, and I could not help but give in to his need.

It is heartbreaking to tell your thirty-year-old son that he has a severe brain injury and that is the reason he is blind, why he cannot walk or talk or go to the bathroom. But it is nothing less than cruel not to tell him these things—to let him lie in a bed in a nursing home trying to figure out where he is, why he is there, and what has happened to him.

One afternoon while I was visiting Nick, he wanted to hear again about what was wrong with his body. I put a blank tape in his recorder and simply taped our conversation. I played it for him whenever he wanted to hear about it. This upset the nurses very much. I know they thought it was an outrageous thing for me to do and were convinced that Nick's restlessness was due to listening to this tape. This was recorded in their notes many times.

I suppose these were normal reactions for the staff. However, I deeply resented their not understanding that I made the tape only after many talks with Nick about the same thing. It was hard for me to keep repeating it to him. Their reaction to it was their own, not Nick's. It disturbed and upset them to hear it more than it did Nick.

What the nurses never charted was the fact that in time they learned that the tape had a calming effect on him, and that they played it for him themselves many times when we were not there. More than once when Mary arrived in the daytime, Nick would be sitting in his chair, quietly listening to the tape.

On one evening when I arrived at the nursing home to visit Nick, no staff person was on duty at the front desk, so I went directly to his room. Nick was turned sideways in bed in a very peculiar position, and he was very wet. When I saw his predicament, I decided to put on his call button so that someone on the staff could see Nick's situation for themselves. When the aide came into the room, she went directly to the wall to press the button turning off the bell, which was ringing in the nurses' station indicating Nick needed help. She barely looked at the bed where he was lying, so I called her attention to him. She glanced at him in the bed and casually said they would be in to tend to him as soon as the supper hour was over.

I proceeded to straighten Nick out in bed and to clean him and his bed. It was charted, "PT's disposable diaper found in middle of corridor." And indeed, that's exactly where I threw it! I knew they couldn't miss it if it was in their hallway and that they would get the message I was sending if they had to pick it up. My patience was at an end but, like Nick, I had no choice but to try to endure.

We knew that if we didn't provide ways for Nick's life to have some normal activities in it, he would live in a never-never land forever. As was often charted, we took Nick to Mass in churches in Watertown and Waterbury. In the beginning, he was always in a wheelchair. However, as he got better at walking, with our assistance, he began to walk into the church and sit in a pew.

On Fridays, there was a Mass at the church in Watertown that the junior high school students attended regularly. They had seen Nick come to church in his wheelchair many times. The first time Nick walked into the church and sat in a pew, the teacher was thrilled. She had been praying for Nick ever since the first time she saw him, and so had some of her students. She felt that her prayers had been answered when she saw Nick, and, indeed, they had.

On another occasion when Nick and Mary were planning to go to Mass, a very unusual thing happened. Mass was at 11 o'clock. Nick did not get his bath until 10:00, so it took a great deal of planning for them to get to the church on time for Mass. Yet going to Mass was more important to Nick now than before he was injured. Any time the word was mentioned in his presence, he would sign, "I want to go," by putting his left hand on his chest and then extending it outward. So the effort was made.

On this particular day, just as they were ready to go, it started to rain, and it became a downpour. Mary had to explain to Nick that they could not go out in that kind of weather. He did not want to hear this and kept signing, "I want to go." Mary suggested that they pray for the rain to stop. Nick liked that idea, and so they did.

Much to their delight, the rain did stop, and they got in the car and went to church. Once the Mass started, the rain came down as hard as it had before. Now Mary was worried about how she was going to get Nick from the church into the car to go back to the nursing home. But once Mass was over, the rain suddenly stopped again.

While Nick and Mary were walking out to the car, the priest, who had become friends with Nick, came over to them and was commenting on what strange weather we were having: rain stopping just before Mass and then again right after it was over. Mary told him about their prayers to be able to attend Mass that morning, and he was as surprised and as impressed as they had been. This story made all of us believers in the power of Nick's prayers to God and how swiftly God answered them.

The more Nick could communicate, the surer we became that his spiritual life had undergone some kind of powerful transformation since his injury. It was hard to define just what this was. Nick had learned a gesture for God, and he indicated many times that he saw him. Our first reactions to this were as varied as one might expect. We felt embarrassment and concern, disbelief and uncertainty. Then we began to tolerate it, and eventually some understanding came to us about this strange happening.

There were other times when we would be strolling with Nick in his wheelchair through the halls of the nursing home and he would stop the chair suddenly, with his left foot. At these times, he would always be *looking over his left shoulder with a terrified look on his face.* He would gesture that he saw someone, and he was very frightened. He would gesture that it was a man.

Of course, we wondered if he was remembering the moment just before he was hit with the baseball bat by Joseph Tramontano. Could this be who Nick was picturing in his mind? We certainly hoped not. However, this was his first real communication with us that he was seeing things or persons he would later describe as angels and devils.

At other times, Nick would sit in his chair with a look of unbelievable rapture on his face. Sometimes he would say he saw Jesus, and other times he wouldn't know who it was, but it gave him such peace that we were just very happy when it happened.

The activity Nick loved the most, though, were the trips he and Mary made to the local ice cream store. These were wonderful opportunities to get out of the environment of the nursing home and be alone with Nick for a short period of time. Nobody was watching, and it felt so good to do something "normal" with him. Many times it was obvious where they had gone, because signs of strawberry milkshake would still be on his beard or coming out of the tube in his stomach. It was always worth the trip no matter what the consequences when they came back.

The staff was so paranoid about Nick's eating that they even talked to Father Filip, the priest who brought Communion to the patients, about not giving Nick Communion. Mary told Father Filip, "There is no better way for Nick to die than by receiving Communion. Give it to him." Thereafter, Father Filip gave him Communion by breaking off a small piece of the wafer and placing it on his tongue. It was enough. When Nick went to church with us, he received Communion regularly.

We considered the staff to be unrealistic many times in their care of Nick. We believed their regular practice of detaching the nurse call button, which we had purchased, was dangerous. John finally found one that Nick could operate. It was attached to the side rail of his bed, and all he had to do was hit it with his left hand.

The result was that he rang it too much, and when they came to his room they could not communicate with him, so they would take it off the side rail and put it in the chair beside his bed where he could not reach it. Of course, it angered us when we came into his room and found the button in the chair. Mary used to tape it on the rail with so much tape that it would take them a half hour to get it off. Nevertheless, they did. It got to be one of the "games" that were played between staff and family, but they nearly always won. We were at their mercy, and we surely felt they were in short supply of that.

Nick continued to receive the services of a physical therapist while he was at the Convalarium. Though she was a registered PT, in my opinion, her treatment of Nick was certainly unprofessional. I believed it was childish in some ways and cruel and insensitive in others. It seemed to me she was a stooge for the staff and no friend to her patient or his family. She did little if anything to get even the smallest necessities for doing her job with her patient. The family had to supply knee pads when Nick was asked to crawl on a bare tile floor without the benefit of a mat.

As far as I know, she made no attempt to try to get the administration to provide an adequate place for her to carry on her treatments or the necessities to function as a professional person. Instead, she reported and charted the silliest events imaginable regarding the family members who were trying to take care of their son and brother in a situation where he desperately needed their help.

John was sure that Nick could walk better if he had the benefit of a brace on his right leg. We mentioned this to the therapist many times, but she ignored our suggestions. We finally made an appointment ourselves to take him to Dr. Vanderwerker at the Waterbury Hospital physical therapy department. The doctor took one look at the pitiful manner in which we were trying to walk with Nick and completely rejected our pleas. However, if we had had a physical therapist who was also an advocate for her patient, this interview might have been different.

She tried to teach Nick, who was blind and had no control of his right arm, to go from a sitting position in his wheelchair to a kneeling position on both knees on the floor. This was a frightful experience for Nick, and he balked vigorously at doing it. She alternately accused him of not trying or of inattention to her directions.

I knew this was putting Nick through an ordeal each time she tried it, and I finally asked her to do it herself, not using her right arm or hand and closing her eyes while she attempted it. (I had tried it!) She just laughed and said they tried things like that in college, too. It seems hard to believe she never tried to do what she was asking of Nick. She certainly never did in my presence.

Many times, Mary deliberately took Nick out somewhere during the time when he was supposed to receive physical therapy. She was often called on the carpet for leaving when the PT session was due, and took the bawling-out rather than have Nick endure another "treatment." This caused the staff to dislike Mary even more than they already did, but it rescued her brother from the "cure" that was worse than the injury.

In many ways, Nick would have been better off without the services of this therapist. He openly showed his dislike of her endless chatter by his uncooperative attitudes. She would spend ten minutes talking to us while Nick was supposed to wait patiently for her to begin his therapy. She seemed disappointed and surprised when he did not immediately respond when she finally decided she wanted to begin.

Why didn't we change therapists? When you are a Medicaid patient in a nursing home, you take whatever therapist contracts with that home to provide services. Only if you are paying your own bill, and are independently wealthy, can you bypass this system. When you are a Medicaid patient, you are tightly restricted in the choices you can make for your own treatment.

We were learning the desperation of having to resort to Title XIX for treatments for our son, but we were in for another shock from the administration of this program.

32
A Threat from Title XIX

When we hired aides with our own money (not our son's) to relieve Mary and me for a period of rest that we badly needed, it was reported to the Department of Income Maintenance that we had these aides on duty with Nick. They were simply performing the chores that the family had been doing for years. Nevertheless, I received the following letter from the Torrington office of the Department of Income Maintenance:

> September 17, 1982
> Dear Mrs. Del Buono:
> I am doing a redetermination of your son John's title 19 eligibility.
> It has been reported to our department that you have hired an aide in-attendance. I will need to know the weekly gross amount that you pay this aide. I also need a copy of all bank accounts in John's name.
> Please have this information to me by 9-27-82."

I responded to this letter on September 24, 1982, in this manner:

> This will acknowledge receipt of your letter to me as Conservatrix for John Nicholas Del Buono dated September 17, 1982.
> As his conservatrix, I have reported to you previously and regularly that the only monies and/or income which John receives on a regular and predictable basis are the Veterans Administration pension of $362.00 per month and the Social Security Disability benefit of $417.00. In accordance with the directive of the Department of Income Maintenance, I pay to the Watertown Convalar-

ium each month $722.70 toward his care in this facility. The balance is spent on clothing, toiletries, haircuts, etc., which he needs. There is always a deficit in this regard.

As his conservatrix, I now report to you again that there are no bank accounts in his name nor any funds held in trust for or by any other person for his benefit. He has no assets other than a lawsuit for his injuries which is in Superior Court in Waterbury. I enclose a copy of the letter from the court with regard to this case. The pretrial conference was held on September 14th but no settlement was effected. The trial is presently scheduled to go forward on October 19th. As you know, your department has a lien on this lawsuit for monies expended by you in John's behalf.

If your department has some regulation based on state statute whereby you may inquire of me personally as to the source or amount of any contribution to provide a traumatic brain injured patient who is blind with an aide in attendance, I respectfully request that you give me a copy of such regulation and the statute upon which it is based. I have previously requested this information and it has not been given to me. Enclosed are copies of letters from Dr. Lucas, Dr. Taylor and Dr. O'Brien setting forth the need for, minimally, an aide in attendance for John. As his conservatrix, I have requested the Department of Income Maintenance to provide this and it has been refused.

As you know, geriatric convalescent home care for traumatically brain injured persons like John is hopelessly inadequate and this has been documented by the Interdepartmental Committee of the State of Connecticut and will be the subject of the inquiry of the Governor's Task Force recently named with regard to traumatic brain injury. No facility exists in the State of Connecticut adequate for the long term care of traumatic brain injured patients and particularly one who is blind, aware and as physically handicapped as is John.

I trust that I have given you all of the information which you need and are entitled to with regard to your letter. I will respectfully comply with any further information which you may request from me as Conservatrix for John Nicholas Del Buono.

Only someone who has lived through the Medicaid maze can appreciate the fear that this type of correspondence brings. Any suggestion that funds will be cut causes tremendous anxiety about how to manage the care of the patient without them. The Department of Income Maintenance continued to press this matter, and we always put them off with letter after letter, hoping the lawsuit would come to trial so that we could be rid of this program and

A Threat from Title XIX

pay for medical treatment ourselves.

However, one of the nicer things that happened as a result of our hiring aides for Nick was his meeting a young, eighteen-year-old girl, Gail St. Mary. Gail is a tall, slim, dark-haired beauty with naturally curly hair flowing down her back in cascades. She could easily pass for modeling material.

Gail is extraordinary in that she has a natural, instinctive gift for helping handicapped people, and Nick became the beneficiary of her many talents. She quickly learned the details of the things we did with Nick and immediately began to find new ways to help him with her innovative ideas. They were invariably good. John, Mary, and I developed a real friendship with Gail, and all of us came to rely on her when we could not be at the nursing home to protect Nick. We never had this feeling with any of the other aides we hired.

Little did we know what an enduring friend this young woman was to become in all our lives, but especially in Nick's. When I had to let all the aides go because we could no longer afford to keep them, Gail worked for no pay just to be with her friend Nick.

We were still at the Convalarium with Nick when Dick Quatrano's criminal case was finally disposed of on November 30, 1981. It was reported in the newspaper that he pleaded nolo contendere (no contest) to five charges of larceny (one in the second degree and four in the first degree), which meant an automatic finding of guilty by the judge. He was sentenced to not less than five years and no more than ten years in prison. Execution of sentence was suspended, with the defendant on parole for three years. He was fined $82,100 and ordered to make restitution of $41,050.

His license to operate the nursing home was suspended for a year. Nevertheless, I never observed any other person in charge of the Convalarium while his license was suspended. The only time I noticed any recognition of the fact that he was under suspension was the day Ken Smith of the State Health Department came with a nurse, a physical therapist, and a recreation therapist to discuss ways in which Nick's care plan might be improved. I had been able to get such a conference through my work with the support group and the governor's Task Force.

On the day of the conference, we were met at the door by another man who acted as though he was the administrator. Dick Quatrano took a back seat throughout the meeting. I never saw this man at the Convalarium again after that day. Once again, the criminal "justice" system had done its mighty nonwork.

I can't say the conference to improve Nick's care resulted in any improvement in his situation, but it did have the positive effect of letting the staff and the on-parole administrator know that I had friends at the State Department of Health, and that I intended to consult with them about Nick's treatment at their facility.

My personality changed dramatically when Nick was assaulted but even more after his admission to nursing homes. I watched helplessly as my son was reduced to a subhuman, inhuman level of living. And it was called health care through the Title XIX system.

Seeing this cruelty inflicted on my son on a daily basis caused me to relinquish any desire I had for wanting to be liked or respected. I discovered that my son was treated better when I was viewed as a nasty, bitchy woman to be disliked and even feared.

33

The Governor's Task Force on Traumatic Brain Injury

October 21, 1982
Dear Mrs. Del Buono:
Earlier this year a study done by the Department of Health Services documented that traumatically brain injured patients and their families needed additional support and services.

As a result of that study and the personal pleas of TBI families, I am establishing a TBI Task Force to develop recommendations that will effectively address those needs.

By this letter, I am appointing you a member of the Task Force. I am also enclosing a list of the membership for your information…

Commissioner Douglas S. Lloyd of the Department of Health Services has agreed to chair the TBI Task Force and to provide staff and support services.

Thank-you for your willingness to serve.

I am confident that with your help the needs of TBI patients and their families will be addressed.
Sincerely,
William A. O'Neill
Governor

I was one of four persons appointed to the Task Force to represent the Connecticut Traumatic Brain Injury Support Group, Inc. (CT-BISG). Also chosen were Charlotte Kane and Grace Cieri, who were also parents of TBI sons. Dr. Stephen D. Sarfaty, neuropsychologist at Gaylord Hospital, was the fourth. Dr. Sarfaty and I were also members of the executive committee and the board of directors of CT-BISG, so we were in positions that required a great deal of work from us. The four members of CTBISG on the Task Force were expected to report to the board regularly concerning its progress.

Other members of the Task Force were from Hartford Easter Seals Rehabilitation Center, a neurosurgeon from Hartford Hospital, a physiatrist from Danbury Hospital, a nursing home representative, a deputy commissioner of the Department of Mental Health, the commissioner of the Department of Mental Retardation, the medical director of the Department of Income Maintenance, the commissioner of the Commission on Hospitals and Health Care, the executive director of the Office of Protection and Advocacy, an associate commissioner of the Department of Vocational Rehabilitation, the executive director of the State Planning Council on Developmental Disabilities, a representative from the Department of Children and Youth Services (who was also the mother of a TBI son), and Ken Smith. Governor O'Neill had put together an impressive group to form his Task Force.

Dr. Lloyd made it clear at the first meeting on October 27, 1982, that this was going to be a working Task Force. He gave brief opening remarks and stated, "TBI persons are a group we have not done enough for." Dr. Lloyd then asked the members of the group to introduce themselves and to state briefly what each hoped the Task Force would address. As he went around the table, Dr. Audrey Morrell of the Department of Mental Health dropped a bombshell on the meeting. "What is TBI?" she asked. "I never heard of it. How do their needs differ from others?"

The room was silent for a long moment. These questions, coming from a care giver appointed to the Task Force, were shocking. We were going to have to educate our own members before we could do anything else! The fact that several TBI patients were in state mental hospitals made her remarks even more outrageous. Her remarks showed that professionals in charge of caring for the TBI population were uneducated and untrained at what they were doing.

When everyone was finished with their remarks, Dr. Lloyd announced that he wanted to hold public hearings around the state in five different regions. He stated that he wanted three to six members of the Task Force assigned to each panel in the five regions. He wanted one or two people on each panel from the public (TBI mothers), the professional community, and government.

Dr. Sarfaty questioned him about whether these hearings would be the life span of the Task Force, and Dr. Lloyd answered that they would not. Dr. Lloyd went on to explain that after the public hearings were held, the Task Force would meet every three weeks. I was appointed chairman of the Public Hearings Committee, and I knew that a great deal depended on these hearings.

After this first meeting, Dr. Lloyd sent all of us a schedule of the dates for the hearings; to our astonishment, five hearings were scheduled to be held in a three-week period. The timing couldn't have been worse, right through the big holiday seasons of the year, Thanksgiving and Christmas.

Some persons in our support group voiced the suspicion that these hearing dates had been deliberately set close together through this season to show that there really was not a sufficient constituency of TBI people to warrant the work a Task Force would require.

Nevertheless, we had to gear up for the hearings, and this meant that the volunteer resources of our board members were stretched to the limits. It would be imperative that the public hearing dates be well publicized so that people could come to them to testify. Newspapers and radio stations would have to be contacted, as we did not dare depend solely on the announcements coming from the governor's office or the Department of Health Services.

I was named chairman of political action for CTBISG, and all members of the board cooperated by attending additional meetings to plan strategy for the public hearings and to help in the work of contacting the media.

The first hearing was held in Norwich, and we were pleasantly surprised when the room was filled with TBI people and their families. They came to the podium expressing the concerns they had in very emotional stories of discrimination on the job and a son's bitter resentment that caring for his TBI brother had killed his father.

In New Haven, television cameras from Channel 8, WTNH, Connecticut's ABC affiliate, were filming the hearings. One particularly pathetic story of a wife caring for her TBI husband and her small children at home was so poignant that the camera crew went home with her and filmed the story for their 6 and 11 o'clock news broadcasts.

In Hartford, the hearing room was jammed with people while others were standing outside. This was Dr. Lloyd's home base, and he was in attendance and had to confront personally the cries for help on every person's lips.

All the hearing rooms had to be wheelchair accessible, but it was not always easy to find such accommodations. In Waterbury, the public library had a room that would hold a hundred people, but it was located in a basement. However, there was an elevator, so we chose to hold the meeting there.

On the night of the hearing, every chair in the room was filled. People were standing along three walls and others were in the hallway. A newspaper reporter was present and heard the testimony of TBI persons as well as their families. Several persons were in wheelchairs, and one young man was wearing a helmet. It soon became apparent why. He began to have seizures while seated in his chair. His father tenderly attended to him and made no move to take him out of the room. It was obvious that this was a common occurrence.

A young brother of a TBI woman approached the microphone and told the story of a beautiful young ballet dancer who had been struck by a snowplow on her way to a rehearsal of the "Nutcracker." The family had been heroically taking care of their daughter and sister for years. He was on the verge of tears as he introduced his sister, sitting in a wheelchair.

A diminutive figure of a girl with an angelic face was wheeled to the microphone. She addressed her remarks to the committee members in a sweet, childlike voice. Her words were difficult to understand, but the message about living with brain injury was beautifully told.

All the family members were fighting desperately to take care of their sons, daughters, and spouses. The TBI persons knew this and expressed their gratitude in stuttering, sometimes unintelligible, heart-warming words. The plea was always the same: "There are no services for us. Please give us help and professionals to work with who are educated about TBI. We have neither now."

I had contacted the mayor about the meeting, and he sent a representative with a written message in support of our cause. Even the nursing director from Nick's nursing home came and talked about the difficulty of caring for these patients in a geriatric setting. The newspaper did follow-up stories.

The public hearings were turning out to be a stunning success. Commissioner Lloyd had attended only one: the Hartford hearing at the Capitol. After Waterbury, he must have been impressed, because he attended the next one in Stamford. The participants' stories were just as dramatic, and each spoke eloquently of the heroism going on in families all over the state trying to cope with brain injury.

A beautiful young girl limped slowly to the microphone with the aid of her cane. She told of trying to go back to work on her job at GTE and being unable to perform her previous duties. She had been involved in an accident in New York City while riding in a taxicab.

A mother told the story of her young son who was injured in a shooting accident; he was confined to the state psychiatric hospital because of behavioral problems. Nursing homes would not accept him as a patient.

I was the only member of the Task Force to attend all five hearings. After they were over, everyone knew we had a huge problem on our hands. No one wondered any longer whether this was a real cause or just a campaign promise Governor O'Neill was trying to fulfill.

While the Task Force was in session, Nick's lawsuit was scheduled for trial in January 1983. Nevertheless, with the staff support supplied by Ken Smith's office, I was able to file the report on the public hearings, and it was given to Dr. Lloyd at the Task Force meeting on April 28, 1983.

From the hearings, we learned that TBI problems fell into four categories:

1. Delivery of services
2. Education of both the public and professionals
3. Funding, which consisted of either insurance, government aid,

or private finances

4. Methods of prevention

The work of the Task Force was divided into these four subcommittees.

The lifespan of the Task Force turned out to be fourteen months. Every subcommittee worked very hard to grapple with the problems it was directed to address. I was appointed to the committee on funding (insurance and government aid). Dr. Claire Callan, medical director of the Department of Income Maintenance, was appointed chairman of this committee. All its other members were either providing finances or services to TBI persons. All were specialists in their fields.

Our first meeting was held on February 9, 1983, and by August 23 we had completed our report. Meetings were sometimes called every two weeks. They were well attended, and each member contributed to a smooth-running, hard-working group. The members were a joy to work with. Each person could voice an opinion, which sometimes differed with others, but there was a real respect and a common interest in trying to develop recommendations that made service on this committee pleasurable.

Ours was the last subcommittee to turn in its report for the perusal and agreement of the Task Force members as a whole. Each committee report was accepted, and the Task Force members had to consider major recommendations as well as those in each subcommittee report.

The Task Force report was an admission by state government that services were not available to this injured population. No longer was it just a few grumbling parents crying in the wilderness. The plight of the TBI persons and their family members was now documented in an official report. We hoped it meant that the wheels of a giant machine called government were now turning in our direction.

The report was accepted and approved by all members except the representative of the Connecticut Hospital Association. He abstained because the report contained recommendations that might require the association's approval to implement, and they did not want to be in the position of already having approved. The report was to be given to the governor at a special public ceremony to which all members of the Task Force were invited.

During the time the Task Force was in session, the four representatives from CTBISG were supposed to report to its board regularly regarding the progress of the Task Force. However, Grace Cieri became disenchanted with the board and resigned long before the Task Force work was completed. Early on, Charlotte Kane announced that she could not attend Task Force meetings because of her personal commitments.

Dr. Sarfaty also resigned from the board of directors of CTBISG due to a conflict with another board member regarding the nomination of New MediCo employees to the board at the annual meeting. This left me as the only board of directors representative of CTBISG on the Task Force who could make reports.

Ken Smith telephoned me the day before the public ceremony and asked me to prepare a short speech in order to hand the Task Force report to the governor. He said that Grace Cieri and I had been selected to present the report to Governor O'Neill. The ceremony was to be televised. I was thrilled, along with my family, and prepared my speech.

On the day the report was to be given to the governor, Ken Smith called me again. He told me that I would not be giving the speech I had prepared, nor would I be with Grace Cieri to present the report to the governor. Instead, Charlotte Kane had been selected for this honor. I was stunned and hurt.

My only comment was, "Well, I see New MediCo got to them." He was quick to deny my accusation, but, right or wrong, I felt sure the word had gone out from New MediCo to get a replacement for me. I believed that New MediCo, as a profit-making corporation, had infiltrated the CTBISG organization with its employees for the purpose of soliciting TBI persons with insurance into the company's facilities while it refused Title XIX patients. I believed New MediCo was acting out of greed and not with compassion for the plight of the TBI persons. New MediCo employees knew my feelings regarding this matter.

I told Ken Smith, "I don't need this kind of treatment. The work of the Task Force is completed. The important job is done. Under these circumstances, I don't want to appear at the public ceremony."

His call had come to my home as an urgent one, and my family called me at the beauty shop where I was getting my hair done to go to the ceremony. The message was to call him back immediately. Therefore, the conversation occurred over the telephone at the beauty shop.

Ken pleaded with me to come to the ceremony, but I replied, "Ken, do you know how much work I did on that report and how little time Charlotte was able to attend Task Force meetings?" "I know, but there is nothing I can do about it. I have tried," he said.

Although I knew he was the messenger of bad news and not the originator of it, I was still adamant. My hurt was too deep, and there wasn't enough time for it to heal in the few hours before the ceremony.

I went home and explained to my family that I would not be going to the ceremony, that the plans were changed and I would not be on television that evening handing the governor the report. My daughters were livid with rage. John was disappointed too, because he knew how many hours away from home, family, and Nick I had spent in order to help make the Task Force report.

John accepted my decision not to go, but our daughters did not. When they couldn't persuade me to go, Mary and Sally went to the ceremony in Hartford and watched as Grace and Charlotte handed the report to Governor O'Neill, without a word being said. No speech at all. I watched on television that night and was dismayed.

Certainly Charlotte and Grace were very instrumental in setting up of the statewide organization of CTBISG Inc., and they truly deserved this honor. However, I could not get past the feeling that I had been asked and then dropped. I knew there was a reason and, whatever it was, my joy at seeing this valuable work come to fruition had been spoiled, not by Charlotte or Grace, but by some unnamed person who would not confront me personally.

However, no amount of personal, momentary disappointment could dim the importance of the valuable report turned in to Governor O'Neill. His letter of thanks to me when he was leaving office more than made up for any resentment on my part. Seeing some of the recommendations implemented, and knowing I had played a part in seeing them come about, was satisfaction enough for me.

34

Support Groups

I chaired meetings of the Waterbury Support Group for three and a half years. We changed our meeting location from John's office to Waterbury Hospital, where some of our best gatherings were those in which we shared stories and information with one another. We also invited guest speakers who had expertise in treating people with traumatic brain injury. All of them gave of their time and talent freely. They were the "caring professionals" and were a joy to work with.

Forty-one people attended our first recreational party held at the Woodmere Nursing Home (a New MediCo facility). One of its employees always attended our support group meetings, and New MediCo offered its facility for our summer outing. Cookies and punch were served by the staff at Woodmere, and we all enjoyed the luxury of relaxation. We met under a large tent that had been erected on the lawn. It was impressive.

Paul Brooks, one of the New MediCo representatives on the board of CTBISG, gave a talk to the group about the programs the company had developed for TBI people. He also mentioned that New MediCo was involved in a lawsuit with the state over the fact that New MediCo would not accept Title XIX Medicaid patients in its facilities or its specialized TBI programs. He asked members of our group to write letters to the Department of Income Maintenance in support of the New MediCo position. It was an easy thing to ask of a group like this because we all knew too well how inadequate the services were and how poorly the nursing homes were compensated for the extra work the TBI patients required.

I will never forget that meeting held on August 29, 1982. It was a beautiful, sunny Sunday afternoon. We had picked Nick up at the Convalarium so that he could go to the meeting with us. We were in a joyous mood, and this did not happen often. It made us realize how few good times we had had since Nick's injury.

However, when we arrived at John's office the following day, there was a court pleading in the mail regarding Nick's case, which quickly brought us back to the realities of living with a TBI lawsuit and the intrigue involved in dealing with New MediCo.

Edward Murphy, administrator of New MediCo's Darien facility, had agreed to testify as an expert witness for the defendant National YMCA. The Wiggin and Dana law firm, which represented the National YMCA in our case, also represented the New MediCo Corporation in its lawsuit against the state, as well as in its other corporate matters.

It must have been very easy for the National YMCA to get this expert witness. The irony of all of this was that while Paul Brooks urged the members of our support group to write letters in support of New MediCo's position that the state paid too little to nursing homes in the case of TBI persons, one of its administrators was going to testify as to how little the cost would be to care for Nick in this nursing home atmosphere.

This pleading was especially inflammatory for another reason. Dr. William Collins, who had tested Nick at Yale-New Haven Hospital, was also going to be an expert witness for the National YMCA against the very patient he had examined at our expense (since Title XIX was eventually paid back monies they had spent on Nick). We had spoken with him and his team openly and honestly about many things involved in Nick's life, including this lawsuit, believing that we had a confidential doctor-patient relationship. John checked the statute and in Connecticut no common law privilege existed between a doctor and patient. (In 1990, the Connecticut General Assembly passed C.G.S. 52-1466, providing a privilege between patients and physicians, surgeons, or other licensed health care providers in civil, probate, legislative, or administrative proceedings.)

I called Dr. Collins's office to voice my resentment, but he was out of the country. Nevertheless, the pleading from the National YMCA stated:

> Dr. Collins is expected to testify as to the type of care which is and will be appropriate to treat John Nicholas Del Buono. Dr. Collins is of the opinion that *Del Buono cannot achieve significant progress;* that his seizures can be controlled with appropriate medication; and that if he is institutionalized in an appropriate nursing home facility, he could be properly cared for without assistance such as around-the-clock personal nurses. Dr. Collins is also of the opinion that Del Buono's life expectancy is approximately twenty to twenty-five years. He also believes that the future cost of physicians and hospital care should be minimal.
>
> Dr. Collins is Chief of Neurosurgery at Yale-New Haven Hospital and his opinions are based on his many years of experience in treatment and placement of persons with neurological injuries, his review of the pertinent medical records of Del Buono and his participation as part of the consultation team which evaluated Del Buono during his stay at Yale-New Haven Hospital [italics added].

I was furious with Dr. Collins for what seemed to me to be a betrayal of the trust we had placed in him. He used the work he did testing Nick to give an opinion to opposing counsel in our case against the YMCA. Title XIX paid the bill for this testing, and we were expected to pay it back through the lien they had on this case. It seemed unreal that this could be happening. But the most devastating part of his testimony was that he expected Nick to remain in nursing homes for the rest of his life and be treated in the inhumane way he was now living.

The same pleading also related how Mr. Murphy would testify:

> Mr. Murphy is expected to testify as to the cost of providing care for Del Buono at the level considered appropriate by Dr. Collins. Mr. Murphy is expected to testify that the cost of such care in a nursing home setting should be between thirty and fifty thousand dollars per year depending on what ancillary services are provided. Mr. Murphy is a Registered Nurse, a Licensed Nursing Home Administrator in Massachusetts, New Jersey and Connecticut, and currently

serves as the Administrator of the Darien Convalescent Center. His opinions are based on his thirty-six years of experience in the administration of care to neurologically impaired persons in institutional settings and his familiarity with the pertinent medical history of Del Buono.

I felt like I had been punched in the stomach by the New MediCo people. I was angry and deeply hurt. It seemed to me the New MediCo people wanted it every which way there was. They came to our meetings with their brochures, obviously seeking patients (so long as they were wealthy, either with insurance or private funds). They defiantly refused the TBI patient on Title XIX because the state did not pay them enough to take care of these patients, but were now willing to have one of their employees testify as to how cheaply they could take care of Nick if he was a private patient content to live on the subhuman level a nursing home provided in accordance with the manner Dr. Collins deemed "appropriate" for him. *What hypocrisy!* Mr. Murphy had never laid eyes on Nick, John, or myself. He was simply going to read a bunch of reports and pronounce his "expert" opinion based on them.

I called the New MediCo employee who usually attended our support group meetings and angrily told her what had happened and that I felt I had been used by her organization. Apparently, New MediCo considered goodwill with our group more important than Mr. Murphy's fee for testimony as an expert, because he declined to testify.

Attorney Zimmerman had the arrogance to complain to the court that I was tampering with his expert witness. I believed he was tampering with Nick's doctor and the doctor was allowing him to do it! Attorney Frank was obliged to write the following letter to him:

Dear Mr. Zimmerman:
My discussions with Mrs. Del Buono indicate that she never spoke to your witness, Mr. Murphy and never indicated to him, or any other person, that Mr. Murphy should not testify in this case.

It might have been very interesting if Mr. Murphy had testified, since it was one of the New MediCo facilities that had refused Nick as a patient based on the fact that he required too much care for the facility to handle. Dr. Lawson would certainly have been subpoenaed to rebut Mr. Murphy and Dr. Collins.

The proposed testimony of Mr. Murphy was my second encounter with New MediCo, and it had turned out to be just as sour as the first. In my opinion this kind of behavior on the part of professionals working with brain-injured persons only serves to keep these people and their families in the hopeless state they are in year after year.

They slam doors in the faces of those too crippled to help themselves, but actually know so little about what is possible for these injured people. Further, they do nothing to help change the inappropriate rehabilitation and long-term care treatment for the very brain-injured people whose lives they save.

Nevertheless, our Waterbury Support Group continued with other professionals who were willing to educate us about TBI. Several TBI persons told their individual stories. It took tremendous courage for each of them to get up and speak. I know, because I received the phone calls before each meeting was to take place. The complaint was always the same, "I just can't do it." Each one of them did, though, and they were courageous and wonderful.

Over one hundred families sought the help of the support group in the years that I chaired it. It is impossible to measure the tremendous education we all received from our guest speakers and from each other.

One overwhelming fact became clear as the meetings went on month after month. TBI family members had developed an expertise and a network of their own in the treatment of TBI because professional help was too often nonexistent after the acute care hospital. This meant that family members were left on their own to improvise as best they could. Many times they did very well, under conditions from which heroes are made. However, we also learned that many TBI persons were left with crippling body conditions that need not have happened if proper rehabilitation and treatment had been given.

We shared the knowledge we had gained with one another openly and honestly, and we profited greatly by it. We also learned that sharing our stories helped relieve that awful feeling of being alone in this tragic situation.

Support groups still exist in Connecticut and all over the country. They are usually run by family members who get help from the state organizations affiliated with the Brain Injury Association, Inc., formerly known as National Head Injury Foundation (see Appendix, BIA). These affiliations exist in most every state; information about traumatic brain injury, resource help, and individual consultations are readily available from the state chapters of BIA.

The addresses and telephone numbers of the national Brain Injury Association and the state organizations and their addresses are included in the appendix of this book.

35

Leaving the State Support Group

After the Task Force had completed its work, I continued to attend board meetings of CTBISG and was the lone dissenter when some of the members wanted to replace Jean Harkins as director. My dissent was based on a belief that this was a direct attempt to hire someone who would be connected with New MediCo.

The position had to be advertised in accordance with stipulations in our grant from DDC. Many resumes were received. One was from Christine Sirignano, who had been an employee at Woodmere when my support group had its outing there. As soon as I saw her resume, I knew that the interviewing process would be a charade and that she would be the new employee.

Many members of the board were anxious to cooperate with New MediCo representatives because they viewed this corporation as the only one doing anything to try to develop much-needed TBI programs. Their view was understandable, but I did not share it. Their profit-making corporation was viewed by me, and a few others, as an opportunity to "use" the TBI persons and their families for their own financial gain.

I believed the influence of New MediCo on our organization was destroying the harmony which had produced so much good work and success in establishing the state support group. Further, I had reason to believe that our support group organization was being watched for a possible takeover by New MediCo, and that if that occurred, it would not be looked upon favorably by state government. I made the mistake of calling the president and warning him of this belief and raised this concern with him.

I thought my message would be held in confidence, but he brought it up at the next board meeting. This caused a tense scene to take place between Paul Brooks and myself. It resulted in Paul using vulgar language, so I told the president if he was going to allow him to use this kind of language at our meeting, then I would leave. He cautioned Mr. Brooks, but the damage was done.

I had watched Paul Brooks at previous meetings make his pitch for Christine to be hired. Further, he sat in on her job interview with the board, which I thought he should not have done. The irony of it was that without his influence, she had qualifications for the position and was one of the serious contenders for the job. But with her New MediCo background, she was anathema to me. Nevertheless, I was sure she would be hired.

In the car going home from the board meeting, I decided that I would resign. I had stayed on the board long enough to see the work of the Task Force completed. The other representatives of the organization to the Task Force had long since removed themselves from this atmosphere. I was taking abuse for opposing the New MediCo influence while volunteering my services. On the way home, I kept muttering over and over, "I don't need this." I wrote my letter of resignation the next day, citing my reasons, and sent copies to each board member.

Jean Harkins was forced to resign, and the office was moved to Rocky Hill to be nearer to the Capitol. This was a most necessary move, and one which I had long advocated. Christine was hired, and she was an excellent advocate on behalf of TBI persons in our state.

The governor included the sum of $125,000 in his budget to the legislature for the funding of three positions recommended in the Task Force report. The legislature approved the governor's recommendation, and a contract was signed between the Department of Health Services and CTBISG to hire a TBI director, education consultant, and resource coordinator. All three are working full time in the office in Rocky Hill.

Four education workshops were designated to be held in different regions of the state for community care givers to educate them regarding TBI. Two of the "highest priority" recommendations were accomplished.

Gaylord Hospital continued to be deluged with TBI patients and always had a long waiting list for admission. New MediCo continued its expansion of TBI programs but still refused to take Title XIX patients into its facilities.

The third "high priority" recommendation for a TBI center to be developed was not realized. We had hoped that Connecticut would develop a TBI center where patients on every level of the Rancho Los Amigos Scale* could be treated.

The RLA Scale was developed at the Ranchos Los Amigos Hospital in California. It depicts the predictable stages through which TBI patients travel on the road to recovery. Not every patient will experience every stage, but rehabilitation services throughout the country are now geared with this scale in mind.

There is, perhaps, no better explanation of a brain-injury victim's journey through a living hell than the description of the eight stages of recovery from coma contained in the RLA Scale. Those who have not been involved in brain injury will want to skim over these or not read them at all. The families who are new to brain injury pore over these descriptions, intently trying to find the road leading to where their loved one is located on their way "home."

Gaylord Hospital would not accept patients in the first two stages of recovery. This meant there was no coma therapy program in Connecticut where any patient might be treated, except a few who had enough insurance or were wealthy enough to be admitted to a New MediCo facility that had developed a coma recovery program. Even those with insurance would not be kept when their insurance funds ran out.

Behavioral management cases became a big concern too, as none of the rehabilitation institutions wanted to handle these patients. Con-

---

* See Appendix.

necticut Medicaid would not pay for them to be treated out of state in schools that specialized in traumatic brain injury behavioral problems. Persons with behavioral problems were generally sent to mental institutions, provided they did not commit a crime first and land in prison without the judicial system ever knowing of their brain-injury condition.

No group homes were available for those who needed permanent housing with supervision. Only the well-funded middle group of patients were receiving the treatment they needed, unless, of course, they developed behavioral problems. Then they too dropped out of the rehabilitation picture.

Professionals dealing with Nick in the early stages of his recovery did not have access to any coma recovery information. His behavior, consistent with the RLA Scale of coma recovery, was misunderstood and misinterpreted frequently. His family was equally ignorant.

It is to his credit alone that he tolerated our ignorance without becoming a behavior problem. He made his way through all of this journey in his own confused state with only the love that all of us could offer to see him through. Though we were lacking in knowledge, love was there in abundance, and it sustained him.

Today, trauma centers exist in most major hospitals, and they are much more capable of properly treating these victims. Also, professionals are becoming more aware of TBI as a special disability and are attending conferences to learn more about it. Therapy and nursing schools are beginning to include courses in brain injury in their curriculums. Newspapers and radio and television stations are presenting stories and programs about TBI, its victims, and their families in order to educate the public. But it must also be said that any victim of a brain injury is still subject to the luck of the draw as to where he/she is sent following the injury.

The CTBISG changed its name to Connecticut Traumatic Brain Injury Association, Inc. (CTBIA), and then to BIAC (Brain Injury Association of Connecticut). The office is still located in Rocky Hill.

The Brain Injury Association puts out a newsletter called *The Signal* each month for its members. In a 1993 issue, there was an article entitled "Remaining New MediCo Facilities Sold in Connecticut":

> The four remaining New MediCo facilities still operating in Connecticut were sold in late April. Woodmere Health Care Center, in Plantsville, Golden Hill in Milford, River Glen in Southbury and the facility in Darien were purchased by Mediplex. They are now known as Mediplex Rehab and Skilled Nursing Center of Central Connecticut (Plantsville), Mediplex Rehab and Skilled Nursing Facility of Southern Connecticut (Milford), Mediplex of Southbury (River Glen), and Mediplex of Darien. The other New MediCo facilities in Massachusetts were also purchased by Mediplex, and are now known as Mediplex Rehab and Skilled Nursing Center of Northampton and the Mediplex Rehab and Skilled Nursing Center of North Shore in Lynn, Massachusetts. As *Signal* goes to press, it is uncertain whether or not Mediplex will continue to do brain injury rehabilitation. As the situation develops, we will provide updated information.

Jeff Cole of Channel 3, WFSB, Connecticut's CBS affiliate, had done an investigative report on New MediCo facilities in Connecticut and New York due to complaints from families of TBI persons. It was a scathing attack on New MediCo's treatment of these people and their families and the high cost of the facilities' services.

I cannot say I was sorry to see New MediCo go. There was a certain amount of "I told you so" attitude coming from me, as I felt vindicated for my long-standing views about New MediCo.

Pat Gilland, a representative of Mediplex, stated that when New MediCo was doing its TBI programming, the majority of its funding was coming from New York patients on Title XIX. New York's Medicaid rate was much higher than that of Connecticut and therefore more profitable for New MediCo to have New York patients in its facilities than ones from Connecticut.

He stated that this is not happening any more in the Mediplex facilities, since New York has successfully attempted to rehabilitate these patients back to New York. The TBI program census has declined drastically in Connecticut from about one hundred patients to two. Therefore, Mediplex has not continued to run its facilities in Connecticut geared to TBI rehabilitation, though it does care for some TBI persons in its facilities. There are some Mediplex facilities in Massachusetts that do continue TBI rehabilitation programs, however.

I had done a necessary job at the state support group organization, and it was now the appropriate time for me to leave and let others take over the work that needed to be done. John and I still look on the Brain Injury Association as our favorite charity and continue to support its work.

Nick's brain-injured life played a most important role in organizing the state TBI association and in getting government as well as professionals to admit how little they knew about TBI. I'm sure he and others like him provided the motivation for them to act to make changes possible.

36

The Trial

Five and one-half years after injury and three and a half years after the suit was filed, Nick's case finally reached trial. Judge John Flanagan came from another jurisdiction, and John was quite sure he had been hand-picked by the administrative judge to try this case because of the National YMCA and the likelihood that any verdict would be appealed.

The trial began with the choosing of a jury, and the young lawyer representing Joseph Tramontano gave us an unexpected break. Because Tramontano had pleaded no contest in the criminal case, his confinement in prison could not be admitted into evidence in our case.

To our astonishment, the lawyer began questioning the prospective jurors and asking them if they would have any prejudice against his client by knowing he had served time in prison! This was the only way this piece of evidence could have gotten to the jury, and his lawyer handed it to us at voir dire (jury selection) on a silver platter.

Judge Flanagan was a tall man with wavy gray hair that still retained streaks of black. He was handsome, with attractive facial features that would have made him a leading man in the movies. His personality was overpowering in the courtroom, and everyone in it knew he was in command. If he had been in the Army, he would have been a strong rival for General George Patton.

Our attorney, Richard Frank, was of medium height, with dark hair and attractive, strong facial features. He had a way of charming you when he wanted to that bordered on the flirtatious. He had the ability to feign cockiness and self-assurance at will. Each day he came to court driving a Porsche, which he parked in one of the metered parking spaces directly across from the courthouse. Each day the police would ticket his car for overtime parking. At the end of the trial he had a wad of parking tickets an inch thick. He stuffed them and a check into an envelope addressed to the Police Department with the comment that it was the cheapest and most convenient parking he had ever paid for.

It was inevitable that Mr. Frank and Judge Flanagan were going to duel over who would control the jury. Mr. Frank courted them openly and honestly. Judge Flanagan devoted himself to them through ten transcript pages of instructions. Mr. Frank then took another eighteen pages to woo them to his side of the court.

Before the trial began, Mr. Frank decided that John and I would be sitting in the courtroom as Nick's parents. John would not be at counsel table, nor would he go into judge's chambers when discussions about the case were going on. When Mr. Frank introduced us to the jury as Mr. and Mrs. Del Buono, Nick's parents, Attorney Robert Danaher jumped up and asked the court to correct him. John Del Buono was an attorney, and Mr. Danaher wanted the jury to know it.

John Del Buono was indeed a lawyer and had been one for twenty-eight years of practice in Waterbury. He is a short, stocky man with dark hair just beginning to turn gray; an Italian immigrant's son, he was born and raised in Waterbury. He is a self-effacing person, gentle on the outside, seemingly meek and mild. Nevertheless, he is a self-assured man of principles, and heaven help the person who tries to attack one of those. One of his colleagues described him as a "bulldog" because once he gets his teeth into a case, nothing can pry him loose. Another lawyer became exasperated with him in court and said, "You are not who you appear to be." Judge Milton Meyers once told him that lightning could strike all around him and it never bothered him.

Mr. Danaher, the attorney for the Waterbury YMCA, was a typical

The Trial

Irish gentleman who turned red in the face when his anger was aroused. He was gentle in manner but a keen businessman. Competence as a lawyer was his trademark, and he dealt fairly and squarely at all times.

Jeremy Zimmerman, the attorney for the National YMCA, was a tall, slender, wiry man who looked like he belonged at the head of the class at Yale. It was easy to picture him on a sailboat or at an exclusive country club. There was nothing warm about his personality, and his offensive air of superiority suggested that he was above the fray in this battle of weightlifters, remaining only out of obligation to protect his sacred client, the National YMCA.

The courtroom was not a big one. There were only three rows of pews for spectators. Most of the time, John and I were the only ones in the front row, but there was one mysterious woman, a lovely young blonde, neatly dressed, who came every day and sat across the room from John and me. Everyone, including the newspaper reporter and the court personnel, tried to find out who she was. We never spoke to her and hardly glanced in her direction. When a reporter asked her to give him her name, she refused. Her identity remained a mystery to everyone in the courthouse to the very end of the trial, except John and me and our lawyer. It was Mary.

Mr. Frank didn't want the family to attend the trial because there would be too much temptation for jurors to overhear remarks we might make to each other, or to get wrong impressions if they saw us laughing in the corridors or even just talking to one another. Mary let him know in no uncertain terms that she was going to attend the trial. She promised not to speak with her father or me or even to go to lunch with us, but she was going to be there. And that's how she became the mystery woman.

The first witness to be called was John Mercier, who was introduced to the jury as president and CEO of the Waterbury YMCA as of October 1, 1973. It took two pages of transcript for him to admit these simple facts. John Mercier was a tall, slender man with dark hair who gave the impression he was always trying to hide something. He came to court with dark-colored glasses covering his eyes.

Mr. Frank had his work cut out for him, as he had to pull every bit of information from Mr. Mercier's mouth. When he did get something, it would take question after question to distill his answer into something resembling the real truth. Pages and pages of transcript were focused on Mr. Mercier refusing to say that most of the part-time staff at the YMCA were volunteers and that they were sometimes given a free membership such as Tramantano got as weightlifting instructor in the Bar Bell Club.

Mr. Frank elicited facts from Mr. Mercier only by using the documents we obtained by disclosure motions, and even then his answers were evasive until the judge interjected at one point, "Wait a minute, just a minute. Now let's get something straight here. He is asking you whether it isn't so that is what the document says. That is what he is asking you."

Mercier got the message. After that his answers were quick and crisp, "Yes" and "Correct." He stopped evading when he was faced with the written word where denial was impossible. As soon as there was no document to hold him in line, he reverted back to his evasion and stalling tactics, with a lot of help from objections by Mr. Danaher.

Mr. Frank was bringing forth evidence that the National YMCA exerted enough control over the local YMCA to be held legally responsible in an agency relationship.

The stage was being set for a monumental argument about the YMCA logos, which were trademarked. The YMCA was on the horns of a dilemma. The trademark law required it to exercise exclusive control over the use of its marks, or it could lose them.

This important argument began when Mr. Frank asked Mercier, "Do you know who owned the name YMCA and the logo that appears in those photographs that was attached to the front of the Waterbury YMCA?"

Mercier never got to answer this question. Objections were flying through twenty-six pages of transcript in which Mr. Zimmerman tried to claim that just because Mercier had admitted in the pleadings the truth of the statements contained in the applications to the Patent and Trademark Office and the genuineness of the documents, they couldn't be admitted into evidence because they were out-of-court statements.

The judge countered, "If you have something that you can point to, I will be more than happy to take a look at it, which says that in a certified copy of a public document such as this is, that a supporting affidavit to what the document stands for is inadmissable."

"I don't have a case specifically on point," Mr. Zimmerman admitted.

"But it is the basis upon which the patent office took certain action, correct?" the judge asked him.

"Apparently, yes."

"Well, you are going to have to give me some authority that says an affidavit that is part and parcel of the certified copy of the records which identifies certain activity taken by the National Board with respect to the local, [cannot be admitted], otherwise I am going to let it in."

"Give me over the lunch hour," Mr. Zimmerman pleaded. The judge agreed to do so.

Mr. Zimmerman was taking a real risk in behalf of the YMCA, and he was about to lose, because the judge told him:

> They are certified copies of public records and as such are admissible. Also, that observation, coupled with it the response to the request to admit dated 11/28/80 and 1/29/81, incline me strongly in the direction of admitting these as full exhibits. I do say, Mr. Zimmerman, with respect to registration 889198, the affiant is the controller of the National Board, which is a high office. And with respect to the registration number 668795, the affiant is the vice president. So that who else can speak for your clients than somebody at that level?...I don't want to belabor the point. But the affidavits were assertions of fact which your clients urged the patent office to consider for the purpose of issuing what it is that you sought...My ruling will be, absent something further, Mr. Zimmerman, these will come in as full exhibits, okay?

As Judge Flanagan said this, he was leaning across his desk overlooking the courtroom, peering straight at Mr. Zimmerman and holding up the certified documents, which were held together with an attractive bright blue ribbon with a seal on it. John's labor in obtaining these documents from the Patent and Trademark Office was about to pay off. John too was leaning forward in his seat as excitement pulsed through his body. These trademarks were one of the most essential elements of our case against the National.

When court resumed in the afternoon, the judge asked Mr. Zimmerman, "Have you been able to come up with anything?"

"I have nothing in addition to add, your honor."

The shining moment arrived as Judge Flanagan said, "All right. Then mark Exhibits Eight and Nine as full exhibits."

This was a red-letter day in the trial.

It was now January 27, 1983, ten days since we had first appeared in court for jury selection. It was our thirty-third wedding anniversary. This was not how we had hoped to celebrate it, but there was no time now for personal feelings and family ceremonies. All our attention and all our strength was tied up in this trial. We were learning a lot about what it means to be a plaintiff in an important case.

Mercier was still on the witness stand, and the testimony had turned to the Waterbury YMCA. He continued to evade questions and only became more responsive when shown a document. Nevertheless, the jury was told by Mercier that Tramantano had been a volunteer on the staff of the YMCA until April of 1976.

A great debate developed over the word "supervise" when it came time to elicit testimony as to who was supposed to supervise activities in the Bar Bell Club room.

"Who was the person who was supervising in the room while the Bar Bell Club was used?" Mr. Frank asked.

"The Bar Bell Club members," was Mercier's response.

"Well, who supervised the weight lifters in that room when the paid staff wasn't there looking in once in a while?"

"There is no supervision in that room," Mercier responded.

As the jury was hearing this, I had a momentary feeling of relief. I guess it was because Nick was finally getting his day in court, even though he couldn't be physically present. The hardest part about this case was the fact that one of the most important witnesses could not give his testimony.

Another telling moment came when Mercier was asked, "Well, was Michael Carter on the volunteer staff of the Waterbury Y in the

The Trial

three-or-four-year period prior to June of '77?"

"At some point he was, yes."

"Was he on June 25, 1977, a volunteer on the staff of the Waterbury YMCA?"

"I don't recall that, I don't know."

For the executive director of the YMCA to have had such a terrible thing happen on the premises of his building and then come into court three and one-half years later not knowing whether or not one of the witnesses to this assault was on his volunteer staff was hard for me to accept.

I looked at the jury, and they were listening intently. I wondered about their reaction at hearing this. What were they thinking? Were they as appalled as I had been when I heard this about Carter? How would they feel when they knew he had asked Nick to let go of Tramantano when he was choking him and then when Nick did let go and started walking back into the Bar Bell Club room, Carter watched while Tramantano got his bat and hit Nick on the head with it several times? Would they feel the hatred I did in knowing he, of all of the men in the YMCA weight-lifting room, should have done something to stop the fight long before it became so serious?

Mr. Frank exploded a bomb in the courtroom when he asked Mercier, "You became aware, did you not, that Mr. Tramantano in April of 1976 assaulted another participant at the Y?"

Mr. Danaher immediately rose to object. Without asking for his reason for the objection, without ruling, before he could blink an eye, the judge ordered the jury to be excused.

When the jury was safely sequestered, the judge said, "The reason that I excused the jury, gentlemen, I assume that we have reached a point that will require some discussion in their absence."

The most important piece of evidence of the trial was now under a doubt as to whether the jury would ever hear about the prior assault by Tramantano on another YMCA participant.

Mr. Danaher was ready and quickly stated the reason for his objection. "If Mr. Frank has evidence that Mr. Tramantano assaulted somebody in the Y in April 1976, and subsequent thereto up to June of

1977, that he did it on other occasions, then I submit that is one thing, and that we now have the first step in the progression of things relative to Mr. Tramontano's assaultive behavior....I think that a person does not prove a tendency by offering evidence of one incident."

At this point, both John and I immediately rose from our seats and went to the cartons of material that we had stored in the courtroom. All eyes were on us, but especially those of Judge Flanagan. He had learned that this kind of action from us meant that we had something material to present in the way of evidence about the subject being discussed. We certainly did this time. Without saying a word to each other, we were looking for Tramontano's deposition.

However, Mr. Frank was ready with his own rebuttal. "I think it is most relevant....to the plaintiff's case. In fact, it forms essentially the heart of the plaintiff's case with regard to imputing knowledge to the Waterbury YMCA and its staff of the assaultive propensities of Joseph Tramantano ....There were other abuses attributed to Mr. Tramantano which the YMCA was aware of as part of a continuing course of conduct."

Judge Flanagan was equally ready with warnings regarding his ruling on this most important matter. "Well, I think, gentlemen, that the ruling with respect to this particular incident does have some far-reaching repercussions as far as this particular case is concerned....If this one incident is to be followed by other incidents chronologically closer to the day of the assault....I might feel differently about it. I would like to suggest that this be done in the way of an offer of proof."

Mr. Frank was fighting for our lives now, and we all knew it. Every muscle in our bodies was tense and our attention glued to this debate with Judge Flanagan. Mr. Frank quickly explained, "Between the two assaults....Mr. Tramantano was using violent and abusive language, was threatening people in the YMCA, was known to be acting up....immediately prior to the assault. And....known by the people at the Y, and that his conduct from the time of the first assault through the time of the second assault was a continuous course of abusive behavior, inappropriate behavior, which should have put the YMCA on notice, and all of which culminated in the assault upon the plaintiff."

Judge Flanagan was impressed. "Well, if you represent to me that

The Trial

you have evidence that between the time of the two assaults that Mr. Tramantano threatened others, that has some appeal to me. What specifically are you talking about?"

"Well, your honor, I find it difficult in an offer of proof to outline my entire case for the benefit of the defendants with the witness on the witness stand."

But Judge Flanagan said, "I can't deprive a lawyer of an opportunity to make an argument. I will expect a more definitive offer of proof. And it is going to be made here in open court."

With that gauntlet laid down, court was recessed for lunch.

This was certainly the worst hour we spent during the course of the trial. The prior assault was such a crucial piece of evidence to get to the jury that we were all devastated that its admittance was in doubt. It was definitely the lowest moment for Mr. Frank. We spent our lunch hour in a private room just off of the courtroom and worked on gathering all the evidence we had concerning Tramantano and his behavior at the YMCA.

John and I immediately directed Mr. Frank's attention to Tramantano's deposition in which he said the prior assault had taken place only a few months previous to when he assaulted Nick. Mr. Frank had been contemptuous of Tramantano ever since he took his deposition and certainly did not believe what he had said.

John and I did, because he had no selfish reason to lie, and because we had never believed in the genuineness of the letter the YMCA said they had made him sign. John and I considered Tramontano's deposition to be our ace in the hole in this tight spot, and we told Mr. Frank this. He didn't agree with us and wanted all the other proof he could muster, so we worked feverishly the entire hour gathering it.

When we returned to court for the afternoon session, action began immediately. Our lawyer's priorities of evidence showed in the manner in which he addressed the court. He reiterated all the statements Paul Ford had made about Tramontano's abusive behavior, and it had an impact on the judge.

Then Mr. Frank turned to the deposition of Bruce MacFarlane and told the court what he had said about Tramontano's temperament.

Mr. Frank had gone through all this testimony and had not yet brought up Tramantano's deposition and this valuable testimony. John and I were getting scared.

Then, hesitantly, almost apologetically, he began to close his argument. "There is also a fact, your honor, that hasn't been mentioned here before. And that is Mr. Tramontano's deposition was taken....And he says that he assaulted a kid in February or March of 1977 at the Waterbury YMCA....The question was, 'It was the same year as the incident with Del Buono, but a couple of months earlier, right?'

"Answer: 'Absolutely.' I have also other extrinsic testimony to support all these allegations, your honor."

Mr. Danaher quickly rose when this date was brought out and said to the judge, "Your honor, going to that last point first, namely Tramontano, I think it is perfectly clear from Mr. Tramontano's deposition that he is talking about the incident that occurred in the gym in March of 1976. And that he was incorrect on his dates. There is no evidence, I submit, to indicate that there was more than one assault by Tramontano."

"Well, excuse me. Let's get that straightened out," the judge said. "The excerpt from the testimony that was read to me was that he said absolutely it was in February of '77. I can't start passing on the credibility or the memory or the recollection of witnesses at this juncture in the proceedings. You may say that he didn't mean that. He meant something else. But that is for the jury."

Judge Flanagan was certainly not going to protect the YMCA from Tramontano when his credibility as a judge was at stake. His position was clear.

It seems clear to us that someone had committed perjury. Both Tramantano and Mercier had given their testimony under oath. Was it Mercier? Or was it Tramontano? Only the jury could decide, and that is exactly the question John and I wanted before them.

Mr. Frank watched this exchange, and his attitude about Tramontano's deposition testimony turned quickly in the direction we wanted him to go. He thumbed through Tramontano's deposition rapidly to the pages where this testimony was given. Mr. Danaher turned to Mr.

Frank. "Is that in issue, Mr. Frank?"

"Yes, it is in issue."

"Is that what Tramontano said?" the judge asked.

"Yes, your honor," Mr. Danaher responded.

"You are saying he meant something else?" the judge asked.

"He was talking about the incident in April of '76," Mr. Danaher responded.

"He did say that he assaulted a kid in February of '77?" the judge asked again.

"Yes, your honor."

"As far as admissibility is concerned, I don't see how I can keep it out," Judge Flanagan said.

What a victory! It was surely the most important one of the trial. We were all limp by this time, and we certainly needed a break to celebrate, but none was granted. Instead, Mr. Frank was immediately pressed into action again with the evasive Mr. Mercier. It was a Friday, and we left the courthouse in a jubilant mood. This was not the kind of gift we had expected on our wedding anniversary, but it was certainly one we enjoyed. John and I celebrated quietly that night after we had taken time to visit Nick in the nursing home.

The next week testimony continued, and Mercier told the jury that he didn't know what had happened to the membership records of Tramontano prior to April 1977. None existed with any notations about the prior assault or his suspension. The one subsequent to April 1977 showed he had had a membership in the YMCA for twenty-three years, yet no records existed?

I imagined the jurors were much like myself. I suspected these records may have been destroyed because they contained information about Tramontano that the YMCA did not want us to have. He had been a member of that YMCA for ten years before he assaulted Nick, and I cannot believe they did not keep a record of his membership and a personnel file on him when he became a member of their volunteer staff.

During the recesses, Mr. Zimmerman was on the telephone for extended periods, and we learned from Mr. Frank that a crack in the wall of resolve of the National YMCA was taking place. They began discussing their participation in a possible offer of settlement of the case. This was the first time in all these years they had conceded anything, and we felt sure it was due to the mounting evidence in open court of their legal responsibility as master in an agency relationship with the Waterbury YMCA.

The last comment on the record for this day was made when the judge said, "I noticed that the visitor from Hartford is here. I don't know why. But we never can tell."

He was referring to someone from the Department of Income Maintenance. They had a lien on this case and had been contacted to come to court to discuss the terms of their lien. This could only happen if settlement negotiations were serious.

Just before 5 o'clock, Mr. Frank came to us with an offer of settlement that would be participated in by both the Waterbury YMCA and the National YMCA. He sat with us at a table in a private room and explained all the hurdles we still had to face in this trial.

Then Mr. Frank left us alone for a while, and John and I just looked at each other a long time before either of us spoke. We discussed the offer, and both of us were disappointed in it. We called Mr. Frank back into the room and told him we were just too tired to make a decision about such an important matter on the spot. He understood and reported this to the attorneys and the judge.

John and I needed time that evening to discuss the settlement offer, but we couldn't get it until we were in our bedroom ready to go to sleep. I think both of us were reluctant because we didn't like the offer. While we talked, we both realized we couldn't accept it, and before we laid our heads on our pillows, we had made our decision. The answer would be, "No."

We hugged each other tightly that night, almost afraid of our decision. We had made it in spite of the fact that we knew the case would be appealed if we won and that appeal could take years to be heard. Moreover, our home had a second mortgage on it because of this case, and the bank was pressing us for more than interest payments on the loan. We were risking a lot and we knew it. We had a sleepless night.

The next morning, before court opened, we told Mr. Frank we couldn't take the offer and why. He went to the judge and the lawyers and reported our decision. When court opened at 10 o'clock, the judge announced, "Gentlemen. I think that the evidential problems are going to take some additional time. I don't see any reason to call the jury in now."

We didn't know what evidential problems he was talking about, but he excused the jury until 2 o'clock. The judge and the lawyers were in his chambers all morning. It became a matter of some concern to me. I sensed that the case was not going to be allowed to go further. John knew what was going on, though he was not in chambers hearing the discussion. Settlement negotiations were in full swing. The judge felt the smell of a successful settlement of this very serious case with so many opportunities for appeal. He was not about to do anything but try to facilitate a settlement.

It is impossible to describe the feeling of being stifled, of waiting with nothing happening in the courthouse. It was the first time in my life I had ever sued anyone, and this time it was in behalf of my son. I considered a court the place of absolute last resort for settling any matter, and here I was stuck in this building, almost choking with anxiety. I couldn't go far away but I did step outside for a while. It helped me get myself under control.

The waiting continued, but the lawyers seemed as busy as they could be whenever they emerged from the judge's chambers. The jury was not called back into the courtroom for the afternoon session either.

Ten days later, at a Lincoln Day dinner, I learned what had happened that afternoon. A member of the YMCA board of directors and a friend from old political days when I was vice-chairman of the Republican Town Committee sought me out. Her tone was friendly and congratulatory. She told me about a meeting of the board of directors of the Waterbury YMCA on that afternoon in which its private attorney, Thomas Brayton, told the board that it had better come up with some money over and above its insurance coverage to settle this case because, in his opinion, the YMCA was losing it.

Late in the afternoon, Mr. Frank came to us with a new offer of settlement. It was not totally what we wanted. However, when John and I discussed it privately, we came to the conclusion that if we accepted it, Nick would receive care for the rest of his life. John said, "Isn't that what this case is all about? With this settlement Nick can get his security and I can get my freedom to practice law again. If you are satisfied, then I will be."

"Well, I want this over and Nick taken care of, and this settlement will do it. He has suffered long enough. Our whole family is suffering over this, and they need relief too. I wish we could get everything we want, but I am willing to say yes if you are."

We took a deep breath, went to Mr. Frank, and told him we would accept the offer of settlement.

The next morning we expected to go into court and have the stipulation read into the record that would finalize the matter. When Mr. Frank arrived, he told us that the stipulation would be read into the record in the privacy of the judge's chambers, not in open court.

We were stunned to hear this and were told that the National YMCA had asked that the settlement agreement concerning our case be sealed and the judge had so ordered. We learned this for the first time as we were told to go into the judge's chambers instead of the courtroom.

We had not been asked if we agreed or disagreed with this arrangement. Nevertheless, we were not going to upset the settlement because of this issue. The sealing of this part of the case was binding on us, and we would be held in contempt of court if we revealed the terms of the settlement.

The newspaper reporter was furious when he learned the final outcome could not be reported. He had attended the entire trial and reported on it daily for his newspaper. He went to his editor to try to get him to intercede but was not successful.

We entered the judge's chambers. All the lawyers and a court stenographer were present. The terms of the agreement were dictated by the judge, and John and I agreed to each one.

When the jury was called into the courtroom, Judge Flanagan sincerely thanked them for their time and attention to the trial. He told them, "I want to impress upon you....that if it wasn't for the fact that you people are here, this [settlement] would never have happened....You, the jury....are the catalyst in the system that makes it work."

Mr. Frank told them, "Thank you all very much for your help in being here. Thank you." As the jury left, I shook hands with each one of them.

John and I were alone in the courtroom, packing our cartons of binders to take with us. Mr. Danaher came in our direction to retrieve his coat from the coat rack. He turned to John and me and said, "You did an excellent job of managing this case." We thanked him sincerely, and he left.

We were finally free of the terrible oppression of this lawsuit and the trial. We had laboriously hacked away at another head of our dragon until it was severed. It had been a mighty foe, but it was gone from our lives forever.

37

Coming Home

I was still serving on the Governor's Task Force on TBI when the civil lawsuit was settled. A representative of the Department of Income Maintenance had been at the courthouse to protect the department's interests in the lien on the case. I went to a meeting of the Insurance Committee, chaired by Dr. Claire Callan, who was medical director in that department. I noticed her and Ken Smith huddled in a corner in animated conversation, glancing in my direction several times. I'm sure they were talking about the settlement, and I suspected that there were few times when the Department of Income Maintenance had ever recovered as much money from a Title XIX recipient as the amount they received from Nick. Ken Smith came forward and congratulated me on the settlement of the case, and Dr. Callan was especially cordial.

At home there was tremendous exhilaration and relief. For the first time since Nick was injured, we could actually discuss alternatives as to how his future care was to be managed. I wanted him to come home where we could exercise complete control of his daily life and medical treatment. However, two very influential people in my life strongly opposed this plan. John and Mary both felt that if we attempted to do this, it would ruin my health and that we wouldn't be able to care for Nick at home.

John favored a plan wherein Nick would have a private room in a good nursing home with personal aides to attend him. Mary agreed. But the only nursing homes that catered to TBI persons were New MediCo facilities. As much as I distrusted New MediCo, it was our only resource, and the closest facility to our home was in Forestville.

An appointment was made for the three of us to tour the facility and meet the administrator. We would be customers with money now, not Title XIX welfare people. I knew how much New MediCo wanted this kind of patient. I had to agree this might be the best place for Nick. We drove to Forestville with high hopes. However, the facility was another nursing home just like the ones I had seen in the past. The nursing station was in the center corridor with rooms to the right and left. The only difference was that most of the patients in wheelchairs were young.

We were shown a room with three beds in it, two of which were occupied by young men. The third bed would be Nick's if we were to admit him. There was no more room here than he had had at the Convalarium, and certainly not as much as at Kimberly Hall. Mary and I searched through the recreation chart on the wall hoping to find some activity Nick could join. Because of his blindness, there was nothing listed in which Nick could participate.

We were ushered into the administrator's office and began to discuss the cost of services in this specialized TBI facility. We were told that the three-bed ward they had showed us would cost $72,000 per year. (This was about double what Mr. Murphy was willing to testify it would cost to take care of Nick in a nursing home.)

In addition, it would cost $25 for every half hour of therapy Nick received. We wanted him to have physical therapy three times a week, speech therapy once a week, and occupational therapy twice a week. This would add $150 a week, or $7,850 a year, to the cost. The yearly total would be a minimum of $79,850.

Nick would be squeezed into a little cubicle of space and have little or no recreation. He would be farther from home than he now was, making it harder for us to be with him as often. This sum would not include any money for a private aide—even for one shift! Our spirits, which had been so high, were dashed to the ground.

All three of us left Forestville in a state of shocked dismay. Mary and John talked while I sat in silence. Finally, John said, "Maybe it's not such a bad idea to think of Nick coming home to live."

"Dad, I think you may be right," Mary agreed.

That was all it took to make my spirits soar! Now I became excited. I told both of them how I thought this could be accomplished.

We all agreed that our present home would not be appropriate for him. We would have to move. John suggested building a new house so that all of Nick's special requirements could be met. I was opposed, because building a house would take a long time. I wasn't willing to wait that long for Nick to come home.

I searched the newspaper the following Sunday, looking for real estate that might be appropriate. It should have separate quarters for Nick and for us. All our children had left home, so there were only the three of us to consider. There was a listing in the newspaper for a home on Academy Hill in Watertown that advertised an open house on Sunday. Mary and I decided to go see the listed property.

We drove up a winding hill, almost to the top, and turned left into a driveway surrounded by a large lawn. Located in the center of the lot was a very big two-story white wood-frame house with black shutters, very typical of old New England homes. The agent on the premises was a lovely elderly woman named Rowena. She began to follow Mary and me from room to room and noticed how attentive we were to every detail of the house. "What kind of home are you looking for?" she asked. We explained about Nick, and I could see her heart melt. She made sure she gave us her card and said to me as we left, "I think I have a place I want you to see."

Rowena called me during the week and insisted I had to see this place she had listed with her agency. I reluctantly agreed to take the time from work to see it. As I followed her directions, I traveled down a tree-shaded street with beautiful homes set far back, with groomed, green lawns sloping toward stone walls. It was an exclusive setting. I drove into the driveway, and Rowena was waiting for me.

She took me into a foyer leading to a country kitchen with a dining area the size of some living rooms. An oversized fireplace with glass doors on two sides was located in the center of the room. The fireplace serviced both the living room and kitchen dining area.

In the living room, there were beams on the cathedral ceiling. It looked huge with the see-through fireplace and double sliding glass doors leading to an above-ground patio. At one end of the room, there was a dining area with floor-to-ceiling windows overlooking two acres of manicured lawn with maple trees surrounding the entire property. Upstairs, there were four bedrooms and two full baths. Each room was more attractive than the last.

Then Rowena took me downstairs to a third level where there was a large room with another kitchen in it. Colonial cabinets filled a U-shape at one end, and there was a two-car garage.

On the fourth and lowest level I became very excited. There was a large, carpeted living room with another brick fireplace, three floor-to-ceiling windows, and a door leading to another patio overlooking the two-acre lawn. Off the living room was a spacious bedroom with two floor-to-ceiling windows, paneled walls, and a full bath. This whole level would be perfect for Nick, and it was already built. The only problem would be how to get him up and down the stairs. I knew there had to be a solution to this one problem.

I tried to contain my enthusiasm with the agent, but once I left her, I went to the nearest phone and called John. "You have a panic-stricken woman on your hands," I said. He laughed, but I was serious. With unbridled enthusiasm, I told him this was the place for Nick. Everything about it was ideal, as if it had been built for us! The problem with the stairs would just have to be solved.

In the meantime, Mary and Sally had found a place they wanted me to see. They were insistent that I go with them, but I would agree only if they saw "my" place first. I made arrangements with Rowena for them to see the property, and they toured it with their mouths wide open.

Mary and Sally forgot about the place they wanted me to see and began pressuring their father to buy this house as soon as possible. However, John insisted that he have time to consider all the problems involved. He continued to be reluctant for several days because of the finances. I could see the turmoil he was in, so I said to him, "It's all right with me to let the place go. We will find something else." It hurt me a lot to say that, and he knew it. From that moment on, he began to figure out how he could solve the problems and purchase the property.

Everything had to be planned for Nick to come home in his present condition. We had plans drawn for a ramp leading into the house. Mary and I investigated chair lifts for stairs, while John got a price on installing an elevator. Everything we considered was very expensive.

On May 1, just fifty-six days after Nick's case was settled, we had a closing and the property was purchased. We spent a month painting, papering, and redecorating the house and moved in on Memorial Day. Mary insisted that John and I take a vacation before bringing Nick home, and we did.

On July 1, 1983, at age thirty-one, Nick left the Convalarium for the last time and came home. What a happy day! John had a bottle of Dom Perignon champagne that had been given to him by Sally as a gift. He had been saving it for a memorable time. He opened it that day, and we toasted each other in honor of the happy occasion when Nick came home to live. My joy at having him home again, never to leave, was exceedingly great.

I had this eerie feeling that God and his angels had led us to this place at this time in our lives. Once Nick's case was settled, everything happened too quickly and too perfectly for it to be mere coincidence. So much good was coming our way that I know God's hand was directing it all!

38

Caring for Nick at Home

Taking care of someone at home in the kind of physical condition Nick was in was an awesome task. He had the gastrostomy tube in his stomach; the tracheotomy was still open in his throat; a large piece of skull bone was missing on his forehead, causing a noticeable indentation; he spoke only with gestures; he couldn't walk; and he was blind. Further, he was still wearing diapers and obviously incontinent. These were just the most prominent of his brain-injury deficits!

Though the work was hard, and sometimes frightening, there was an eagerness and a thrill to it that none of us had experienced since his injury. We were in control now, without the constraints that doctors, nurses, hospitals, and nursing homes had put on us in the past. We didn't need permission from anyone to experiment with our own ideas about how to care for Nick and rehabilitate him at home. We were anxious to prove Dr. Collins wrong and make Nick far more comfortable and happy than Dr. Collins could imagine.

We obtained a hospital bed from the VA, but we put it in one of the upstairs bedrooms because I was too frightened to have Nick sleep downstairs. The distance from our bedroom was too great for me to feel secure about his safety.

His room was decorated with wallpaper of gold and black with furnishings to match the decor. The dresser and chest were a shiny black onyx with white hardware, and he had a large closet for his clothes. Now we could buy attractive clothing and never have to worry about its being lost or stolen. Even though Nick couldn't see the wallpaper or furnishings, we could tell him about them and hope he would visualize the room in his mind's eye.

It made me feel good that Nick was in his own room attempting to live as normal a life as his injuries would allow. Obviously, "normal" in this sense would be a far cry from the life other people lived, but it made me feel proud for him, and I had not experienced that emotion in a long time.

I purchased a gerichair and had a special headrest built onto it because Nick could not easily hold his head up without some support. We put bells on the bed rails so Nick could ring whenever he needed us. He was never restrained, day or night, and never medicated with sleeping pills.

The sensation of having Nick home was so exciting I found it hard to sleep. One morning Nick was up early too, so I helped him get dressed and into the gerichair in his room. I told him, "I'll be back with your breakfast soon." I was frying bacon in the kitchen when I looked up and saw Nick immediately in front of the stairs. *Another six inches and the chair would come crashing down those steps with him in it!* I screamed with all my might, *"Nick!"* He stopped dead in his tracks as I ran to him. My heart was pounding as I pushed his chair back into the room and hugged him tightly.

John came running, wondering what in the world had happened. He and Nick both looked confused. I explained to both of them the danger Nick had been in. Nick did not seem to fully comprehend what had happened, but John did. We looked at each other, and the unspoken question showed in our eyes: "Can we really handle this?"

Nick had maneuvered the gerichair out of his room and into the hallway and was heading toward the sounds in the kitchen where I was preparing his breakfast. Not once since his injury had Nick been placed in a position of jeopardy involving the danger of falling downstairs. He would have to learn about stairs all over again. This caused me to move his bedroom downstairs immediately. I slept on his living room couch because I was too frightened to leave him alone so far from our bedroom.

A TELEVISION MONITOR. John solved the problem by getting the television camera he had always wanted to monitor Nick at night. He had a camera located on the wall in Nick's bedroom directed toward his bed. The picture from the camera was transmitted to the television set in our bedroom. With the aid of an intercom system, we could see and hear Nick all night long while he was in his bed.

Only after the television camera was installed could I relax enough to sleep in my own bed. Still, my nervousness was reflected in the fact that for over a year I slept with the television set on all night because I wanted to see Nick any time he called. It finally dawned on me that if I was asleep, I couldn't see the television anyway, so I turned it off. With a remote control set on the proper antenna and channel for his camera, I could turn on the set and view Nick in his bed any time I wanted.

HIRING AIDES. Mary decided to work with Nick as his aide from 8:00 AM to 2:00 PM. With this kind of schedule, she could help her brother and be with her children when they came home from school. Gail came home with Nick as his other aide from 2:00 to 9:00 PM. It was my responsibility to supervise his daytime activities and to be his aide from 9:00 PM to 8:00 AM. We became his new team for rehabilitation.

I became a real employer for the first time in my life. Now I had to deduct withholding taxes, Social Security and Medicare taxes for each employee I hired. In addition, unemployment compensation had to be paid to the state, and quarterly reports were required by the state and federal government. Workers' compensation insurance was a requirement, and this added to the expense of hiring employees.

In the years to come I would hire many people, most of whom did not work out at this kind of home care. But the ones who did became long-time employees and friends. Angels are few and far between in this business of TBI, but they are out there and are frequently directed onto Nick's path.

DAILY SHOWERS. When Nick arrived home from the Convalarium, he had a very bad groin rash. I believed that daily showers would help cure the rash. Also it was an important change in his routine that I wanted to implement immediately. I bought a shower chair that fit inside the bathtub with a seat on the outside for transfer. We had to tape clear plastic wrap over the opening in his throat and do the same over the gastrostomy tube in his stomach. This way he could have the much-needed showers instead of bed baths without getting water in the tracheotomy hole or the gastrostomy tube in his stomach.

These showers were a wonderful sensation to Nick. He would gesture with his left arm, "I love it, I love it." We could wash his hair and let the warm water run over him for as long as he wanted. They made a wonderful difference in his skin care, and the rash was soon cured.

DAYTIME CONTINENCE. We knew Nick could indicate the need for a urinal, but he had never been able to do this on a regular basis. We did not know if he would be able to tell us each time he needed to use the bathroom. Therefore, we continued to use diapers, but found that they were always a problem. Besides their high cost, there was the odor of urine. The urine on the skin caused rashes; the diapers were disagreeable to change; they never protected the bed entirely, and the sheets always had to be washed.

With all these problems, we were anxious to help Nick use the bathroom as a regular routine. We began by asking Nick several times a day if he needed to go to the bathroom. He would often say "no"; nevertheless, the thought was placed in his mind. Sometimes we took him in spite of his objections. Occasionally, he would have an accident, and this upset him. We then stopped using diapers, and the accidents upset him even more.

With our reminders, there were fewer and fewer times when he urinated in a chair, and he began to gesture that he needed to go to the bathroom. Sometimes he would be upstairs and have to travel down six steps, yet he was able to control himself until he got to the bathroom. This was quite an accomplishment considering how slowly he walked, especially downstairs. We finally put another bathroom on his kitchen level so that he would not have the problem with the long walk. His success pleased us, and we complimented him profusely.

Nick had enough presence of mind to be quite humiliated when the accidents occurred, and would repeat over and over, "I'm sorry. I'm sorry." He was never scolded or chastised when he was unable to make it to the bathroom. On the contrary, we told him it was not his fault, and we quickly cleaned his skin. This solved the skin irritation problems we were having. Within three months of his coming home, Nick was telling us when he needed to go to the bathroom, and we were happily rid of diapers.

NIGHTTIME INCONTINENCE. Nighttime urinary problems were quite different, however. Nick slept so deeply that he would urinate while he was sleeping and then wake up. I would have to help him out of bed, clean him, and then change the sheets. This could happen more than once a night. It began to seriously affect my ability to sleep.

We tried several methods for solving nighttime incontinence, and finally found that the use of an external catheter, combined with a two-sided tape wrapped around his penis, worked best. The catheter was attached to a plastic tube that conducted the urine flow into a drainage bucket placed on the floor next to his bed. Commercial drainage bags were not big enough for the amount of urine collected during a whole night.

However, there were times when Nick would pull off the catheter; or, if the tape was wrapped too tight, an erection would cause it to come off. Such erections are normal for all men and may occur several times a night. Most times, though, Nick just pulled the catheter off.

I sought the advice of Dr. Sarfaty, and he recommended a plan wherein Nick would be told at bedtime that if he pulled the catheter off, the bed would be wet and he would have to sleep in a wet bed until morning. This was a difficult solution for me to accept, since I didn't want Nick to sleep in a bed with urine next to his skin. However, I knew the situation had to change.

We became very careful about putting the catheter on and used the two-sided tape to ensure the catheter would stay on. After a few months Nick stopped pulling off the catheter. This method for nighttime management of Nick's need to urinate is still in use today. Urine never touches his skin, and he rarely has a groin rash as a result.

Nick's call for help in the middle of the night usually meant he thought he had to have a bowel movement. Sometimes he did, and sometimes not, but I would always get him out of bed and let him try to use the bathroom. In the nursing homes, Nick's only privacy and release from the restraints he always wore was when he was sitting on the toilet. It became his place of peace and meditation. To this day, he still uses the "throne" as his sanctuary for prayer and may say he needs to have a bowel movement as an excuse to have that time alone.

A WATERBED. We decided to purchase a king-size water bed so that Nick would have warmth on his muscles all night long. This would help prevent skin breakdown, and he could move about on the bed as much as his ability to maneuver would allow him to. In addition, he could not get out of the water bed without assistance, so he did not need side rails.

This turned out to be a very good idea in that it solved other problems as well. Nick was no longer confined by the hand rails that always had to be in the up position on the hospital bed. Also, the hospital bed was narrow with a hard mattress that was not comfortable, and it made him think he was in an institution whenever he awoke. Sometimes he would shake the rails violently, making a lot of noise.

Nick's brother, Joe, devised an ingenious way to further protect Nick while he was in the water bed at night. With a crocheted line of ropes on either side of the bed attached to switches that would trip an electric talking clock, we would be made aware, through the intercom system, that Nick was trying to call us or get out of bed. I could then turn on the television set in my bedroom and see if he needed help. I could talk to him on the intercom, or I could go to his room if I thought I needed to.

It has turned out to be a marvelous convenience and one that Nick likes because sometimes he just wants to know what time it is. There are times when I think the familiar voice saying, "The time is 4:10 AM," is his nighttime friend. On these occasions, he will ring it over and over, three or four times.

A LONG-LEG BRACE. We desperately needed a method to get Nick up and down stairs. John was sure he needed a leg brace on his right leg to assist him in walking, so one of the first things he did was to make an appointment with the VA hospital in Newington. The therapists in the physical therapy department were cooperative even though they too were skeptical about his being able to use a brace. Nevertheless, they fitted him with a metal hip brace with six notches at the knee for adjustment, hoping he would be able to extend his leg over the course of time.

It worked beautifully right from the start. With the brace, Nick could walk with only one person to guide him for the first time. He would put his left arm on the right shoulder of his guide and walk wherever he was led. He could climb stairs by putting his left foot on the stair and lifting the right one up to the same step. Even though he had to do it slowly, he could climb an entire flight of stairs like this and descend the same way. In fact, having to put his full weight on the right leg when he lifted the left one to the next stair was the best exercise for strengthening the muscles in his right leg.

We were elated. Our plans for ramps, elevators, and lifts were no longer needed. All this was possible because there was no need now for everything to be done in a hurry to fit into the time schedule of a nursing home. Now we could make schedules to fit Nick's needs. The slow-slow world of brain injury became our world too. This simple adjustment made all the difference in Nick's ability to recover as much as he could of his damaged life.

Gail, Mary, John, and I were overjoyed with the effect the leg brace was having on Nick. His greatest wish, that he could walk again, was coming true. The fact that a blind man's most fervent desire would be to walk might surprise some people, but this was certainly the case with Nick. More than anything else, he yearned to get out of his chair and walk. I know because I had asked him one day at Kimberly Hall: if he could have only one wish—to talk, to walk, or to see—which would he choose? He quickly gestured, "to walk."

Gail was always pushing Nick to his limits with the brace. She would sit him on the floor with his back to the couch and extend his leg in the brace as far as it would go. She played tapes of music and talking books, read stories and Bible passages he loved. This kept his mind off the pain while his leg was being stretched in the brace.

In the parallel bars we had obtained from the VA, Nick would walk for an hour at a time with Mary, Gail, or I always holding his hand, walking backward as Nick came forward. Within six months, Nick's leg had been stretched to the last notch on the brace, and he would soon need a new one.

Caring for Nick at home has become a joy and not the sorrow we experienced before. We look forward to each new day and the progress and hope that it may bring to his life. As we do this, our own lives experience a new sensation. We are helping another human being to live, and it feels good. The work is hard and sometimes grueling. There are setbacks and disappointments, but they are quickly forgotten as more progress occurs. Nick's coming home has been the best thing that has happened to him and to us.

39

Home Rehabilitation

At last we were in charge and could hire therapists to teach us how to help Nick recover as much of his lost abilities as possible. Dr. Collins had said it would be cruel to do this to him, but I did not believe this. Nick exhibited all kinds of signs that he wanted help, and he was thoroughly motivated to do any therapy we asked him to perform.

No institution can do the things we have done and are doing with Nick. Time is a big factor in the work of rehabilitation, and institutions are set up in such a way that time becomes the enemy rather than the friend. Time was our friend, and now we could use all of it we needed to help Nick come back to some kind of life that was meaningful. I was in charge of Nick's recovery now, and I wanted all the help we could get, so I started hiring the loving angels of brain injury—the therapists.

SPEECH THERAPY. Speech therapy was continued at home with Lisa Golymbieski. Each of us in charge of Nick's care learned the speech lessons and would practice them as Nick's ability to tolerate them would allow. Speech muscles are some of the most finely tuned ones in the human body. They work in beautiful unison to form sounds and words. It takes thirty-six muscles to orchestrate the word *church*. Therefore, when the brain is injured in the area controlling speech, it is more difficult to regain the ability to speak than most any other function.

Nick could not make all the sounds of the letters of the alphabet. Some were very hard to pronounce, especially the "k" and "f" sounds. Gail worked tirelessly with him on each and every one, but the "k" sound eluded him for many months. The first day he was able to say it, Gail, Mary, and I shouted and danced with joy. This is what it is like to work with a brain-injured person. Each small accomplishment is greater than any Olympian feat.

Gail made up cards with letters and words to be practiced daily. Exercises on sheets of paper were given to us by Lisa. Some of these exercises tested his ability to think, as they would require him to come up with the right answer to a question. For instance, What do you use to clean your teeth? What keeps your hands warm? What has pages? Still, Nick had trouble speaking in a discernable manner.

Lisa suggested a muscle stimulation treatment at St. Mary's Hospital. Electrodes were attached to his facial muscles as short bursts of electricity were sent to his face to encourage reaction from these muscles. After only a few treatments, Nick had a grand mal seizure, so these were discontinued. Lisa investigated the use of a computer for Nick with experts in the field. However, not even a voice computer was adaptable to him.

The time finally came when Lisa told us the speech therapy sessions had to come to an end. Nick was simply not making progress. However, the great thing that had been accomplished was that we were now able to communicate with Nick both verbally and with gestures. Not every word is understandable, but we can always figure it out by asking him to spell it. We learned that he spells words phonetically but can only remember about four letters in sequence when trying to spell. Even with this much spelling ability and the content of the rest of the sentence, we rarely miss his meaning.

PHYSICAL THERAPY. Through the Visiting Nurses Association, I contracted with a physical therapist, Stephanie Berry, to come to the house to work with Nick and teach Mary, Gail, and me exercises to do with him on a daily basis. She was dismayed when she saw the condition of Nick's ankle. John used to say the ankle had the consistency of a brick. To her credit, though, Stephanie did not give up on him. She taught us various kinds of heel, toe, hip, and ankle exercises to do with him in the parallel bars.

Mary, Gail, and I quickly learned from Stephanie how to get Nick from a chair to a kneeling position, and then from kneeling to a prone position on the floor for arm and leg exercises. In this position, Nick accomplished movements with his right arm that we never dreamed he could make.

The right arm, which was so contracted, would relax enough for him to voluntarily move it from the floor to his shoulder and then to the other shoulder. In a sitting or standing position, he couldn't do this. Therefore, it was a thrill to watch. Nick caught our enthusiasm and tried any exercise we asked him to do, including kicking a ball that we threw in the direction of his left foot while Nick was lying on his

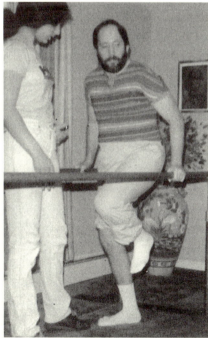

Left: Nick standing on the deck with his father—notice the right leg bent at the knee in a contracted scissorslike position. Right: Nick—about ten years later—standing on the same right leg with his full weight on the foot. This miracle is the result of home rehabilitation which he could not get anywhere else.

side, leaning on his left arm with his feet stretched out on the floor. Despite being blind, he was very good at it.

Nick began with an hour of physical therapy on the floor of his living room, or on an exercise table, five days a week. His legs were bent at the knee and stretched to the opposite side for hip rotation. He did leg lifts, and we watched in fascination as the right leg slowly began to straighten when he would lift it from the floor. Lifting his right leg from the floor and maintaining it in midair in a straight position was the hardest exercise he had to accomplish. We did rolling exercises by holding his hands over his head and helping him roll along the floor. It was slow, tedious work, but we were all happy to do it. Nick finally had productive activity in his life and not the dull routine carried out in the nursing home.

Nick doing floor exercises leaning on contracted right arm and able to kick a ball with his left leg even though he is blind.

We enlarged Nick's bathroom to include a walk-in shower and a two-person hot tub. In the beginning, it required two of us to help Nick into the hot tub, and then one of us got in the spa with him. We could exercise his ankle in the 104 degree temperature to a ninety-degree angle. Nick enjoyed this immensely. We would turn on the bubbling action and Nick would say over and over, "I love it, I love it." It has become a permanent part of his routine.

I had two sections of plywood cut the same size as the top of the hot tub. I covered one side with foam and made imitation leather covers for the plywood pieces. These two sections could be placed on top of the hot tub, and thus we had a very good exercise table for him.

Nick continues to do physical therapy routines three or four times a week. Mary has learned many exercises that are invaluable in keeping his physical condition in the best shape possible.

MASSAGE THERAPY. I hired Elaine Ferris, a massage therapist, to come to the house once a week to give Nick a complete body massage. I watched as she manipulated every nerve ending in his body, from his head to his toes, for an entire hour. When she first began her treatments, Nick's back muscles were so tight and tense he couldn't bear to have them touched. As the weekly massages continued, he not only relaxed, he began to fall asleep during the treatment.

His body muscles and nerve endings were kneaded like dough until he was limp and relaxed. As I watched, I too felt the tension go out of my own body as the special oils were poured over Nick and the soothing music filled the room. After a while, I had to get up and move about in order to keep from falling asleep myself. These professional massages were continued for about a year.

OCCUPATIONAL THERAPY. I also contracted with an occupational therapist, Marty Mahon, to come to the house and help Nick with arm exercises. She made a splint brace for his right arm and hand in order to extend the fingers, which were tightly closed in a forced grasp. She taught us how to help Nick balance himself on a large gymnastic ball to improve his ability to walk.

Gail was marvelous at doing these routines with Nick and got hip movements from him that none of us could duplicate. With the exercises Marty taught us, combined with the ones the physical therapist gave us, we were busy all day.

NEUROPSYCHOLOGY. Though I had left CTBIA and the Governor's Task Force, my friendship with Dr. Sarfaty continued. He came to our house to visit Nick and to have a counseling session with our family. We gathered around the dining room table, and he asked each of us to talk about Nick and what each family member expected in the way of progress in Nick's life.

The session revealed a great deal of unreality on the part of many of us. Joe felt that Nick was being babied too much and not pushed hard enough to become an independent person. Debbie still wanted the brother she knew before he was injured and was very upset at any suggestion she might not get him back. Sally insisted that Nick was not given credit for being more intelligent than he was treated. She asked

Dr. Sarfaty point blank, "Where do you think his mental IQ is at?"

Dr. Sarfaty was reluctant to answer this question and explained the difficulties involved in trying to test Nick's cognitive abilities. "In actuality, it's impossible," he said. Nevertheless, when pressed by Sally, he gave us an opinion that in some respects Nick was probably at a two-year-old level and, in others, perhaps at sixteen years. (Even Dr. Sarfaty has had to change this opinion as he continues to monitor Nick from time to time and realizes how much more mental ability Nick has than any of us ever imagined.)

Mary and John and I were more realistic than the others because we cared for Nick on a daily basis. Reality was something we had to face every moment. My own assessment is that you cannot put a limit on Nick. In some respects, he is childlike. In others, he astounds me with his mental, physical, emotional, and spiritual abilities.

Dr. Sarfaty explained to the family that Nick would always require twenty-four-hour care. He told the family that there was absolutely nothing Nick could accomplish completely by himself. While Nick possessed the basic instincts to tell us when he wanted to get out of bed, when he wanted to eat, when he needed to go to the bathroom, he would never be able to initiate much more than these daily routines in his life.

Even this assessment is not entirely the case. More and more Nick is beginning to tell us what he wants to eat, how he feels, when he is feeling pain, and to turn off the TV when he doesn't like a program or a cassette tape if he doesn't like the music.

Dr. Sarfaty explained that a very structured lifestyle would be an essential part of his living, and we would have to supply the structure. With structure, Nick could learn and accomplish simple routines to stimulate his physical, mental, and spiritual needs. In this regard, Dr. Sarfaty gave us a method for teaching Nick any new task. His "General Principles of Learning for Nick" consisted of four steps:

1. Direct and simple structure
2. Consistently repeated structure
3. Generalized structure
5. Gradually diminishing structure

For instance, we were having a problem with Nick's pulling off the catheter at night. When he was ready for bed, we would tell him each evening why he wore the catheter. After about a month, the information would be phrased in the form of a question: "Why do you wear a catheter?" If Nick could tell us why, then the information had been learned. If not, we had to return to the first step of telling him why he wore the catheter. This system worked with everything we tried to teach him. The more stimulation he received, the less the time required for learning any new information. It was not long before the month of repetition became a week, and Nick was learning any new routine.

Dr. Sarfaty came to our house for another visit in 1986. We were trying to determine some cause for an angel/devil phenomenon that Nick visualizes. Dr. Sarfaty observed Nick while he was eating when Nick suddenly dropped his spoon and pushed away his table because he saw some kind of vision.

This was the most exasperating part of taking care of Nick because we didn't know what to do for him. He was obviously disturbed by this, and he couldn't explain to us what was happening except in terms of angels and devils, heaven and hell, life. This drove us crazy.

On this visit with Nick, Dr. Sarfaty became determined to find the answer to what was happening to Nick during these episodes. His determination never let up and kept us from giving up on this problem many times.

OPERATIONS: GASTROSTOMY AND TRACHEOTOMY. On Nick's first day home, I ordered that nothing ever be poured into the gastrostomy tube again. I knew he could swallow and eat and I was determined to prove it. For nutrition's sake, we continued using the supplemental drink, but he sipped it through a straw!

However, the gastric juices continued to overflow from the opening onto his skin and caused terrible rashes. The first time the visiting nurse came to change the dressing and the tube, we had to show her how to do it because it had been so long since she had any experience with one.

Lisa Golymbieski, Nick's speech pathologist, told us about a swallow test that could be done. She recommended Dr. Neil M. Lindenman, and we took Nick to him for an examination. He not only wanted the swallow test but suggested the tracheotomy opening in his throat be closed as well.

The test was scheduled, and as Nick drank a colored liquid, his swallowing was viewed on an x-ray machine known as a cineesophogram, which moved downward as the liquid descended into his body. The same routine was done with solid food. The test showed no evidence of any aspiration or choking, so there was no problem with his swallowing liquids or solids. This test could be viewed by any doctor who wanted to see it. As a result, an operation was scheduled for September 14, 1983, to remove the gastrostomy tube. Two operations and two surgeons were required for the procedures. Dr. Gedeon closed the gastrostomy opening, and Dr. Lindenman closed the tracheotomy.

He returned home a week later minus two man-made openings in his body. He had lived with these for six years. As these and other changes occurred, it seemed more and more that Nick was returning to us as the son we had lost, even though we knew his return would never be complete.

CRANIOPLASTY. On one of Dr. Sarfaty's visits to Nick, he cautioned us that Nick should get something done about the piece of skull bone missing from his head. As he watched Nick walk through the parallel bars, he advised us that if Nick were to fall and hit his head near that particular spot, the effects could be disastrous.

I explained to Dr. Sarfaty that Dr. James Finn had examined Nick two months after he came home on August 29, 1983, and determined that "cranioplasty in this man is not necessary from the point of view either of cosmetic or protection." Dr. Sarfaty countered with the fact that Nick had become much more mobile since that time. He recommended a neurosurgeon we might take Nick to for an examination.

We made an appointment with Dr. Yarob N. Mushaweh and went to his office on March 19, 1986. He was in the same office as Dr. Finn, and we were told that it was their office policy that once a patient was seen by one doctor, another doctor in that office would not see that patient. I became very upset at this and told them that my appointment was with Dr. Mushaweh, and if we couldn't see him, we would leave. The secretary asked me to wait and quickly returned with the message that Dr. Mushaweh would examine Nick.

We were ushered into an examining room and questioned about Nick while Dr. Mushaweh carefully felt the area of Nick's head where the indentation was located. He stated that Nick's significant recovery over the past two years warranted a cranioplasty operation primarily for brain protection and secondarily for cosmetic reasons. He explained our options and the potential risks of performing the cranioplasty, including the risk of infection.

We had been through this so many times before that it was easy to say, "Yes, go ahead with the operation." An x-ray and CT scan were ordered. The operation took place on April 9, 1986. A substance called methyl methacrylate was mixed and laid over the defect until it became hard. Dr. Mushaweh fashioned this material and contoured it to make Nick look as normal as possible. He did such a magnificent job that I cried when the bandages were removed from Nick's head. He looked so much like he did before the injury that it touched me deeply. What a wonderful change in his appearance!

Now that we are used to Nick's new look, pictures taken of him before the operation shock us. I shall always be grateful to Dr. Sarfaty and Dr. Mushaweh for this transformation in Nick's appearance and for the protection it provides.

Years later, Nick decided he wanted to shave off his beard and Mary did it for him. When I walked into the room and saw him, I broke down and cried again. It seems like the grieving will go on forever. The son I once knew was staring me in the face with unseeing eyes. Sometimes it is more than I can bear, and tears are my only relief.

A SHORT-LEG PLASTIC BRACE. The occupational therapist, Marty Mahon, told us about an orthotist from Massachusetts, Bob Drilio, who was making a new kind of leg brace—very lightweight, with a hinge at the ankle so the ankle could move when the person walked.

The thought of trekking to Massachusetts with Nick in a car caused me to pause and seriously ponder the idea of this brace. Marty arranged for me to visit another one of her clients who had the brace, and I agreed to go and see it.

The brace was certainly better than anything I had seen before. It fit inside a regular shoe and was very lightweight. The hinge on the ankle really sold me, though. Nick's bricklike ankle was beginning to move. We worked on it daily and were succeeding in getting it to a ninety-degree angle. We wanted more.

We decided to travel the three hours by car with Nick to see Bob Drilio. This was no easy task. We had to stop midway for lunch and take Nick into a busy highway restaurant. He was fidgety after sitting in the car so long and asked over and over again where we were going. When we arrived, he was stiff from the long hours of sitting in the car, as were we, but his stiffness was more pronounced.

When we arrived at Case Surgical in Reading, Massachusetts, we found Bob Drilio to be a personable young man and not a bit intimidated by Nick's injuries. He was obviously used to dealing with handicapped people, but members of his staff were a bit more formal in their attitude. The shop was crowded, and bathroom facilities were difficult to get to.

Nevertheless, Bob began the task of making a cast of Nick's foot from which the brace could be made. It was very important to get Nick's foot in the right alignment for the impression to be made. After several attempts and some very hard work on Bob's part, the job was successfully completed. Next, the cast had to be cut from Nick's leg with a noisy electric saw. It took some explaining to prepare him for what he was going to hear but could not see. He was amazingly cooperative and patient.

Once we were on the road again, we had another three-hour trip home, with a stopover at another restaurant. This time we chose one of John's favorites, the Publick House. It was a fancier restaurant than the one we had stopped at on the way to Massachusetts, and the stares as we walked Nick in the door were more apparent. I had to help Nick eat, and it is understandable that the patrons were a bit curious to watch a mother feed her adult son his meal. But the waitress was pleasant and patient, and we managed the meal quite well.

Home Rehabilitation

Nick fell asleep in the car, and when we arrived home he was ready for some exercise. We were exhausted from the trip and thankful to have someone take over when we arrived, eight hours after leaving home.

In a couple of weeks, we had to make the same trip again to pick up the precious new brace. It was worth all the trouble we went through because it was easier for the aides to put on and, more importantly, Nick walked much better in it.

Still, Nick's right ankle was very tight. Sometimes we let him try to walk barefoot so we could watch what was really happening with his foot as he walked. The heel of Nick's right foot could not yet touch the floor, so he could not make a flat-footed step.

I will never forget the night when I was preparing Nick for bed and he was barefoot while going from the bathroom to his bed. I watched his foot and could not believe my eyes. For the first time, he landed solidly on his right foot as he took each step! The brick ankle resembled a sponge! I called John to come and see the miracle. If all miracles are as hard to come by as this one, then hard work is the key to success in receiving one. This was especially pleasing to John, as he thought this an impossible accomplishment. Nick's eyes gleam every time he is pleased and excited. This night he caught our enthusiasm, and his eyes fairly dazzled.

JOAN FAULKNER AND MYOFASCIAL RELEASE. Marty also told us about someone in Massachusetts who did something called myofascial release, which she thought might help Nick restore some of the formation of the muscles that she could not obtain through her standard occupational therapy. We took Nick to him, and he agreed with Marty's assessment of the situation. However, he felt we would be better served by someone in Connecticut and gave us the names of two physical therapists who did this treatment. We chose Joan Faulkner because she was in Wallingford, close to our home. Or was it because angels were guiding us again?

Joan Faulkner is a small woman with dark-brown hair and eyes who takes command of a room the moment she walks into it. Her smile spreads across her face, her eyes light up, and she beams as she begins every conversation. Her voice is firm and her manner exceptionally pleasant. She explains myofascial release as relieving abnormal pressure on nerves, bones, and organs caused by a breakdown of the fascial system due to trauma, posture, or inflammation.

Joan watched as Mary and I removed Nick's shirt and helped him get onto the examining table, and then she took charge. With obviously experienced hands, she felt her way along the muscles in his arms, neck, chest, stomach area, and legs. She inquired about the operations he had and felt along the lines of the scars on his stomach and neck where the gastrostomy and tracheotomy were located.

Joan Faulkner, the miracle therapist in Nick's life.

When she finished her examination, she told us she thought she could help Nick with the release of fascia, especially where scar tissue was involved. Joan added that in her opinion, Nick would benefit from craniosacral therapy as well, which would relieve the binding down of the fascia within the dura of the craniosacral system.

We were now on the road to a new kind of treatment for Nick. We started taking Nick three times a week to have Joan lay her hands on his skull and move parts of his body underneath the skin that were hardly discernable to the naked eye.

As the treatments continued, Nick's facial appearance improved. Joan overcame his usual apprehension about any person related to medical treatment, and she was the most instantly liked person in Nick's life. That old attribute of his of sizing up adults he met was used favorably in her case. Nick was eager to go to the sessions when told we were going to see Joan, and he was very pliable and content as she moved her hands along his body all the way down to his legs.

As Nick lay stretched out on the table, she took his right arm and slowly worked it out further away from his body than I have ever seen. Only when Nick grimaced in pain did she stop. She had promised the treatments would not be painful to him, and she kept that promise. As a result of her treatment, Nick's right arm is more relaxed than it has ever been. Most of the time it now rests below his waist. It was previously contracted in a position bent at the elbow with his hand touching his chest.

Two large bumps on Nick's forehead bothered us greatly when they first appeared. They were diagnosed as cysts, and we were advised to do nothing about them. After Joan's treatment, both cysts disappeared and have never returned.

Mary picked up new techniques for physical therapy throughout all these sessions with Joan. She was very interested in these treatments and asked Joan a lot of questions. Joan took Mary's hand and showed her the release she was getting while she worked on Nick. Mary felt the "wobble" or bubble as it passed through Nick's muscles underneath the skin above and below his kneecap and his thigh. Joan taught Mary how to properly rotate the knee by holding the leg above and below the kneecap and moving it inward until there was resistance. At the first sign of resistance, she was to stop and wait until he released the muscle again, and then she could continue with the usual rotation.

Nick's hip had become rotated outward when he lay in bed so many months with his right leg in a scissorslike position. Physical therapy sessions with Stephanie helped us learn exercises to do with Nick to release some of this rotation. Now, as a result of Joan's treatments, when you ask Nick to rotate his own knee inward, he can do it. Also, when he is walking and turning his foot outward from the hip down, you can go to him, touch him in the right spot on his hip, and actually feel the release that immediately takes effect.

Going to Joan's was such a pleasant experience for Nick that it was the only time I have ever allowed Nick to travel in a car with only one other person, usually Mary and sometimes myself. Joan was always animated in her talks with Nick as she laid her hands on his head and body. During one of her sessions with Nick, he was trying to tell her something. We were able to understand the first part of the sentence, but the last word eluded us. Finally, we asked him to spell it. He was saying, "Joan, you are a wizard." We all laughed, and thereafter we have referred to her as the "Wizard of Wallingford."

One of the most dramatic things about these sessions with Joan was Nick's attitude. He would leave the Carriage House, where her office was located, in a mellow, relaxed, happy, peaceful mood every time. His body was almost like Jell-O as he would walk out to the car.

The change in Nick as a result of her treatments was hard to explain unless you were there and you knew Nick. He didn't all of a sudden get off the table and start walking by himself. However, there was a distinct difference in him. There is no question about the fact that Nick's sense of well-being has improved greatly with Joan's treatments.

The entire staff in Joan's office treated Nick, and us, as special guests who were always welcome. Nick was talked to, not at or about. He was always given a hug before he left, and at Christmas time he got a plate full of cookies Joan had baked herself. She was more than a therapist, she was our friend. Yet there was never a moment when she did not maintain total professionalism in her treatment of Nick. What a rare quality that is!

After several months of sessions with Joan, the visits were limited to twice a week, then once a week, and finally monthly, to make sure his improvements were holding. We still call her when Nick is having a special problem, and she often leads us in the right direction for treatment that will help him. He still sees her every few months for follow-up to see that he is maintaining the effects of her treatments. No matter how many months in between his visits, he recognizes her voice immediately, smiles, and opens his left arm to give her a hug.

I will admit there is a certain mystique to what she does, but I also know the results are real. We are so glad our angel led us to her.

A word of praise for therapists everywhere is in order. They are truly the angels in this world of brain injury because they have the temperament and patience to move slowly and appreciate accomplishments that other professionals would not consider significant.

We are very grateful for the marvelous therapists that we were able to get to work with Nick at home. They deserve much praise for his accomplishments, but none of their work would have been possible without Nick's marvelous cooperation and motivation to regain as much of his life as he could.

ASSOCIATION FOR THE BLIND. Nick had progressed to the point where Mary and I began to think that he needed to learn to live in his home as any blind person would do. With this in mind, I contacted the Association for the Blind. They sent a representative to our house to see his quarters and make recommendations to make it adaptable to a blind person.

We learned how to take Nick around a room and let him feel everything in it and try to memorize where everything is located. He is able to go to the kitchen counter and, by touch, name the stove, the sink, the microwave, the coffee pot, the bread box, the toaster, and the refrigerator. He remembers them each time he does this. He counts steps from the door of his living room to his parallel bars, and he counts the number of stairs from his living room to his kitchen.

Another person from the Association for the Blind came who was partially sighted. She watched as we went through our routines with Nick and told us that as far as she was concerned Nick was doing as well as, if not better than, most blind persons. She had very few suggestions. Her one surprise was that Nick had never developed any of the characteristics of a blind person. He never put his hand out in front of him when he walked. He just trusted us that we would be his eyes for him. I believe her good report was due to the imagination, skill, and perseverance of Mary and Gail in working out every detail of his daily routine.

Yet none of Nick's progress would have been possible without his total cooperation. I have never asked Nick to do a single exercise that he did not try to accomplish with all his might. Many of the things we did with him, and still do, would be very scary to an ordinary blind person who did not have TBI. But not to Nick. The spirit and motivation he displays is an inspiration for anyone who has the eyes and ability to see it. Home rehabilitation proved to all of us what an incredible fellow Nick really is.

40

A Cocoon of Love

Walking was Nick's most fervent desire, and once he accomplished the ability to stand on both feet and move them in a walking pattern, it became his favorite pastime. Nick could use only his left hand to hold onto the parallel bar, so we split the bars, securing half to his living-room floor and anchoring the other half to the deck outside. When the weather permits, he prefers to be outside. Sometimes we have breakfast on his deck so he can enjoy the outdoors and be close to his beloved walking bar. His nephew and godson, Michael, gave him a birdhouse, which we attached to the ceiling of his deck. Wrens built a nest in it and hatched baby birds. They became so used to Nick that, without fear, they would bring worms and bugs to their family when we were having breakfast or Nick was walking in his bar.

The walking bar is not Nick's only source of walking exercise, though. Gail and I have accompanied him on treks all around the two-acre lawn surrounding our house. Gail plans picnics for the two of them at the end of the yard. She makes it seem like they are going to a park. I had lawn chairs placed in several locations so they would have a place to sit if Nick ever grew tired while they were going for their walks.

We started accompanying Nick for walks down the street where we live, and sometimes passersby in cars who knew Nick would stop to say hello and chat for a few minutes. Nick enjoyed these walks, and I soon became confident enough to allow Gail and Nick to go alone. A horse was stabled at one of the homes, and it often stood right next to the stone wall near the street. Gail would take Nick up to the horse and let him pet it. It was not long before they were stuffing carrots and apples in their pockets as they set out on their afternoon walks down the street.

Nick walking in his beloved walking bar. This is his favorite pastime and it shows in the peaceful, contented look on his face.

For years I walked with Nick as he held onto the parallel bar, holding his hand so I could catch him if he were to trip. Eventually, he was walking so well that I let go of his hand but stayed near him in case he needed me. After many months of doing this, and never touching him, I decided to sit down in a chair while he walked holding the bar. My heart was in my mouth as I talked to him from the chair. He walked perfectly well alone. I continued this for weeks.

When I was finally convinced that he was safe, I told Mary and Gail about this. They tried sitting down while he walked too. They experienced the same success that I did, and it opened up a whole new world for Nick, because we could entertain him while he walked by reading books. He enjoys every minute of this. Sometimes he becomes so engrossed in a story that he stops walking and stands still to listen. When he really likes a story, he will even give up food for it! He keeps up on the latest and best novels this way.

When we first began reading stories to him, Nick's attention span was very limited. Short magazine articles, such as those in *Reader's Digest* and *Guideposts,* were all we thought he could understand. Then one day Gail decided to try an audio book on tape. They would listen to part of the book, and the next day she would refresh his memory as to what the story was about and the point where they had left off the day

A Cocoon of Love

before. To our astonishment and pleasure, Nick was able to remember the story and would nod his head "yes" when asked if he remembered what it was about. Soon the volume of books being read to Nick was increasing, and everyone was becoming an expert at reading aloud.

Nick likes to have Bible passages read to him too. The Christmas before Nick was injured, John and I invited several of our friends to an open house party at our home. One friend in particular, Sam Longo, had studied the Bible for many years, and he got to talking with Nick who, at twenty-five, astounded him with his knowledge of the Bible and his enthusiastic way of talking about it.

As children, Nick and Mary, along with the rest of our family, observed the season of Lent from Ash Wednesday to Easter. It was a time of making special sacrifices for love of Jesus for dying on the Cross for us. The children would often choose to give up some special food they liked or an activity they enjoyed. It was more important, however, to add some spiritual readings or prayers to our daily life at this time. Sometimes the whole family would attend daily Mass before the children would go to school.

With this kind of background, it's understandable that one Ash Wednesday Mary and Nick resolved to start reading the Bible at Genesis and finish at Revelation by Christmas. It was an awesome challenge. Mary had to read every word aloud but they did it.

Reader's Digest Condensed Books became our favorite ones because they were edited before we got them and we didn't have to worry about explicit sex scenes, which were very embarrassing to read, or excessive violence, which none of us wanted to read to Nick since he was living proof of that kind of crime. He now has a valuable library of over one hundred of these books.

Mary's husband, Tom, and their son, Peter, are both great lovers of books and often go to flea markets and old-book stores looking for rare volumes. One time Peter got two paper bags full of *Reader's Digest* books for Nick for about fifty cents. What someone else considered flea market material was a treasure to Nick when Peter proudly presented them to him.

Gail established a custom each Christmas by starting early in December to read Charles Dickens's *A Christmas Carol*. They would finish it right before Christmas.

It was always difficult to think of new things to get Nick as presents. On his fortieth birthday, we planned a big party and invited many of our old friends who knew Nick.

We let everyone know that Nick was starting a collection of Charles Dickens Village houses, and he received many for his birthday. Each Christmas he has the set lighted on a table in his room while he and Gail read their annual story. Though he cannot see them, he knows they are there, and his young nieces and nephews are enraptured with the small figurines, the sleds, the street lamps, and the snow. He picks up their enthusiasm and smiles as they talk about the little Christmas town with people in it in Uncle Nick's room.

The habit of reading books to Nick taught us that he could understand some complex material. All the reading is done at a normal pace. Sometimes, when an aide stumbles over a word, Nick will correct her by saying the word himself.

On one occasion, I began reading a book to him and started to wonder if it was too deep for him to understand. It referred to polytheism, so I paused and asked him if he knew what that word meant. He stopped walking and stammered out the words, "A belief in many gods." Pleased and proud of him, I continued the reading.

After a while I began to realize that as Nick walks round and round through his parallel bars, listening to adventure after adventure in the stories that authors bring to him, he is transported to another world where he is not the crippled, handicapped, brain-injured Nick who cannot see. While he is walking and listening to a story, he travels in his imagination to other lands, brought there by authors who live on another plane. In this world of make-believe, Nick is *free:* free from brain-injury, free from blindness, free from the prison of his body. His imagination can visualize the scenes in the story, and he is no longer blind.

While reading to Nick one night when both of us were awake at 4 o'clock in the morning, I came across a poem by Emily Dickinson entitled "A Man." As Nick drifted back to sleep, I sat reading the poem over and over. Tears began to roll down my cheeks as I thought of all

A Cocoon of Love

he had been through, and his father with him. Her poem described beautifully the two marvelous men with whom I live.

Fate slew him, but he did not drop;
She felled—he did not fall—
Impaled him on her fiercest stakes—
He neutralized them all

She stung him, sapped his firm advance,
But, when her worst was done,
And he, unmoved, regarded her,
Acknowledged him a man.

With the advent of speech, we could more readily test Nick's memory, but he still forgets where he is and what has happened to him. Also, he cannot remember what he has had for lunch an hour later. His short-term memory is poor.

On the other hand, he can remember many of his childhood activities, like skating on the ice rink at Murray Park and grabbing girls' hats and never being caught because he was the fastest kid on skates. He laughs and his eyes sparkle when this is mentioned.

Nick remembers being in the Air Force and can tell us where he was stationed for basic training, about his term of duty at the Air Force photography school in Denver, and about the time he spent at George Air Force Base in California. The closer the conversation gets to the time he was injured, the dimmer his memory becomes.

Gail loves hearing these stories because it gives her an insight into Nick's life she longs to know. She lost a brother when she was very young, and I think in some ways Nick has become that beloved brother she never got to grow up with. She tries in every way possible to get Nick to the point where he is "normal."

Gail met Nick when she was only eighteen years old. On her twentieth birthday, she was bemoaning the fact all day long that she would never again be a teenager. Finally, tired of listening with his usual patience, Nick stammered, "Gail, Gail, please, grow up!"

She laughed and told us about the good advice Nick had given her!

Gail is a heroine to her friend Nick. She conceived new ways to help him on a daily basis. She tried built-up spoons so that he could hold a utensil and feed himself. She experimented with cups of every type until she found one with a spout he could easily hold in his left hand and get to his mouth without assistance. She bought terry-cloth mitts for him to use in the shower so he could try to wash himself. For the benefit of all the aides, she catalogued his books so that all of them would know which books had been read to Nick. Peter put this on the computer so that we could constantly update it. She made speech cards with letters, words and phrases for him to practice. All these things stimulate his body and mind and make his life pleasurable.

We soon learned that Nick is a man of few words, but oh, how mighty they are. Speaking is difficult for him, so when he has something to say, he makes it short and profound. (There is much to be learned by caring for someone with Nick's limitations.)

Obviously Nick receives a lot of attention and demands a great deal of care. This is a need of all TBI persons, but not all get it. When I was asked to write an article for the *CTBIA Professional Reference Guide,* from the perspective of a parent, I remember writing that the TBI person seems to become another appendage, and this is certainly true. In many respects, the TBI person needs more care and concern than an infant. You are in the awkward position of trying to care for a grown adult, but certain aspects of the infancy stage will never pass. For instance, just as an infant can never be left alone, neither can Nick. The infant will grow out of this stage, but Nick never will.

However, there is a blessing that is received by his caregivers that others do not see. He is a very wise advisor in times of trouble to all of us who seek his advice. No matter what the problem, he is willing to patiently listen and talk. His counsel is always to the point and very appropriate. In a family as large as ours, problems always arise, and they are discussed freely with Nick. When he is able to talk very slowly in a one-on-one conversation, he reveals an understanding, a compassion, that is rare to behold. At times like these we realize that the twenty-five-year-old young man who was injured has grown and

A Cocoon of Love

matured to a forty-five-year old adult man with all the wisdom that any other maturing adult acquires.

Nick always handles problems with children, spouses, business, and politics competently and honestly. His honesty is probably his most outstanding quality. Honesty many times means telling someone what they do not want to hear, yet he is able to do this in a compassionate way that others cannot accomplish easily.

On one occasion, Joe was scolding one of his nephews in a brusque, offensive manner. Nick stammered out his assessment of the situation in concise terms: "Joe, I don't like your attitude." He didn't disagree with the substance of Joe's remarks, only the manner in which it was said. Nick's comment stopped the action immediately.

Mary has raised her two children by daily advice from Nick on nearly every facet of child-rearing. He has heard intimate details of their daily lives in school, and they have been unaware of their uncle's influence with their mother over many instances in their lives. Nick always advises patience, prayer, and loving God in any situation. He says it in gestures or stammering it out one word at a time, but the message is clear. If people loved God, their problems would be solved.

Gail "dancing" with Nick at her wedding. The song especially chosen was *Wind Beneath My Wings*.

Gail too took advantage of Nick's wonderful counsel as she grew from a teenager into a young woman. He listened attentively as she discussed her boyfriends and what she hoped for in the future. When she finally found the love of her life, Nick approved after meeting her future husband, and he does not give his approval casually.

As she planned her wedding, Gail and Nick practiced dancing, because she wanted a special song sung just for them. She chose "Wind Beneath My Wings" made popular by Bette Midler. At her wedding she was dressed in a beautiful white gown, and Nick in a new suit. They were alone on the dance floor as the song was played. Some in the audience cheered while others cried. (I was among the teary-eyed ones.)

Gail has become Nick's treasured friend and our "adopted" daughter. Each year on July 5, Nick and Gail celebrate the anniversary of their meeting by having a special dinner together to which we are always invited. Gail had special shirts made with the name "Champ" on his and "Coach" on hers. The shirts are old and worn now, but they still express the meaning of love in their relationship.

Angels take care of Nick. Mary (his sister) with Nick.

Gail has coached Nick from a wheelchair onto his feet and worked every muscle in his legs to enable him to walk again. She has spent hours figuring out routines for him to do to improve his ability to walk, to talk, to listen to books on tape, records, and reading aloud. They have made pizza together as she holds his hand while he kneads the dough. They have planned Christmas presents and made cakes together for family and friends. Nick has stood at the sink with his hands in dishwater, trying to learn to help himself in every way possible. She alone is allowed to manicure his nails and take care of his feet.

We all cried with Gail when her first-born son died at only five months of age, and we rejoiced when she became preg-

Nick's angel: Gail Duffany with Nick.

nant again and gave birth to a new son, Zachary. Nick would feel her stomach when the baby kicked, rejoicing in the new life she carried. Her son calls me "Grandma D," and John is referred to as "Grandpa Dude," because he dressed in a cowboy outfit to go to one of our special dances. She has given birth to a third son, Spencer, and a fourth, Brendan. Nick has held each one on his lap and bounced him up and down on his knee. Angels do exist, and Gail is Nick's personal angel.

No other person in Nick's life, though, means as much to him as does his sister Mary, unless it is his father and me. From the moment he was injured, she has been by his side. The love that has grown between them over these years is profound. Without Mary's enduring love and help, Nick would not be where he is today. John and I consider ourselves very fortunate to have the company of our two oldest children with us on a daily basis. We are loved deeply by them and they are much loved in return.

Nick's angel: Debra Vienneau with Nick.

Mary Ann (as Nick calls her) taught Nick how to paint ceramic figures at the Convalarium. Now they can do it at home whenever they want. Nick chooses the colors he wants and holds the brush in his left hand to paint the object. He feels the cool ceramic figure with his left hand, and with Mary's help he makes the brush strokes on the figure. After several strokes his arm becomes relaxed and the brush moves easily over the object. Joan Faulkner always felt that if Nick was to get back the use of his arm and hand it would start with reflexive movements. Painting these objects proves her point.

One Christmas he painted beautiful figurines for each of his aides. It took him six months to complete them. His great pleasure is in the reaction of those who receive them. They were ecstatic with their gifts, and his eyes glistened with pleasure as he was complimented on his great achievement.

Many young women and a few young men have come into our home as aides to Nick, and most have gone on to other jobs. In one year I sent out thirty W-2 forms to people who had tried to work with Nick. Not everyone can handle such a job. It requires very special qualities of caring, loving, and being able to be around a severely handicapped person.

Michelle Minicucci is one of those special persons. She helped cook dinners with me, and we enjoyed her extroverted personality. Nick loved her cheerleading him along to accomplish his evening and night activities. She too married and invited Nick and us to her wedding. His dance with her was special too, and though she no longer works with him, she is very dear to Nick, John, and me.

Nick at the beach—his balance is incredibly good.

Debbie Vienneau brought her special charm into our home too. She taught us all to love country music and all that goes with it. She worked on Saturdays when the "American Gladiators" shows were on television, and got Nick so interested in them that he knew them by name and would place bets with her on who would win the games. Nick could not see the show, but he could often pick the winner!

When Debbie Vienneau left to move to Maine, we were all saddened to lose the vitality she brought into our lives. We wrote to her, and she kept in touch with letters and phone calls. On one occasion when I wrote to her, I suggested she pack her bags and come back, as we needed her. I got a phone call from a teary-eyed Debbie right after she read the letter. She and her family did not like living in Maine, and this was just the impetus they needed to decide to move back to Connecticut.

She worked with Nick while she attended school to become a medical technician. He often listened to her lessons and sometimes helped her study. When she graduated she got a full-time job in her chosen field, but we still treasure her as a friend. She still returns to work with Nick for a day or evening each week.

With all these people to help, Nick finally has the structure that

Dr. Sarfaty said was so necessary for his well-being. We have created a cocoon of love to surround him every day. But it must be remembered that for love to be true it is not just received, it is given, and Nick gives it to all of us in abundance.

His love is most often expressed in appreciation. Many times a day we hear him say, "I appreciate it, I appreciate it." He cannot buy us gifts or take us to events he wants to share with us but he can say, "I love you," and when he does you know he means it. When Nick takes your hand and kisses it, his charm warms you, and when he gives you a hug, you know it is special. How lucky John and I are every morning when Nick refuses to sit in his chair for breakfast until we both get our morning hug. He never passes up a chance to say, "God bless you."

Another one of Nick's pleasures is to sit and listen to John talk, mostly about his cases, but also about politics. He also likes joking with him. Their very special relationship is a quiet one. John is best with Nick when no one else is around. He will read the Sunday paper to him and they will talk about the articles. Mary says Tom does this with Nick when we go away on vacation. Everyone needs this "alone" time with Nick to be able to talk with him.

Nick likes to listen to tapes of Bishop Sheen and the Bible. He especially likes the Gospel of St. John. All this gets pretty serious after a while, and

Nick, the rebel (he was born in Oklahoma), and John, the Yankee. They like to joke with each other, and Dad is the only one to indulge him man to man.

John will break it up by kidding Nick. "Nick, you are living in a state of grace. When you die, you will go straight to heaven. There is only one way you can commit a sin. That is by coveting a woman. So don't covet a woman, and you can spend eternity in heaven."

Nick replies to this with the half-laugh that he is able to muster. Then John will say, "If I knew how much you were going to eat, I might have reconsidered your coming home." John knows how much Nick prays the Our Father prayer and comes into his room in the morning and says, "Nick, this is your father who art on earth." John is the only one to joke with Nick in this manner, and he smiles and his eyes twinkle when he does.

John sincerely believes that everyone has an immortal soul that will one day escape the bonds of the body. He believes that though Nick is forced to live in a crippled body now, when he dies, his spirit will be set free to soar heavenward, where he will spend an eternity with God, his most beloved friend, and he will not be hindered there with the effects of the terrible sin committed against him.

Nick was a normal young man insofar as his sexuality was concerned. He was the only one of my eight children whose choice of friends I never had to worry about. His girlfriends were all young ladies I would love to have had for a daughter-in-law. Though I don't know what his life was like in the Air Force, I'm sure he was as normal as any young man regarding sex. I do know about his sexuality since his injury.

He is constantly cared for by women who are not related to him. They have to bathe him, help him in the bathroom, and put a catheter on his penis every night. He has never displayed any untoward attitude or gesture to any of them regarding sex. Just the opposite is true. They must be clean in their speech and actions toward him. I asked him one day how he was able to handle the emotion of sex when he was around all these women. He slowly said to me, "Mom, Mom, I am a man who has a soul as well as a body and I don't want to hurt anyone, especially God." His answer was so profound it brought tears to my eyes. Crippled? Brain damaged? Only in body, not in spirit!

We have kept in contact with Father Fulton in Oklahoma all our married life. He is much more than a priest, he is a dear friend. So I felt comfortable to ask him to record his Mass on a cassette tape for Nick. On December 6, the Feast of St. Nicholas, he did, and this tape is played over and over, year after year, when Nick wants to hear the Mass. Father Fulton made a personal dedication during this Mass for Nick, so it is very special to him. Sometimes it is a wonderful relief for Nick when he needs something to take his mind away from the angel/devil visions he sees.

Our daughter Sue had a sleigh she used in winter time for sleigh rallies and for family pleasure. She invited Nick to her house for a sleigh ride, and we took him. It was a bit of a trick to get him into the sleigh, but once in, he had a wonderful time riding around the track and listening to the jingle of the bells attached to the sleigh. Nick was leading as "normal" a life as we could make it, and it filled my heart with joy to see it happening.

Nick was a teenager and young adult in the sixties and seventies, so he was familiar with many of the rock groups. He remembers the names of some of these and their music. He had been to many concerts before he was injured, and since Mary was only a year older than Nick, they had much in common in this regard.

Mary wanted to take him to hear their favorite group: the Moody Blues. She traveled to Springfield, Massachusetts, with him, his sister Debbie, and an aide. Nick was in his wheelchair,

Nick on a sleigh ride with sister Susan.

neatly dressed in white pants and white shirt with a white cap on his head. The handicapped section was in a favored spot right next to the stage. When Nick especially liked a song, he would clap his left hand on the contracted right one and then tip his white hat to the musicians. The flute player noticed him tip his hat. The group then dedicated a song to "a special person," and the flute player saluted Nick as this was announced. They played the song, "Question," which contains the lyrics, "Looking for a Miracle." Tom and Mary have taken Nick to four Moody Blues concerts.

When our daughter Debbie was pregnant with Nicole, Nick carefully followed her through the pregnancy. When she was due to deliver, she was on the couch in the family room at our home and experiencing labor pains. Nick suddenly said to her, "Debbie, go to the hospital, now." She did, and I stayed with her, holding her hand, until Nicole was born.

Nicole was named after Nick and lived in our house for over a year. He held her in his lap, she ate next to him in her high chair, and he felt the first tooth come through her gums.

Nick's only brother, Joe.

Nicole is a most unusual child, as sweet and as kind as is possible to be. Because she was named for him, Nick has arranged to buy her pearls for a necklace each birthday and Christmas. She is thirteen years old now, and the pearl necklace is getting to be a very fine piece of jewelry. She loves her Uncle Nick very much and never leaves our home without giving him a hug and kiss.

Sally chose Nick to be the godfather to her son, Michael. He went to the church and was able to do everything necessary at the baptismal ceremony. Father De Carolis was very proud of him, as were all of us.

Our daughter Joan got married, and Nick accompanied me down the aisle at Immaculate Conception Church. He walked straight and tall dressed in a white tuxedo. She had her two brothers and five sisters in her wedding party, and we had a wonderful day of celebration.

Cathy too was married, and Nick attended her wedding. Gail, Debbie, Mary, and I took turns dancing with him. He cannot maneuver himself around the dance floor as others do, but he can keep rhythm to the music by swaying his body and making small steps with his partner. Only those who work with Nick are trusted to do this with him, because he could so easily fall with someone who is unfamiliar with how to walk with him. He ate and enjoyed the festivities just like the rest of us.

A Cocoon of Love

Nick's six beautiful sisters, Mary, Joan, (on her wedding day), Susan, Sally, Debbie and Cathy.

He has made a profound impression on more than a few of his nieces and nephews. Young Kyle, Sally's four-year-old son, was a favorite companion of Nick's, walking behind him in the parallel bars and talking to Nick about all kinds of four-year-old topics. Nick learned about Ninja Turtles, Spider Man, X-Men, Star Wars, and all the latest video characters from him.

Uncle Nick as godfather to nephew Michael.

Nick's young nieces and nephews loved to watch Nick do his exercises, and then they too would lie down on the floor and try to do what he was doing. Nick was often the role model for the young grandchildren, even when they were in high chairs. They would watch how Nick held his spoon and try to imitate him. When Nicole was just a baby, she was a very slow eater. When her high chair was placed next to Nick's table, she often gained a healthy appetite by trying to keep up with Uncle Nick. The grandchildren all loved to drink from Nick's cup with a spout on it instead of their own "learning cups." They often watched through his speech lessons and sometimes learned to talk by pronouncing the words along with Nick.

Kyle would sometimes stay with Nick and Mary while his mother worked. He would bring his books for Mary to read to Nick and make up games to play with his uncle. He would ask Nick to name an animal; then Kyle would imitate the sound of the animal while he either ran, crawled, flew, or walked through the room, just as the animal would do. He'd say, "Nick, do you want it to be a fast animal or a slow one?" He would stand directly in front of Nick and talk to him and wait patiently for Nick to answer him in the slow manner he has to use. If someone tried to answer for Nick, Kyle would get very upset and want Uncle Nick to speak for himself.

Uncle Nick with his niece, Nicole. She was named after her uncle Nick and never leaves him without a hug and a kiss.

Nick has had trouble throwing a ball since his injury because he cannot release the fingers of his left hand quickly enough to accomplish this simple feat. Kyle had a bright idea that helped Nick overcome this problem. Kyle placed a Nerf ball in Nick's open left hand, closing the fingers around it for him. Then Kyle ran across the room and shouted, "Ready." Nick was able to release the ball and throw it at the sound of Kyle's voice. Kyle had provided the opportunity for Nick's reflex to throw a ball to take over. Oftentimes Kyle

Uncle Nick with his nephew, Peter, who was only four years old when he was injured. Peter grew up visiting him in nursing homes until he came home.

would catch the ball, to the delight of both of them. Nick had tried to play this kind of "catch" with both his older nephews, Peter and Jason, but had been unable to do it.

Kyle would also play kickball with Nick while Nick was standing, holding onto the parallel bar. Mary would put the ball right in front of Nick's left foot, and Kyle would stand at the end of the bar. When Nick kicked the ball to Kyle, Kyle would kick it back to Nick. Soon all the grandchildren were joining in this game. It was good for Nick because it helped him with his balance. It intrigued the children that Nick could do such things, and they loved to join him in this activity. Kyle was especially gifted at understanding Nick and was able to appreciate the kind, considerate, loving person he is. This is a very rare quality in a four-year-old child.

Nicole reads books aloud to her Uncle Nick. He touches her head and follows her long brown hair all the way to her waist to get a picture of what she looks like in his mind. She was especially pouty one day, and he gave her the same advice he gave Gail: "Grow up, Nicole." She was surprised and smiled, the first smile we had seen on her face that day.

Nicole's eleven-year-old brother, Johnny, has a hard time believing Nick actually can't see and tries to

Uncle Nick with Kyle who loved to play games with him. He taught Nick how to turn loose a ball and throw it.

figure out what it means to be blind. Mary puts a blindfold on him and lets him feel his way around the room, but he soon takes off the blindfold. Yet Johnny does have some understanding of Nick, because when Nick holds out his cup after he is finished with his coffee, Johnny will take it from him and when it is refilled, go to him and carefully place it in his hand and tell him just how to hold it so he won't spill.

We believe in the guidance of angels in Nick's life very sincerely. So much good comes his way that it cannot be all by chance. Just recently we discovered a place for Nick to swim that is on the street behind our house. A wonderful woman, Joyce Smillie, has built a place where handicapped and elderly persons can enjoy the benefits of her beautiful indoor pool, in which the water is heated to ninety-six degrees for the benefit of these people. She calls her nonprofit organization La-Paloma, Inc., dba The Open Space. She allows many organizations to bring handicapped and elderly people to The Open Space for the benefits of swimming, horseback riding, and exercise. It takes two to three people to manage Nick in the pool, but he loves it. Maybe horseback riding will be next on his list of activities.

Nick's cocoon of love is a very large one, and though none of us can take away the agony he suffers daily by being so handicapped, we can make his life as pleasurable as possible in the limited way that is available to us. This is what makes us truly human. We love and take care of each other.

41

Dancing on the Dragon

John and I have had to make many adjustments in our lives since Nick came home to live with us. One of the greatest losses is the freedom to do as we please in the later years of our lives. We must be home each night by nine o'clock when the aide leaves or hire one of them to stay late. Vacations must be carefully planned in advance. It is not possible for us to spontaneously decide on a weekend that we will go away for some event or pleasure. Dinner engagements with other couples always have to be made early in the evening so that we can be home by the time the aide is scheduled to leave.

Time alone in our own home is very hard to realize, and interruptions on an hourly basis are something we have learned to accommodate. It is difficult to have people in our home from 8 o'clock in the morning until 9 o'clock at night every day of the year. However, we lived with the alternative to this arrangement, and it is much worse. As John frequently reminds me, "What else would we be doing with our lives that is more worthwhile?"

For thirteen years after Nick was injured, I could not bear to be with groups of people. The noise level in a room where many conversations were occurring was such that it upset me, and I could not stand the social chitchat that goes on at such events because it was so trivial. I turned down all invitations for this kind of gathering.

I grew used to this feeling and thought it would go on forever until our friends, Margaret and Joe Rossi, invited us to their fortieth wedding anniversary. This was an invitation we could not refuse. While there, we met Louise and Ed Petrusiewicz, who invited us to a dance club they belong to, the Cha Rum Bo Dance Club. I was opposed to going and wanted John to decline the invitation, but when Louise called him at his office and made a point of a second invitation, it was hard for him to refuse.

Mary dancing with Nick at our 40th wedding anniversary.

I went out of obligation but was surprised at how much I enjoyed the evening. We were invited back again and had just as much pleasure the second time. Week after week, we began to go out to ballroom dances on Saturday night, and the enjoyment began to grow to the point where we wanted to take dance lessons.

We began private ballroom dance lessons with Bob and Marge McEnerney, who are first place winners in both American and International ballroom dance styles as well as finalists in the United States national competition for ballroom dance. After winning these prestigious awards they decided to turn professional and began teaching ballroom dance to students. They taught us the joy and freedom there is in being able to spend three minutes on a dance floor doing different steps to music and really having fun doing it. Unconsciously, we were beginning to accept our situation and the fact that our lives could go on in spite of the tragedy that changed it.

I still feel guilty every time I leave Nick, knowing he cannot have this in his life. However, I have learned that most of the time he is content at home and does not seem to miss going out on a weekend. He frequently tells us to have a good time. All of us try very hard to provide him with as much entertainment as we can. Once when we went on a trip, Gail planned a vacation at home with Nick. They had a Mexican night, an Italian night, and a Caribbean night, and planned food and music to fit the mood. When we came home, they had more to tell us about their vacation than we did about ours. They stayed at "La Casa Del Buono" and had soap and shampoo wrapped in paper with the name on it.

It is Mary who gives us the freedom to go out on Saturday nights, and she and Tom come to our home and stay day and night when we go on a vacation. We can leave knowing someone is in charge of Nick's care who is knowledgeable about him and his routine. They are a lifeline for John and me because respites from home are truly a necessity.

One of the very special occasions in our lives was the celebration of our fortieth wedding anniversary. We had an anniversary Mass said by Father John Blanchfield at Immaculate Conception Church and a reception at the Elton Hotel in Waterbury afterward.

I wrote a poem for our book, *When Two Become One,* which appears on the back cover of the book. John asked me to put the poem to music. With the help of an arranger, I did. Our song, "Love Me And I Will Love You," was sung during our anniversary Mass. It was a very poignant moment for me as Donald Gauvin sang:

> *When you come to me with your love*
> *I'll join you with mine.*
> *We'll blend our lives in one wonderful life*
> *That will be sublime.*
>
> *I'll see what you see and I'll feel what you feel*
> *As I walk with you.*
> *I'll know what you believe and I'll understand,*
> *And you'll know me too.*
>
> *Our spirits will soar to the highest heights*
> *As we live our love.*
> *We'll conquer each sorrow that's sure to come*
> *With love from Above.*

Love me and I will love you,
Our whole lives through,
    Our whole lives through.
Love me and I will love you,
We're one, though two,
    We're one, though two.

All eight of our children and their families attended, along with many friends. Nick sat at a table with several of the aides who worked with him, and he feasted and danced along with the rest of us. The grandchildren were all there and took their turn on the floor as the song "We Are Family" was played. John and I danced a waltz to the song I had written, and we had a wonderful time.

Our daughters had taken photographs from our albums of the times when they were all growing up in our home. They had slides made and showed them at the anniversary party. Nick Reynolds is a friend and professional photographer who had photographed several of our daughters' weddings, and we asked him to take pictures at our anniversary. He took the slides our daughters had made and put them on a videotape for us with beautiful background music and presented the video tape to us as a gift. I was overwhelmed and still cry each and every time I see the tape. It is my life passing before me as I watch Nick and the children grow and memories flood into my mind.

John and I celebrating our 45th wedding anniversary.

John and I have been able to do some of the things I thought we could not do while taking care of Nick. I believed it might interfere greatly with our ability to be good grandparents to our grandchildren. Fourteen years later, I do not believe it has. We have thirteen grandchildren now and four great-grandchildren.

The greatest tragedy we have suffered since Nick was injured was the loss of our grandson, Jason. He is Susan's oldest child and the one born just one month before Nick was injured. He was nineteen years old and had just graduated from high school. One evening as he was trying to enter the driver's side of a car, a drunk driver hit him, and he died of brain injuries a few days later. Seeing him in ICU was a very difficult thing to endure. It brought back all the memories of Nick. We miss Jason greatly.

Perhaps the most satisfying aspect of our lives, though, has been the revival of John's law practice since Nick came home. John is no longer burdened with the conflict between the lawsuit to help Nick and practicing law. In 1990 he moved his office to Watertown, just a few miles from our home. The space was designed especially for him, and his new offices are magnificent. He has no plans to retire because he loves what he is doing, is proud to be a lawyer, and enjoys his career more than he ever did.

He decided to specialize in personal injury law. He has handled several traumatic brain-injury cases and is able to bring a dimension to this type of case that few lawyers can. The personal injury his son suffered, and the resulting lawsuit against a national organization, have widened his ability to appreciate what his clients are going through.

On August 1, 1993, we received a letter that surprised and pleased us greatly. It was on the TBIA stationery from Kathleen Ryan, the executive director. It said in part:

Dear Barbara and John,
You are important to TBIA. Your support of TBIA's programs and past initiatives has made a difference in the lives of persons with TBI and their families. In grateful acknowledgment of your efforts, TBIA's Board of Directors has named Barbara and John Del Buono as recipients of the 1993 President's Award.

This means a great deal to both of us. We traveled to Camp Hemlocks in Hebron, Connecticut, for the award ceremony, and Nick, Mary, and our granddaughter, Nicole, accompanied us. We stayed for the day's festivities and met many other TBI persons and their families. One of the great realities I faced that day was how well Nick was doing compared to others. He walked so well, with just a slight limp.

Acknowledged a Man

The TBI Award John and I received.

Though his right arm is contracted, it is not more so than others. His speech is difficult to understand, but so is that of other TBI persons. His appearance is good and his understanding of what is going on around him is amazing considering the serious injury he suffered.

John and I recently attended another TBI function that gave us great joy. Twice each year, the Connecticut TBI Association holds a Big Band Ball. We invited four couples of our dancing friends to accompany us to the ball which was held at the University of New Haven. Mary and Jim Brancati, Valerie and Louis Berardi, Beverly and Bill Hanna, and John and I were dressed in tuxedos and gowns. We had a wonderful time that evening.

When it came time for the dance contests, we entered the one for Cha Cha participants. As we danced, we looked at each other with gleaming eyes and realized we were *dancing on the dragon* in our lives and stomping it for all we were worth. *We were living again and having fun!* TBI is a monster in any person's life, but it can be subdued, and we had done just that. We won first place!

42

Solving the Mystery of Angels and Devils

The phenomenon in which Nick says he sees angels and devils or heaven and hell plagued him night and day and was, by far, the most difficult problem for him, and us, to cope with. When this occurred, he would turn his head to the left and look upward, and his eyes would become fixed on something he saw. I believe this has been occurring since he had his first seizure and was probably the cause for it. Only after he became able to communicate what was happening has he been able to tell us what it is he sees.

I have asked Nick to describe these angels and devils, and he says angels are white in the area of the head and everything from the head down is golden. They have large white wings on their backs and they fly about. He describes devils as black, also with gold from the head down. He does not know if they have wings, but they are smaller than the angels, and they have smiles on their faces that he sometimes describes as mischievous grins. He has said on occasion that devils look like bugs. They do not speak to him.

We considered the fact that Nick's religious background might be affecting him. He had attended a Catholic grammar school, and we were and are a traditional Catholic family. Perhaps he remembered angel/devil pictures from his Catholic education at home and school.

We also thought that because Nick has some light perception coming through one tunnel of vision in one eye, he might be seeing shapes through it that appeared to him as angels and devils. Or, perhaps, it could be related to his loss of sight.

Nick's blindness has really hurt all of us deeply, and we know it has had a profound affect on him, so we try to find ways to help him in daily acceptance of this fact. One evening while he and Gail were walking in his parallel bar, Gail said to him, "Nick, what if you are never able to see again in your whole life. What will you do?"

His answer was utterly profound. "Then that will be my cross and I want to carry it with honor and dignity." It made Gail cry.

I cried too when she told me about it.

Because this angel/devil phenomenon caused Nick so much anxiety and pain, Dr. Sarfaty brought up the idea of using a psychiatric drug in very small doses, closely monitored. I was immediately opposed to this suggestion, knowing what Valium and sleeping pills had done to him in the nursing home. I said I would rather put up with the angel/devil problem than with the side effects of psychiatric drugs.

However, as the years went by with no solution, I finally came to the point where I agreed with Dr. Sarfaty and asked Dr. Bobowick to prescribe Haldol. He explained the side effects to me and told me to be especially careful of Nick going into a catatonic state in which his body might become rigid. He explained that this condition might have to be stopped by medication administered in the hospital. We remained very alert. After only two doses, Nick's body did become rigid on the right side while walking in the parallel bars. We were able to get him to a chair and wait for the condition to subside. Though he did not have to go to the hospital, the drug was discontinued immediately.

Under Dr. Bobowick's supervision, we conducted twenty-four-hour EEG tests on Nick twice at our home with no resolution to the problem. A stressful forty-eight-hour admission to the Seizure Control Clinic at Yale-New Haven Hospital revealed through test after test that "the visual hallucinations do not appear to be epileptiform events." There were no internal seizures causing these episodes.

Then on Saturday, April 23, 1994, an ordinary event took place that turned into an extraordinary one. I shall never forget it. Nick and I were having our first cup of coffee of the morning. We sat talking about the sunshine streaming through the windows and how good it felt on our cool bodies. The weather outside was still cold. I remarked about how wonderful it was to experience such peace and quiet in the house. We were the only ones awake, and the first aide of the day would not arrive until noon.

Nick was solemn but calm, and obviously deep in thought. I left him alone in his reverie for a while because he seemed so tranquil. Finally, I couldn't resist asking him what he was thinking about and slowly, without turning his head, he said, "Life."

"Do you mean your life?" I asked.

He nodded his head affirmatively.

This small exchange of conversation prompted a fruitful dialogue. His comment about "life" made me think about the movie *It's a Wonderful Life* with James Stewart and Donna Reed. We talked about the angel who came to Jimmy Stewart when he was about to jump off a bridge to show him how important his life was to everyone he touched with it.

I told Nick about the many times we had been told he was going to die while he lay comatose in the hospital. I particularly recalled for him the night when Dr. Sturman called and asked for his kidneys. I related to him how his father just fell to pieces and started crying, so I took the phone from him and told the doctor John was afraid Nick was going to die. I told Nick that the doctor said, "Well, I'm afraid he will live."

Nick immediately asked, "Why?"

"I'll tell you exactly why. He thought your life would be so miserable if you lived that you would be better off dead."

Nick quickly shook his head "no" and said, "I love life."

"I know you do, Nick, and your life since you were injured has influenced many, many people."

I named Gail and Michelle and Debbie and others who had come into his life to help him and how their lives were changed by his influence on them.

"You know Nick, your life since your injury has changed completely."

He nodded "yes" over and over.

"It must have been very frightening for you to slowly wake to an entirely new world and life."

He nodded "yes" again and said, "I love life, I see life."

Suddenly a new possibility dawned on me and I asked, "Do you mean when you say 'I see life,' you see your life?"

His eyes sparkled and he said, "Yes."

"You mean you see your new life, the one you have had since you were injured?"

Again, the twinkle was there in his eyes as he nodded "yes." I was beginning to feel like we were nearing the end of a mystery and the solution was about to be revealed.

"Well, what about these angels and devils you see? What do they mean?"

He pointed upward for his gesture meaning God.

I didn't understand this response so I questioned him further. "What do you mean by saying 'God'?"

"I see angels and devils, heaven and hell, and I see life, and God working on me."

It's very unusual for Nick to say so much in one sentence. Because he used gestures to indicate each word, I knew what he meant immediately without going through the tedious process of asking him to spell a word that I couldn't understand.

After this exchange, Nick sat in his chair slowly rocking back and forth, smiling, eyes gleaming. I sat on the couch pondering what had just been said because there was something different in this conversation from any I had before with Nick. Soon, a theory began to dawn on me, and I expressed it.

"Nick, do you mean when you say you *see life* that you are thinking about *your life since you were injured?*"

He rocked back and forth and nodded "yes."

"Do you mean when you say you see devils and hell that you are trying to describe what it was like to wake up to this new life and not understand what had happened to you?"

Nick smiled and laughed that half-laugh he has. I felt that strange sensation, something like a sudden chill that overcomes us when light is shed on a long-standing mystery. The solution is so simple when it's finally revealed.

"It must be like going to hell to wake from coma and not understand what has happened to your life."

His eyes were shining as he said, "Yes, yes."

All of a sudden I tried to think about all of this from his point of view. Nick had slowly emerged from a comatose state as a blind person, but we didn't know he couldn't see. All his life he had known what it was to see, and now, without sight to guide him through this tunnel of darkness, he heard and smelled and touched persons coming in and out of his room in a hospital or nursing home. They appeared as the misshapen figures which his slight tunnel of vision that only sees shapes and colors provided.

These people must surely have appeared to him as devils as they performed their painful routines on his body and strapped him in a bed or chair twenty-four hours a day. Even when he would be pleading for help by turning sideways and upside down in a bed, his begging was misunderstood. He could not talk; he could not ask for an explanation of what had happened to him. Everyone was so afraid to tell him the horror story about his injury that he got no information with which to help guide him through this terrible period, even the fact that the reason he could not see was because he was now blind! What confusion must have engulfed him in this brain-injured state! What fright he must have endured! Surely it must have seemed to him that he had died and gone to hell!

Then other persons would appear with kind voices and soothing hands who would talk to him, who would hold him sometimes and brush his teeth and comb his hair and tend gently to his daily needs. He must have perceived them to be angels coming to rescue him from hell. He must have thought he was in heaven and hell at the same time! And somehow he must have always felt the presence of God working on him and being with him. What salvation and hope this must have been!

When Nick says, *"I see life,"* it is now clear that the life he sees is his own *brain-injured life!* And it is not as frightening now as it first appeared to him. The fear has slowly subsided. The solution to the mystery of angels and devils, heaven and hell, in Nick's life was not an earth-shattering event or a complicated medical problem. *All it took was looking at brain injury from Nick's point of view.* Brain injury is so frightening that we run from its reality and don't want to think about it. We have to force ourselves to travel a very long way to understand what brain injury is really like to the victim.

The psychological impact it causes in those of us who are only close to it can never be compared to the enormous mental disturbance the victim endures. Now I can only ask myself, "Why didn't I *see* this before? Why didn't I *understand* sooner?"

I read these thoughts to Nick the same morning I wrote them as he was walking around his parallel bar. He agreed with all that I've said by nodding "yes," and stopping to raise his hand in approval, sometimes uttering his half-laugh to indicate we are understanding each other and agree. We are both more at peace because of this *understanding* between us. "Mom, I think this is a God-blessed day!" Nick said. He is so right!

After this dialogue, I helped Nick get out of bed one morning, to put on his robe and slippers, and to walk from his bedroom through his living room to the kitchen, as he has done many times before at the same time of day. He asked me, "Where am I?"

Instead of answering his question, I asked him,

"Nick, where do you think you are?"

"I feel like I have come from hell."

Since our special conversation that Saturday morning, I understand what he is trying to convey. He is in bed every night until someone comes to *help* him out of bed. When he awakes, he has to come to the realization all over again that he cannot *see*. That is why he asks, "Where am I?" Getting up and going to the kitchen for breakfast makes him feel that he has come from hell to heaven. These feelings still occur, but he is not frightened by them now. Sometimes, however, he becomes obsessed with this "thing" that has changed his life,

Solving the Mystery of Angels and Devils

and he *must* have time to think about it and ponder it. At these times he will usually tell us, "God is working on me."

The mind's eye is a very peculiar thing, and who can say what it sees in a brain-injured person other than that person? Have you ever awakened from a terrifying dream and found it hard to come quickly into reality? Have you ever had trouble trying to interpret a dream and come to some understanding of what it means? A coma brought on by brain injury is not a dream. It is a terrifying reality that does not go away. The nightmare never ends. How long would it take any of us to come to that reality and try to interpret it with an injured brain?

Sometimes Nick still says he sees angels and devils, but his question is different now. He asks, "Mom, what should I do when I see angels and devils?"

To my great relief, I can now help Nick. It's always related to something he used to be able to do that he now has to have help doing. If he is eating, I ask him, "Why is someone helping you with your meal?"

"I don't know."

"Can you see your food?"

"Yes."

Then I ask him to find his fork and get his own food on it. He tries very hard. I say to him, "Nick, can you *really* see your food?"

"No."

Then I start to question him. "Well, Nick, was there a time in your life when you could see the food and eat by yourself?"

"Yes."

"What happened to change that, Nick?"

He will move his left arm up to his head and say, "I was hit." "Right, Nick, and that caused a serious brain injury to occur, and you can't see the food on your plate or prepare it for yourself like you used to do. That is what brain injury has done to your life, Nick. You have to try to remember that when you see these angels and devils. It is really brain injury you are seeing."

On another morning, Nick asked again, "Mom, what should I do when I see devils and angels?"

"Nick, we have to talk about it, and I need to ask you some questions. What are you thinking about right now?"

"My life."

"Well, what part of your life are you thinking about?"

"My body."

"What's happening to your body?"

Nick shrugged his shoulder and said, "I don't know."

"When you were born, was your body a normal, healthy one?"

"Yes."

"Could you do a lot of things with your body?"

"Yes."

"Can you tell me some of the things you could do with it?"

"I could swim, I could dance, and I could eat."

"Can you swim now?"

"No."

"Can you dance like you used to?"

"No."

"Can you eat by yourself?"

"No."

Now I had to get to the heart of the matter that is so difficult for all of us.

"What happened to your body, Nick?"

"Devils came and took it to hell."

"What happened to your body there, Nick?"

"God came and took it to heaven, and He is working on it."

I praised him truthfully by saying, "Nick, your description of what happened to your body is a very good one. But I wonder if you can give me another description of what happened. Can you think of another way to describe it?"

"Yes," he said, "brain injury."

"Yes, Nick," I almost shouted, "that's right! Brain injury is the 'devil' that came and took your body to hell. You know, Nick, there was a time when we could not have had this conversation because you could not talk. You are right about God working on you, but you should also know how hard you worked with God to learn to speak again. There was also a time when you couldn't walk, but now you can, and you and God worked very hard to accomplish this. You should also remember that God can work on you anytime, anywhere, so you don't have to sit still in a chair for this to happen. Would you like to walk now?"

"Yes."

And I helped him to get up, and we walked away.

Each time this occurs, I am now able to relate it to the activity taking place, and it is invariably something Nick cannot understand why he cannot do without help. Angels and devils are part of his nightmare of brain injury, as is the loss of short-term memory that prevents him from remembering why life has changed so dramatically for him.

Nick rarely complains about this phenomenon today. If he does, it usually means that he is bored with what he is doing and needs to get up and move about. We have used Dr. Sarfaty's Steps to Learning for Nick, and by repetitious explanations Nick can quickly tell us what is happening and change the picture by changing the activity.

Recently, Nick asked me to look in his eyes.

"Why do you want me to do that?"

"Because I can't see."

"Why can't you see, Nick?"

He replied by using his gesture for devils.

I asked him immediately if he had another word to describe what he meant by devils, and he responded quickly. "Joseph Tramontano. He hit me in the head with a bat, and because of it I lost my vision."

As tragic as this conversation was, I could have shouted for joy. Nick came up with the right answers to his own questions about himself, and he did it in the wink of an eye.

I told Nick what his father so often says to him. "Nick, you have better vision with your heart and soul than most people have with their eyes. It is better to have both, but if you can have only one, then you are better off to have it in your heart."

I know that Nick will never cease asking God to restore his sight. Perhaps he will take heaven by storm and nag God into giving him the only cure: a miracle. And as Nick persists in his prayer, so will his father and mother and all of his friends.

I went to see Dr. Sarfaty after all of this occurred. His first question was, "How have things changed since you discovered this?" When I told him what an astounding difference there was in all our lives, he really believed it was the answer to the mystery. He congratulated me for discovering it and asked permission to use this story. I quickly said yes. He explained that Nick's limited language skills caused him to speak in metaphors that we were all unable to understand.

The Nick we know and love. This picture was taken after a shopping trip to pick out his own music tapes. I think he likes them.

I think about the artistic, dramatic person Nick was before he was assaulted and realize how apropos it is that he used the metaphors of devils and angels and heaven and hell to describe the reality of brain injury. I have read a lot of material on the subject of head injury since Nick was injured, and I have never come across a more apt description than his. It is so like his old self to use this vivid, poetic language to describe his condition.

God bless you, Nick, for finally getting through to me. I'm sorry it took me so long to understand your beautiful language of metaphors. My relief is almost as great as yours in finally understanding what it is you are trying to say to me.

Nick is a prince among men whom only a few people truly know. Those who do have traveled a long, hard road through forests and thorn bushes to arrive at his castle. As a result of his extraordinary personality, he has life's most treasured gifts: a loving family and true friends. These are the people who know the brain-injured Nick, the loving human being, the gentleman who always kisses a lady's hand. And there are the special nieces and nephews who come to visit him who never knew Nick before injury. He is their handicapped loving uncle, and they accept him for who he is now.

John and I too love the beautiful son we are privileged to share our life with and are so thankful that he did not die and that we have had this chance to know and acknowledge him a man. We know that Dr. Collins was very wrong about Nick. Rehabilitation has not taught us what he cannot do. It has taught us not only what he *can* do, but what a *true man* is. And it has not been cruel. The treatment he endured before home rehabilitation was the true cruelty.

Our ordeal leads us to believe that the medical profession has written off people like Nick because they don't want to get involved in offering the type of long-term therapies and care they need. Too expensive, they say. They consider only the physical being in front of them and give no value to the spirit of a human being that is far more valuable than the body in which it is encased.

To those who think like Dr. Sturman and Dr. Collins (that Nick would be better off dead), I say: I have learned that Nick's life is not worse than death, and so has he! Nick asked me recently when I was helping him to get out of bed, "Mom, how do I know what God's plan is for my life?" The question stunned me for a moment because it was so penetrating in its inquisitiveness. It is the question all of us who believe in God should ask. We talked about the answer for quite a while and then Nick said, "Mom, I think God's plan for me is to love life." At times like this I cry because the answers are so profound. And then I realize that Nick's life is beautiful in every respect, even though his physical and mental limitations are great. On this morning, as on almost every morning, Nick stood up and hugged me and said, "Mom, Mom, I want God to bless you and me and our life. I LOVE LIFE!"

Epilogue

Death for Nick was a real fear on December 24, 1997, as I held him in my arms in the middle of the night. His breathing was so shallow I thought he could not manage to inhale one more time. But he miraculously caught another breath and the flow of air into his lungs became more regular. I was so concerned, though, that I called Mary to come over because I did not know if this was to be his last night on earth.

He stabilized through the night and we were able to have Christmas dinner the next day. He participated by waking long enough to eat at dinner time and again when the desserts were served. The next morning it was obvious that he must have medical help. I called 911. The ambulance and attendants arrived, and I accompanied Nick to the emergency room.

Nick was admitted to the cardiac unit after tests were concluded in the emergency room. It was thought he had congestive heart failure but monitoring of his heart revealed that this was not the case. Further tests showed that he was aspirating. Food and liquids were getting into his air passage and lungs. As a result he was suffering from respiratory failure. It was also determined that sleep apnea (a condition caused by the temporary cessation of breathing caused by upper airway obstruction during sleep) was a factor in this hospitalization.

Dr. Tate had left private practice at this time and Dr. Stephen Rubenstein had taken over Nick's care. He has turned out to be one of Nick's finest care-givers. He indulged me in my personal rule that

Nick will never be left alone in a hospital. Therefore, I, our daughters Mary and Debbie, and Nick's aides took shifts staying with him twenty-four hours a day for the next five days. It was a very tense time for all of us, and his father, as we had to consider the fact that he might die. He recovered well enough to be discharged home and we were all relieved to have him back in familiar surroundings.

On Nick's return home, a C-pap machine and oxygen were ordered. At night Nick must wear a mask over his nose to receive the air and oxygen this machine pumps into his lungs at a steady pace. During the day another machine supplied oxygen to him through a clear plastic tube but his oxygen level soon rose to a degree which indicated he no longer needed the oxygen during the day.

Another significant change was the introduction of pureed foods with Thicket added so that all his food and drinks are the consistency of pudding. This makes it easier for Nick to swallow food and liquids without getting them into his lungs.

When Nick came home from the hospital, he was so weak that he could only transfer from chair to bed. He was not strong enough to walk even a few steps. Within two months Nick utilized his extraordinary reserves of strength and will power and got back on his feet again. His desire to walk is phenomenal and he is strolling in his beloved walking bar as well as he ever did.

Spring is coming. All the earth is being renewed and our spirits along with it. Nick teaches us constantly how precious life is, and that the body is only the temple of that most marvelous part of our life — our spirit. Nick still says every day, "I LOVE LIFE," and oh, how he means it!

Appendix

Brain Injury Association, Inc.

The National Head Injury Foundation originated in 1980 in the state of Massachusetts under the leadership of Marilyn Spivak, whose daughter sustained a serious brain injury. It is now known as Brain Injury Association, Inc. (BIA). Its offices are located at 105 N. Alfred St., Alexandria, VA 22314. The telephone number is (703) 236-6000 or Fax (703) 236-6001.

    This organization is a nonprofit one encompassing a national network of forty-four state associations and 800 support groups. It is dedicated to acting as a clearinghouse of community service information and resources, participating in legislative advocacy, facilitating prevention awareness, encouraging research, and hosting educational programs.

    This organization of people concerned with traumatic brain injury encourages research and provides resources through innovative developments for brain-injured persons, particularly through computers. They strive to educate the public by increasing awareness of brain injury as a serious disability and stressing the need for prevention. "Prevention is the only cure for brain injury."

    TBI is defined as an insult to the brain, not of degenerative or congenital nature but caused by an external physical force that may produce a diminished or altered state of consciousness, which results in an impairment of cognitive abilities or physical functioning.

The organization's latest brochure notes, "This 'silent epidemic' claims 50,000-60,000 lives each year." It says, "Every year in the United States, two million people sustain a brain injury—one every fifteen seconds." It explains, "Approximately 373,000 of those individuals require hospitalization, and the 99,000 who experience lifelong debilitating loss of function will incur treatment costs of more that $4 million during their lifetimes." It warns, "In this age of high speed cars, adventure sports and a staggering increase in the incidence of violence, the risk of brain injury is greater than ever before."

Brain injury is the leading cause of death and disability in children and young adults. It is the leading cause of mortality among Americans under forty-five years of age, and TBI is responsible for the majority of these deaths. It has been estimated that TBI claims more than 56,000 American lives annually. A startling fact is that after one traumatic brain injury, the risk for a second injury is three times greater; and after a second TBI, the risk for a third injury is eight times greater. An individual with severe brain injury typically faces five to ten years of intensive rehabilitation, with cumulative costs exceeding $48 billion annually.

Vehicles are the leading cause of TBI, as they account for 50 percent of all injuries. Twenty percent are caused by falls, and firearms are currently causing 12 percent. Sports, recreation, and abuse account for the remainder. Alcohol is very significant in the incidence of brain injury, as more than 50 percent of persons with brain injury have been intoxicated at the time of injury.

The Brain Injury Association has produced the *1997 National Directory of Brain Injury Rehabilitation Services*. It contains vital information about all types of services available to people with brain injury. It is the most comprehensive directory of its kind and can be obtained by contacting the Brain Injury Association in Alexandria, Virginia.

State resource information is available from the BIA also. Comprehensive lists of government and private organizations that may be of help to TBI persons and their families may be obtained by contacting the office in Alexandria, Virginia. For instance, the state resource listing for Connecticut contains more than thirty agencies that families may contact for possible assistance.

The Brain Injury Association is, of course, the favorite charity of John and myself. It deserves the support of every American, because brain injury infects every community with its terrible consequences. I believe it is the least understood of all injuries because it is so horrible in nature, and those who must care for the survivors have little strength left after care-giving to advocate for TBI.

It is my hope that this book will help educate many people with regard to TBI and help families who are new to this world where few people want to tread.

State Brain Injury Associations Addresses and Telephone Numbers

(National) Brain Injury Association, Inc.
105 N. Alfred Street, Alexandria, VA 22314
Telephone: (800) 444-6443
Telephone: (703) 236-6000
Fax: (703) 236-6001
E-mail: familyhelpline@biausa.org or www.bia.usa.org

State Brain Injury Associations
Address written inquiries to Brain Injury Association of [state].
(Following addresses and telephone numbers as of January 1999)

Alabama
3600 8th Avenue South, Birmingham, AL 35222
Telephone: (800) 433-8002 (in state)
Telephone: (205) 328-3505
Fax: (205) 328-2479

Alaska
1251 Maldoon Road, Suite 32, Anchorage AK 99504
Telephone: (888) 945-4323 (in state)
Telephone: (907) 338-9800
E-mail: www.alaskanet/drussell/bia.ak

Arizona
4545 N. 36th Street, Suite 125A, Phoenix, AZ 85018
Telephone: (602) 952-2449 (Phoenix)
Telephone: (520) 747-7140 (Tuscon)

Arkanas
P.O. Box 26236, Little Rock, AR 72221
Telephone: (800) 235-2443 (national)
Fax: (501) 227-8632

Appendix

California
P.O. Box 160786, Sacramento, CA 95816-0786
Telephone: (800) 457-2443 (in state)
Telephone: (916) 457-2443
Fax: (916) 442-7305
E-mail: biac@juno.com

Colorado
6825 E. Tennessee Avenue, Suite 405, Denver, CO 80224
Telephone: (800) 955-2443 (national)
Telephone: (303) 355-9969
Fax: (303) 355-9968

Connecticut
1800 Silas Deane Highway, Suite 224, Rocky Hill, CT 06067
Telephone: (800) 278-8242 (in state)
Telephone: (860) 721-8111
Fax: (860) 721-9008

Delaware
P.O. Box 9876, Newark, DE 19714
Telephone: (800) 411-0505 (national)
Telephone: (302) 537-5770

Florida
North Broward Medical Center, 201 E. Sample Road,
Pompano Beach, FL 33064
Telephone: (800) 992-3442 (in state)
Telephone: (954) 786-2400
Fax: (954) 786-2437
E-mail: info@biaf.org

Georgia
1447 Peachtree Street NE, Suite 810, Atlanta, GA 30309
Telephone: (888) 334-2424 (national)
Telephone: (404) 817-7577
Fax: (404) 817-7521

Hawaii
1775 South Beretina 203, Honolulu, HA 96826
Telephone: (808) 941-0372

Idaho
P.O. Box 414, Boise, ID 83701-0414
Telephone: (888) 374-3447 (in state)
Telephone: (317) 356-7722 (Twin Falls)
Telephone: (208) 336-7708 (Boise)

Illinois
1127 S. Mannheim Road, Suite 213, Westchester, IL 60154
Telephone: (708) 344-4646
Fax: (708) 344-4680

Indiana
5506 E. 16th Street, Suite B-5, Indianapolis, IN 46218
Telephone: (800) 407-4246 (in state)
Telephone: (317) 356-7722
Fax: (317) 356-4241
E-mail: suec@iquest.net

Iowa
2101 Kimball Avenue, LL7, Waterloo, IA 50702
Telephone: (800) 475-4442 (national)
Telephone: (319) 272-2312
Fax: (319) 272-2109
E-mail: glauer@blue.weeg.uiowa.edu

Kansas
1100 Pennsylvania Avenue, Suite 4061, Kansas City, MO 64105
Telephone: (800) 783-1356 (in state)
Telephone: (816) 842-8607
Fax: (816) 842-1531

Kentucky
113 S. Hubbards Lane, Louisville, KY 40207-3937
Telephone: (800) 592-1117 (national)
Telephone: (502) 899-7141
Nationwide Center 113: (502) 899-7123
Fax: (502) 899-7106
E-mail: www.braincenter.org

Louisiana
217 Buffwood Drive, Baker, LA 70714-3755
Telephone: (504) 775-2780
Fax: (504) 775-2780

Maine
211 Maine Avenue, Suite 200, Farmingdale, ME 04344
Telephone: (800) 275-1233 (in state)
Telephone: (207) 582-4696
Fax: (207) 582-4803
E-mail: www.biausa.org/maine/bia.htm

Maryland
Kernan Hospital, 2200 Kernan Drive, Baltimore, MD 21207
Telephone: (800) 221-6443 (in state)
Telephone: (410) 448-2924
Fax: (410) 448-3541

Massachusetts
Denholm Building, 484 Main Street, Suite 325, Worcester, MA 01608
Telephone: (800) 242-0030 (in state)
Telephone: (508) 795-0244
Fax: (508) 757-9109

Michigan
8137 W. Grand River, Suite A, Brighton, MI 48114
Telephone: (800) 772-4323 (in state)
Telephone: (810) 229-5880
Fax: (810) 229-8947

Minnesota
43 Main Street SE, Suite 135, Minneapolis, MN 55414
Telephone: (800) 669-6442 (national)
Telephone: (612) 378-2742
Fax: (612) 378-2789

Mississippi
P.O. Box 55912, Jackson, MS 39296-5912
Telephone: (800) 641-6442 (national)
Telephone: (601) 981-1021
Fax: (601) 981-1039
E-mail: biaofms@aol.com

Missouri
10270 Page, Suite 100, St. Louis, MO 63132
Telephone: (800) 377-6442 (IL, MO, KS)
Fax: (314) 426-3290

Montana
52 Corbin Hall, University of Montana, Missoula, MT 59812
Telephone: (800) 241-6442 (in state)
Telephone: (406) 243-5973
Fax: (406) 657-2807

Nebraska
P.O. Box 124, Gothenburg, NE 69138
Telephone: (308) 537-7875
Fax: (402) 761-2219
E-mail: bil3135@Navix.net

Nevada
2820 West Charleston Boulevard, Suite D-37, Las Vegas, NV 89102
Telephone: (702) 387-2318
P.O. Box 2789, Gardnerville, NV 89401
Telephone: (775) 782-8336

New Hampshire
2 1/2 Beacon Street, Suite 171, Concord, NH 03301-4447
Telephone: (800) 773-8400 (in state)
Telephone: (603) 225-8400
Fax: (603) 228-6749,
E-mail: nhbia@nh.ultranet.com

New Jersey
1090 King George Post Road, Suite 708, Edison, NJ 08837
Telephone: (800) 669-4323 (national)
Telephone: (732) 738-1002
Fax: (732) 738-1132

New Mexico
1100 Candelaia NE, Suite 113W, Albuquerque, NM 87112
Telephone: (505) 292-7414
Fax: (505) 292-7414

New York
10 Colvin Avenue, Albany, NY 12206
Telephone: (800) 228-8201 (national)
Telephone: (518) 459-7911
Fax: (518) 482-5285
E-mail: info@bianys.org or www.bianys.org

North Carolina
P.O. Box 748, 133 Fayetteville Street Mall, Suite 310, Raleigh, NC 27602
Telephone: (800) 377-1464 (national)
Telephone: (919) 833-9634
Fax: (919) 833-5415
E-mail: biaofnc@aol.com or cbgreene@aol.com

North Dakota
No BIA at present.

Ohio
1335 Dublin Road, Suite 217D, Columbus, OH 43215-1000
Telephone: (800) 686-9563 (in state)
Telephone: (614) 481-7100
Fax: (614) 481-7103
E-mail: ohiobia@infinet.com

Oklahoma
P.O. Box 88, Hillsdale, OK 73743-0088
Telephone: (580) 635-2237
Fax: (405) 635-2238

Oregon
1118 Lancaster Drive NE, Suite 345, Salem, OR 97301
Telephone: (800) 544-5243 (national)
Telephone: (503) 585-0855

Appendix

Pennsylvania
St. Andrews Church, 304 Moorewood Avenue, Pittsburgh, PA 15213
Telephone: (412) 682-2520 (W)
33 Rock Hill Road, Room 310, Bala Cynwyd, PA 19004
Telephone: (800) 837-5640 (E)

Rhode Island
Independence Square, 500 Prospect Street, Pawtucket, RI 02860
Telephone: (401) 725-2360
Fax: (401) 727-2810
E-mail: BuckleUp1@aol.com

South Carolina
Peace Rehabilitation Center, 651 South Main Street,
Greenville, SC 29601
Telephone: (864) 241-2600
Fax: (864) 241-2621

South Dakota
No BIA at present.

Tennessee
699 W. Main Street, Suite 203-B, Hendersonville, TN 37075
Telephone: (800) 480-6693 (in state)
Telephone: (615) 264-3052
Fax: (615) 264-1693
E-mail: biat@juno.com

Texas
1339 Lamar Square, Suite C, Austin, TX 78704
Telephone: (800) 392-0040 (national)
Telephone: (512) 326-1212
Fax: (512) 326-8088

Utah
1800 SW Temple, Suite 203, Box 22, Salt Lake City, UT 84115
Telephone: (800) 281-8442 (national)
Telephone: (801) 484-2240
Fax: (801) 484-5932
E-mail: biau@sisna.com

Vermont
P.O. Box 1837, Station A, Rutland, VT 05701
Telephone: (802) 446-3017

Virginia
3212 Cutshaw Avenue, Suite 315, Richmond, VA 23230
Telephone: (800) 334-8443 (in state)
Telephone: (804) 355-5748
Fax: (804) 355-6381
E-mail: dana@visi.net

Washington
16315 NE 87th, Suite B4, Redmond, WA 98052
Telephone: (800) 523-5438 (national)
Telephone: (425) 895-0047
Fax: (425) 641-9319
E-mail: biawa@biawa.org

West Virginia
P.O. Box 574, Institute, WV 25112-0574
Telephone: (800) 356-6443 (in state)
Telephone: (304) 766-4892
Fax: (304) 766-4940
E-mail: biawv@aol.com

Appendix

Wisconsin
3505 N. 1024th Street, Suite 100, Brookfield, WI 53005
Telephone: (800) 882-9282 (in state)
Telephone: (414) 790-6901
Fax: (414) 790-6824

Wyoming
246 S. Center Street, Suite 16, Casper, WY 82601
Telephone: (800) 643-6457 (national)
Telephone: (307) 473-1767
Fax: (307) 237-5222

Nova Scotia
P.O. Box 8804, Halifax, NS B3K 5M4
Telephone: (902) 425-5060

Federal Programs that Help
TBI Persons and Their Families

It is estimated that each year, 5,000 individuals in the state of Connecticut alone sustain a TBI that is severe enough to require hospitalization. A further estimate is that 50 to 100 of those so injured cannot return to their homes or communities. Each year this figure means that 50 to 100 *more* people need to access services for the TBI population.

At present, the only option is placement in a long-term care or rehabilitation facility where financial resources from private funds or insurance programs are quickly depleted. At this point, these individuals or their families must turn to the state for support.

The only two sources of government funding presently available are the Medicaid program and Social Security. A long-term TBI patient will almost certainly need to apply to the state for Medicaid assistance.

MEDICAID (OR TITLE XIX) This is a federal program of medical assistance for persons who have no medical insurance and who have limited assets that can be used for this purpose. It is commonly considered a welfare assistance program. It is administered by a specific department in each of the fifty states. For instance, in Connecticut the Department of Social Services administers this program.

Each state has specific guidelines for access to this program. The rules are very complex and change from time to time, so it is important to contact the correct department in each state for information regarding how to access the Medicaid program. It may also be necessary to contact an attorney or other professional who has expertise with Medicaid to protect your rights under this program.

Medicaid will fund the cost of care in a nursing home or chronic disease hospital, but it will not fund community-based services, and many TBI persons need these in order to attempt to return to their homes. Federal regulations that govern the Medicaid program contain provisions which allow states to provide nonmedical services by applying for and implementing a Home and Community Based Services (HCBS) Waiver.

Fourteen states have implemented these waivers for persons with acquired brain injuries. These waivers allow the state to offer an array of services designed to enable these persons to avoid costly institutional care.

The states, the date of approval by the federal government of their application for waivers, the name of a contact person, telephone number, and the services available under the Medicaid waiver are:

COLORADO—pending; Contact: Jay Kaufman, (303) 762-4590
Personal care, respite, environmental access modifications, specialized medical equipment and supplies, substance abuse counseling, transitional living, independent living skills training, and behavioral programming.

CONNECTICUT—2/12/97 Contact: Lauri Di Galbo, (860) 424-4861
Service coordination; homemaker; personal care assistance; respite; day rehabilitation; prevocational; adult companion; community living supports; cognitive/behavioral programs; transitional living; supported employment; environmental accessibility adaptations; transportation; specialized medical equipment and supplies; chore; personal emergency response systems; family training; home-delivered meals; substance abuse programs/hour; substance abuse programs/day; independent living skills training/group; independent living skills training/individual; and vehicle modifications.

KANSAS—7/1/94 Contact: Evelyn McCormick, (913) 296-3981
Case management, transitional living services, respite, home health, personal care, skilled nursing and personal emergency response systems to head injured patients for a maximum of 75 persons.

LOUISIANA—10/1/93 Contact: Virginia Lee, (504) 342-1400
Personal care, habilitation, respite, adult day health, environmental modifications, special medical equipment and supplies, personal emergency response systems, chore, extended home health, PT,

OT, speech, hearing and language and extended psychological testing and explanation of findings, and other services to the disabled, any age with TBI and related conditions.

MINNESOTA—4/1/92 Contact: Debra Wesley, (612) 297-3462
Case management, personal care, homemaker, respite, adult day health, environmental modifications, transportation, specialized medical equipment and supplies, chore, companion, home health, PT, OT, speech, hearing and language, mental health services, independent living skills, structured day program, cognitive rehabilitation therapy, behavioral programming, family support services, foster care to individuals with TBI.

NEW HAMPSHIRE—11/1/93 Contact: Jacquelyn Felix, (603) 271-5035
Case management, personal care, respite, day habilitation, and environmental modifications to individuals with TBI from age 22 to 65.

NEW JERSEY—7/1/93 Contact: Judith Johnson, (609) 588-2733
Case management, personal care, respite, environmental modifications, transportation, chore, companion, extended PT, OT, speech, hearing and language, community resident services, night supervision, behavioral program, structured day program, supported day program, counseling, and cognitive rehabilitation therapy to persons 18 to 65 with TBI.

NEW YORK—6/95 Contact: Bruce Rosen, (518) 474-8645
Respite, environmental modifications, transportation, special medical equipment and supplies, independent living skills, training and development, living skills training and development, structured day programs, substance abuse programs, intensive behavioral programs, therapeutic foster care, transitional living programs, home and community support services, services coordination and community integration counseling to disabled individuals with TBI after age 22 and some age 18 to 21.

NORTH DAKOTA—4/1/94 Contact: Muriel Peterson, (701) 221-5454
Case management, personal care, respite, habilitation (prevocational

and supported employment), environmental modifications, transportation, special equipment and supplies, chore, behavioral management, training for family caregivers, transitional living, TBI residential care, and substance abuse counseling to TBI individuals.

SOUTH CAROLINA—7/1/95 Contact: Ann Dodd, (803) 737-6450
Habilitation, respite, prescription medications, PT, OT, communication, psychological services, attendant care services, private nursing, personal emergency response systems, specialized supplies and adaptations for persons with head and spinal cord injuries.

UTAH—pending; Contact: Sue Marquardt, (801) 538-4199
Case management, homemaker, respite, supported employment, environmental accessibility adaptations, specialized medical equipment and supplies, chore services, personal emergency response systems, companion services, family training, structured day program, community supported living, counseling, behavioral programming, and rehabilitation therapies to 100 persons with TBI.

VERMONT—10/1/94 Contact: Lorraine Wargo, RN (802) 241-3186
Case management, respite, day and residential rehabilitation, environmental modifications, and assistive technology for individuals with TBI who demonstrate a potential for independent living.

WASHINGTON—5/1/94 Contact: Allen Shanafelt, (206) 493-2544
Personal care, adult day health, respite, resident and day habilitation, skilled nursing, assisted living, congregate care and adult family care to disabled with TBI.

WISCONSIN—1/1/95 Contact: Sonja Stoffels, (608) 267-9840
Case management, supportive home care, respite adult day care, habilitation (alternative living arrangement, day services, prevocational, supported employment, and transportation), home modifications, specialized transportation, personal emergency response systems, adapt aids, communication aids, daily living skills training,

and extended counseling and therapeutic services to individuals with TBI.

Lauri Di Galbo, creator and long time advocate of the Medicaid waiver, and education consultant, Bureau of Rehabilitation Services, Department of Social Services, 25 Sigourney St., Hartford, CT 06106, states that the earliest these programs will be implemented in the state of Connecticut is in the Fall of 1998.

She further reports that Connecticut has a budget of $1,100,000 to be spent for brain-injury support programs, and this money is allocated to various institutions and groups helping TBI persons in community-based programs as well as to support the Brain Injury Association office in Rocky Hill. She credits the Governor's Task Force on Traumatic Brain Injury for being the catalyst for obtaining this money from state government.

Information from the *Executive Summary of the Acquired Brain Injury Home and Community Based Services Waiver* states that "neutrality is assured by limiting the number of persons to be served and by instituting an aggregate cost cap of 75% of the categorical institutional cost." In Connecticut, a maximum of 500 persons may receive these waiver services.

SOCIAL SECURITY For information regarding Social Security benefits that might be available to TBI persons, telephone 1-800-772-1213.

Persons under sixty-five years of age who are permitted to access Social Security benefits must be:

1. disabled prior to age 22, living at home and dependent upon a parent; or

2. eligible under a needs-based welfare program (Supplemental Security Income [SSI] or Social Security Disability Insurance [SSDI]).

In Connecticut, disability determination for the programs under (2) are determined by the Bureau of Rehabilitation Services. Each state will have a department covering this funding, and that department must be contacted by the TBI person or his/her guardian or conservator in that state for a determination hearing.

MEDICARE This program is administered under the Social Security Department and pays for necessary medical services. It may be accessed in three ways:
1. person disabled, receiving benefits for two years;
2. person on kidney dialysis; or
3. person 65 years of age or older.

TBI persons generally fall in the first category and may apply to obtain a Medicare card if they meet the requirements after they have been disabled for a two-year period, receiving benefits. Benefits are determined by the number of quarters during which a person has paid into the Social Security system from payroll deductions. This information is available at all Social Security offices by personal application.

OTHER PROGRAMS TBI persons may have access to other government programs designed to help disabled persons, such as government housing for the handicapped; energy assistance programs; Food Stamps; surplus food; nutrition programs; employment and training programs; and emergency assistance.

All these programs are administered in each state through a department of state government.

PRIVATE AND CHARITABLE ORGANIZATIONS

CONNECTICUT
Gaylord Hospital (nonprofit)
BIAC Family Night Education and Support
Contact: Peter Talbot, (203) 284-2843

NATIONAL
National Rehabilitation Information Center, 1-800-346-2741. Resource and research center for persons with disabilities.

Abledata, 1-800-227-0216. Assistive technology for disabled persons. Provides information on products for disabled or handicapped persons. Lists 2,500 manufacturers under 1,700 major headings.

Heath Resource Center, 1-800-544-3284. 1 Dupont Circle N.W. Suite

800, Washington, D.C. 20036-1193. National clearing house for secondary education information and referrals on postsecondary education and adult training programs for people with disabilities.

PREVENTION AND STUDY Public Law 104-166 was enacted by the Congress of the United States July 29, 1996. This is commonly known as the TBI Act and will be administered through the Centers for Disease Control and Prevention.

In its announcement about this act the Centers for Disease Control stated:

> Among all types of injury, traumatic brain injury is most likely to result in death or permanent disability. The incidence and prevalence, severity and cost indicate that these injuries are important public health problems. TBI is also preventable.
>
> Some estimates and studies of incidence have indicated that traumatic brain injuries may result in 260,000 hospitalizations and 52,000 deaths each year.
>
> The severity of the nonfatal injuries is shown by estimates that each year 70,000 to 90,000 people sustain TBI resulting in permanent disability.
>
> The costs of TBI; acute care, rehabilitation, chronic care, and indirect injuries, impose an annual economic burden of $37 billion in direct and indirect costs. These estimates of cost fail to account for the extraordinary losses experienced by the families and friends of those who have died or sustained disability from TBI.

Section 393A of this act provides for:

1. the conduct of research into identifying effective strategies for the prevention of TBI; and

2. the implementation of public information and education programs for the prevention of such injury and for broadening the awareness of the public concerning the public health consequences of such injury.

For the purpose of carrying out this section Congress has appropriated $5 million for each of the fiscal years 1997 through 1999. In collaboration with appropriate state and local health related agencies, studies may be conducted:

1. to determine the incidence and prevalence of TBI; and

2. to develop a uniform reporting system under which States re-

port incidents of TBI if the secretary determines that such a system is appropriate.

Studies may also be conducted to identify common therapeutic interventions that are used for the rehabilitation of individuals with such injuries, and shall, subject to the availability of information, include an analysis of:

1. the effectiveness of each such intervention in improving the functioning of individuals with brain injuries;

2. the comparative effectiveness of interventions employed in the course of rehabilitation of individuals with brain injuries to achieve the same or similar clinical outcome; and

3. the adequacy of existing measures of outcomes and knowledge of factors influencing differential outcomes.

Not later than eighteen months after the date of the enactment of this act, the secretary shall submit to the Committee on Commerce of the House of Representatives, and to the Committee on Labor and Human Resources of the Senate, a report describing the findings made as a result of carrying out the prevalence studies. Not later than three years after the date of the enactment of this act, the secretary shall submit to these committees a report describing the findings made as a result of the rest of the studies.

The composition of these advisory boards shall be representatives of the corresponding state agencies involved; public and nonprofit private health-related organizations; other disability advisory or planning groups within the state; members of an organization or foundation representing TBI survivors in that state; injury control programs at the state or local level if they exist; and a substantial number of individuals who are survivors of TBI, or the family members of such individuals.

To access the funds available through the TBI Act, states must agree to make available, in cash, non-federal contributions toward such costs in an amount that is not less than $1 for each $2 of federal funds.

It will be imperative on TBI persons and family members to advocate for their state to come up with the matching funds to successfully apply for one of these grants.

Glascow Coma Scale

	Examiner's Test	Patient's Response	Assigned Score
Eye Opening:	Spontaneous	Opens eyes on own	4
	Speech	Opens eyes when asked to in a loud voice	3
	Pain	Opens eyes when pinched	2
	Pain	Does not open eyes	1
Best Motor Response:	Commands	Follows simple commands	6
	Pain	Pulls examiner's hand away when pinched	5
	Pain	Pulls part of body away when examiner pinches patient	4
	Pain	Flexes body inappropriately to pain (decorticate posturing)	3
	Pain	Body becomes rigid in an extended position when examiner pinches victim (decerebrate posturing)	2
	Pain	Has no motor response to pinch	1
Verbal Response (Talking):	Speech	Carries on a conversation correctly and tells examiner where he is, who he is, and the month and year	5
	Speech	Seems confused or disoriented	4
	Speech	Talks so examiner can understand victim but makes no sense	3
	Speech	Makes sounds that examiner can't understand	2
	Speech	Makes no noise	1

Scores are determined as response is tested. Total score is determined by adding the three categories. Highest possible score is 15. This score would indicate a person who is awake, oriented, and following commands. Lowest score is 3. This score would indicate a person deeply unconscious. A score of 8 or lower generally indicates a person with severe brain injury.

Appendix

Rancho Los Amigos Levels of Cognitive Functioning

The Rancho Los Amigos Levels of Cognitive Functioning (RLA) were designed to measure and track an individual's progress early in the recovery period. They have been used as a means to develop "level-specific" treatment interventions and strategies designed to facilitate movement from one level to another. A RLA level is determined based on behavioral observations. The RLA scale designates eight levels of function:

I. NO RESPONSE
The individual appears to be in deep sleep and is completely unresponsive to any stimuli.

II. GENERALIZED RESPONSE
The individual reacts inconsistently and nonpurposefully to stimuli. Responses are limited in nature and often the same regardless of the stimuli presented. Responses may include gross motor movements, vocalization, and physiologic changes. Response time is likely to be delayed. Deep pain evokes the earliest response.

III. LOCALIZED RESPONSE
The individual responds specifically but inconsistently to stimulus. Responses are directly related to the type of stimuli presented. For example, an individual's head will turn toward a sound or his/her eyes will focus on an object when presented. The individual may follow simple commands and may respond better to some people (i.e. family and friends) than others.

IV. CONFUSED–AGITATED
The individual is in a heightened state of activity with severely decreased ability to process information. Behavior is nonpurposeful relative to the immediate environment. Attempts to climb out of bed, remove restraints, and hostility are common. The individual requires maximum assistance to perform self-care activities. An individual may sit, reach, or walk, but will not necessarily perform these activities upon request.

V. CONFUSED–INAPPROPRIATE

The individual appears alert and responds to simple commands fairly consistently. Agitation which is out of proportion (but directly related) to stimuli may be evident. Lack of external structure results in random or nonpurposeful responses. Inappropriate verbalizations and high distractibility are common. Memory is severely impaired, but the individual may self-feed with supervision and requires only assistance for self-care activities.

VI. CONFUSED–APPROPRIATE

The individual shows goal oriented behavior, but is dependent upon external input for direction. Response to discomfort is appropriate. Responses are incorrect due to memory problems, but are appropriate to the situation. Simple commands are followed consistently and carry-over for relearned activities is evident. Orientation is inconsistent but awareness of self, family, and basic needs is increased.

VII. AUTOMATIC–APPROPRIATE

The individual appears appropriate within hospital and home settings, goes through daily routine automatically but is robot-like, with shallow recall of activities performed. Has absent-to-minimal confusion and lacks insight. The individual frequently demonstrates poor judgment and problem solving and expresses unrealistic future plans. With structure the individual is able to initiate tasks or social and recreational activities.

VIII. PURPOSEFUL–APPROPRIATE

The individual is alert and oriented, able to recall and integrate past and recent events and is aware of and responsive to the environment. Independence in the home and community has returned. Carry-over for new learning is present, and the need for supervision is absent once activities have been learned. Social, emotional and cognitive abilities may still be decreased.

Selected Reading List

Injured Mind, Shattered Dreams: Brian's Journey from Severe Head Injury to a New Dream by Janet Miller Rife. Brookline Books, P.O. Box 1046, Cambridge, MA 02238. ISBN: #0-914797-95-6

Return to Ithaca: A Woman's Triumph over the Disabilities of a Severe Stroke by Barbara Newborn. Element Books, Inc., P.O. Box 830, Rockport, MA 01966. ISBN: #1-85230-944-X

Blessed Tragedy: Restoring New Life with Hope and Faith After a Head Injury by Karen Wells. Rhodes & Easton, 121 E. Front St., 4th Fl., Traverse City, MI 49684. ISBN:#0-9649401-7-5

Brain Injury: A Family Tragedy by Patt Abrahamson with Jeffery Abrahamson. HDI Publishers, P.O. Box 131401, Houston, TX 77219. ISBN: #1-882855-56-6

Flying Without Wings: Personal Reflections on Being Disabled by Arnold R. Beisser. Doubleday, 666 Fifth Ave., New York, NY 10103. ISBN: #0-385-24770-2

Still Me by Christopher Reeve. Random House, Inc., New York, NY 10022. ISBN: #0-679-45235-4

Man to Man—Surviving Prostate Cancer by Michael Korda. Random House, Inc., New York, NY 10022. ISBN: #0-679-44844-6

Tears of Rage by John Walsh. Simon & Schuster, 1230 Avenue of the Americas, New York, NY 10020. ISBN: #0-671-57754-9

No Mercy by John Walsh. Simon & Schuster, 1230 Avenue of the Americas, New York, NY 10020. ISBN: #0-671-01993-7

Love, Medicine & Miracles by Bernie S. Siegel. Harper Collins, 10 East 53rd Street, New York, NY 10022. ISBN: #0-060-91983-3

Prescriptions for Living by Bernie S. Siegel. Harper Collins, 10 East 53rd Street, New York, NY 10022. ISBN: #00-60191-961

About the Author

Barbara Del Buono became involved in victims' rights after her son's injury. She helped start the Brain Injury Association in Connecticut and served on its first board of directors. She was chair of the first brain injury support group in Waterbury and served on the first Governor's Task Force on Brain Injury in the United States.

She has written and spoken about the effects of brain injury on many radio and television programs. She is the author, with her husband, of *When Two Become One*, a book about marriage that won an award from the National Catholic Press Association.

The mother of eight, grandmother of thirteen and great-grandmother of four, she lives in Watertown, Connecticut. She has served on numerous school, political and social committees in her community.

ORDER FORM

To purchase copies of *Acknowledged a Man*,
order direct from The Ellingsworth Press, LLC,
by any of the following methods:

Credit card orders:
Toll Free 877-ELL-PRES

Or fax your order to:
860 274-9755

Or order on line:
www.braininjurydragon.com

Or mail your order to this address:
The Ellingsworth Press, LLC
680 Main Street, Suite One, Watertown, CT 06795

	Price	Amount
___ copies of **Acknowledged a Man**	$22.95 ea.	$
Sales Tax (CT residents only)	$ 1.38 ea.	$
Shipping and handling	$ 4.00 ea.	
Total payment due	$	

Send my order to:

NAME (PLEASE PRINT) _____

COMPANY/ORGANIZATION _____

STREET _____

CITY/STATE/ZIP _____

Method of payment:

❏ Check or money order enclosed

❏ VISA   ❏ MasterCard   ❏ Discover   ❏ American Express

CARD NUMBER _____

EXPIRATION DATE _____

CARDHOLDER'S SIGNATURE _____